D1486030

# EXPLORATIONS IN SOCIOLOGY
*British Sociological Association conference volume series*

\* *also published by Macmillan and St. Martin's*

† *also published by Macmillan*

# The Social Construction of Social Policy

## Methodologies, Racism, Citizenship and the Environment

Edited by

**Colin Samson**
*Lecturer in Sociology*
*University of Essex*
*Colchester*

and

**Nigel South**
*Senior Lecturer in Sociology*
*University of Essex*
*Colchester*

First published in Great Britain 1996 by
**MACMILLAN PRESS LTD**
Houndmills, Basingstoke, Hampshire RG21 6XS
and London
Companies and representatives
throughout the world

A catalogue record for this book is available
from the British Library.

ISBN 0–333–63089–0 (hardcover)
ISBN 0–333–63090–4 (paperback)

 First published in the United States of America 1996 by
**ST. MARTIN'S PRESS, INC.**,
Scholarly and Reference Division,
175 Fifth Avenue,
New York, N.Y. 10010

ISBN 0–312–12717–0

Library of Congress Cataloging-in-Publication Data
The social construction of social policy: methodologies, racism,
citizenship and the environment / edited by Colin Samson and Nigel
South.
p.   cm.
Includes bibliographical references and index.
ISBN 0–312–12717–0
1. Great Britain—Social policy—1979–   2. Great Britain—Social
conditions—1945–   I. Samson, Colin.   II. South, Nigel.
HN385.5.S575   1996
361.6'1'0941—dc20                                            95–13607
                                                                CIP

10   9   8   7   6   5   4   3   2   1
05   04   03   02   01   00   99   98   97   96

Printed and bound in Great Britain by
Antony Rowe Ltd, Chippenham, Wiltshire

# Contents

## PART III   CITIZENSHIP, RIGHTS AND INEQUALITIES

## PART IV   ENVIRONMENT, PLANNING AND BUREAUCRACY

# List of Figures

# List of Tables

# Notes on the Contributors

**Waqar Ahmad** is a Senior Research Fellow at the Social Policy Research Unit, University of York. He is editor of *The Politics of 'Race' and Health* (Race Relations Unit, Bradford University, 1992) and *'Race' and Health in Contemporary Britain* (Open University Press, 1993).

**Mel Bartley** is a contract researcher in medical sociology. She studied at Bedford College for her MSc in Sociology as Applied to Medicine, and at Edinburgh for a PhD in Social Policy. Since then she has worked on projects funded by the ESRC concerning women's health, and the relationship between social class, unemployment and health in men and women.

**Kate Burningham** is Lecturer in Sociology of the Environment in the Department of Sociology and the Centre for Environmental Strategy at the University of Surrey. Her research interests are in the area of local environmental change and the social construction of environmental impacts.

**Bob Carter** is a Senior Lecturer in Sociology at Worcester College of Higher Education. He has published a number of articles on immigration, national identities and racism in post-war Britain and is currently working on a realist critique of race thinking within sociology.

**Karen Evans** is a Research Fellow in the Department of Sociology at the University of Salford. She is working on a study of 'Community Safety, Personal Safety and the Fear of Crime' under the ESRC's 'Crime and Social Order' initiative. She has previously worked with Ian Taylor and Penelope Fraser on the 'Public Sense of Well-Being in Public Space'. She has also worked at Liverpool University's Centre for Community and Educational Policy Studies on a project funded by Leverhulme, 'The Educational Implications of the 1988 Housing Act'. She has also worked for Lancashire County Council's research department and as a housing adviser in Manchester and Nottingham.

**Janet Foster** is Lecturer in Sociology at the University of Warwick. Her research on attitudes to crime and law and order was published as *Villains* (Routledge, 1990). Her recent work has included a participant observation study of two hard-to-let housing estates, published (with Tim Hope) as

*Housing, Community and Crime* (HMSO, 1993). She is currently writing a book on the subject of a community in transition in London's Docklands.

**Penelope Fraser** is a Research Fellow in the Department of Sociology at the University of Salford. She is currently engaged in a study on 'Community Safety, Personal Safety and the Fear of Crime' under the ESRC's 'Crime and Social Order' initiative with Karen Evans and Sandra Walklate. Her previous work, with Ian Taylor and Karen Evans, was concerned with the 'Public Sense of Well-Being in Public Space'. She is also working towards a PhD on the negotiation of safety and risk by young teenagers in an inner city.

**Marci Green** is a Senior Lecturer at the University of Wolverhampton. Her PhD was on the role of the Americanisation Movement in the racialisation of immigrants. Her current research is on the state, racialisation and unfree wage labour.

**Gill Jones** is a Senior Research Fellow at the Centre for Educational Sociology, University of Edinburgh. She has published widely on transitions to adulthood and inequalities in youth, and on the relationship between young people and their families of origin. She is co-author (with Claire Wallace) of *Youth, Family and Citizenship* (1992) and author of *Leaving Home* (1995), both published by the Open University Press. Before becoming a research sociologist she was a social worker.

**Ray Pawson** is a Senior Lecturer in Sociology at the University of Leeds. He is author of *A Measure for Measures* (1989). He is President of the Research Committee on Methodology of the International Sociological Association and the UK Director of the International Forum for the Study of Education in Penal Systems.

**Carlo Ruzza** is a Lecturer in Sociology at the University of Essex. He has researched different types of social movements including peace, environmental and nationalistic movements with particular reference to issues of institutionalisation. Currently, he is working on a European Union funded study of the impact of the environmental movement on policy-making in Brussels.

**Colin Samson** is a Lecturer in Sociology at the University of Essex. His main intellectual interests and publications are in the areas of privatisation, health and mental health, including most recently 'The Fracturing of Medical Dominance in British Psychiatry?' in *Sociology of Health and Illness*, March 1995. He is currently working on a study on the health of indigenous people in Canada.

**Elizabeth Shove** is a Senior Lecturer in the School of Social and International Studies at the University of Sunderland. Although a sociologist, she has much experience of government-funded building research, having previously worked at the Institute of Advanced Architectural Studies, University of York. Participation in the ESRC's Global Environmental Change Programme has created further opportunities to pursue interests in the sociology of building and in the organisation of social and technical research.

**Nigel South** is a Senior Lecturer in Sociology at the University of Essex. He has published widely on social policy and drug problems, and on privatisation and criminal justice services. His latest book is (with V. Ruggiero) *Eurodrugs: Drug Use, Markets and Trafficking in Europe* (UCL Press, 1995).

**Nicholas Tilley** is Reader in Sociology and Co-Director of the Crime Reduction Research Unit at Nottingham Trent University. He is presently seconded as a research consultant to the British Home Office, where he is working on crime reduction.

**Charles Watters** is Lecturer in Mental Health at the Tizard Centre, University of Kent at Canterbury. His PhD research explored the relationship between the assumptions of British mental health services and Asian communities. His current research interests include the development of community care policy in respect of black and minority groups in Britain.

# 1 Introduction

## Social Policy isn't what It Used to Be – The Social Construction of Social Policy in the 1980s and 1990s

### Colin Samson and Nigel South

SOCIAL POLICY, THE WELFARE STATE AND 'PRIVATISATION'

Social policy is not what it used to be. Changes in the form and content of what we have come to call 'social policy' have rendered problematic and possibly archaic, the accounts produced in the heyday of British social policy analysis (Cahill, 1994, p. 1–7). While the writings of T. H. Marshall (1950) and Richard Titmuss (1958), for example, are both eloquent and humanistic, they portrayed social policy as a phenomenon that could be understood empirically in terms of the rules regarding citizenship and the rights of the individual and social collectivities within the 'classic' welfare state (Lowe, 1993). This tradition, inherited by the 'social administration' studies of the 1970s and early 1980s, emphasised the study of various political processes that established the legislative framework, implementation and social impact of particular policies. This volume does not seek to engage in a critique of this earlier tradition of social policy study; rather, one of our aims is to show through a number of illustrations how cultural and political changes in Britain under Conservative administration have complicated discussions of social policy and have made it necessary to consider issues that would have formerly lain outside of social policy analysis. Hence, the cases examined here include critiques of methodologies underpinning certain policy measures and debates; the expansion of the world of research contracting; racism and health care; citizenship, housing rights and use of public space; and environmental politics as a greatly expanded arena for social policy decision-making.

A number of preliminary, inter-related observations can be made about the issues these papers raise. First, the world of social policy in the 1990s reflects the imposition of the market values that the Government has so assiduously (and dogmatically) promoted. 'Agencies', 'Trusts', managers and fund-holders represent a way of delivering social policy ser-vices somewhat removed from earlier visions of the welfare state. In this climate, it is unsurprising that 'research' has itself become a commodity, bought and sold in a contracting process where 'bids' are invited and tend-ered and the entrepreneurial researcher will build in 'added value' (i.e. something for nothing) to get the grant. Social policy 'knowledge' that supposedly underpins policy decision-making is 'contracted' (perhaps in both senses of the word) within a political process (which usually desires research to confirm the wisdom of decisions already taken) and influenced by commercial (market) interests. For example, as of 1994, both the Leverhulme Trust and the Economic and Social Research Council, each of which are vital to social science funding, have prioritised issues such as 'wealth creation', the 'business ethic' and entrepreneurialism. These are indeed important sociological topics, but they also represent ideological stances that legitimate a narrow and conservative neo-liberal world view.

Throughout the 1980s, the diverse constituencies for whom social policy has traditionally developed to provide assistance, faced ever-greater social and economic pressures at the same time as state support was eroded and notions of eligibility and obligation were re-defined. By the 1990s, welfare services have become not rights of citizenship but consumer goods, distributed to targeted groups of clients/customers and policed by increas-ingly zealous welfare officials.[1] The extreme social polarisation that has occurred as a result of the 'privatisation' of welfare and other services in the 1980s and 1990s (see Samson, 1994; South, 1994) has exploded any consensual belief in the status of the welfare recipient as 'full-citizen'. In response to this, as well as pursuing the tradition of empirical analysis of the politics, economics and social impact of policies, we now need to ques-tion what 'social policy' *is* because its parameters are no longer as self-evident as they might have been in the past. If the 'new' social policy is anything tangible, then to us, the emerging themes seem to be difference and exclusion (see Morris, 1994; Scott, 1994).

In this volume of papers from the 1993 British Sociological Association Conference held at the University of Essex, the contributors provide con-crete examples of the emerging policy-processes which are being con-structed around these themes of exclusion and difference.[2] While no-one would deny that what are termed social policies have effects on or for people (that is, after all, their purpose) the thrust of the papers in this volume is to deconstruct social policies as empirical facts. The authors probe for hidden agendas and embedded, covert assumptions in the organ-isation and delivery of services, and also highlight the various iniquities and inequalities that have followed from the pursuit of particular policies.

THE SYMBOLIC FACE OF SOCIAL POLICY

Policies are not simply unambiguous mandates that lead to courses of action. They are also symbolic gestures, channelled through the legislative process and amplified in political rhetoric. The intention, as suggested by policy-makers, may be the solution or attenuation of some pre-defined social problem. But the problems themselves, as with so much of the current privatisation agenda in Britain, may be raised only so that a particular 'solution', such as cutting welfare expenditure, can be put forward. Although symbolically and semantically associated with an attack on a social problem, such a solution, of course, may well not be a solution. Examples of such symbolic policies include the New Deal in the USA, analysed by Edelman (1987) and anti-discrimination legislation in Britain, discussed by Solomos (1987) and Gregory (1987). Both of these policies failed in important respects to engineer the assistance and intervention implied in their political and legal constructions. Yet, what is important is the *name*. The ideas of the 'New Deal' or 'anti-discrimination' are a different phenomenon – semantic constructions which offer grounds for ignoring inconsistencies and assuming an identity of language and reality, ideas and practice. These solutions may well exacerbate the problem that they are intended to tackle. For example, the Conservative emphasis on greater judicial punitiveness has generally correlated with an increase, not decrease, in crime-related problems, including (ironically) an increasing *fear* of crime (Young, 1992; Downes and Morgan, 1994, p. 199).

These observations reflect recent trends in critical policy analysis which emphasise the importance of examining not only the substance of policies, but also their ideological intentions and linguistic presentation. For example, as well as being symbolic in form, welfare policies are expressive of political agendas intended to influence patterns of social activity and social stratification, or cultural expectations about the appropriate role of the state. As Esping-Andersen (1990) has reminded us, the nature of a state's welfare benefit system and provision has a direct effect on the form that social stratification takes and not the reverse. The re-definitions of welfare provision and constrictions or eliminations of eligibility in Britain under Mrs Thatcher and Mr Major, have sharpened the liberal (in the nineteenth-century sense) characteristics of the welfare system and brought it closer to the model existing in the USA than the systems of Britain's European partners. This is well illustrated by the notions of the 'deserving' and 'undeserving' poor which underpin the recent Government crusade against 'dole cheats' (David Hunt, Employment Secretary, October 1993) and 'young ladies who get pregnant just to jump the housing list' (Peter Lilley, Social Security Secretary, October 1992), and by various other pronouncements at annual Conservative Party conferences, such as Michael Howard's telling judgement of 1993 that

> Social security benefits all too often appear as an entitlement rather than something which should be earned.[3]

## BROADER INFLUENCES AND THE RECONSTRUCTION OF SOCIAL POLICY

Of course, there is more to the de-/reconstruction of social policy in Britain than the decline of the welfare state, and the context in which the recent radical changes in social policy have taken place is broader than the domestic political and economic environment. As Cahill (1994, pp. 1–2) observes:

> the post-war consensus on welfare (and on so much else) has disappeared. There have been numerous accounts of the way in which Thatcherism restructured the politics and policies of the UK, yet this is to take too narrow a view of the changes which have occurred, and accords Thatcherism too great an importance. What has happened to the British economy and society is part of a global pattern of economic and social transformation affecting all the western industrial countries. . . . New global problems have appeared: principally the environmental crisis which puts a question mark over the future of the human race.

The papers in this volume address social policy issues at both these levels – that of the restructuring of politics and policies in the UK, as well as the impact of broader transformations on consumption, urban space, labour markets, environmental politics, and so on. Today, more than ever before, the problems of domestic policy connect to the experiences of other countries and new responses must be sought. For example, unemployment as a domestic social problem, which has been worsening in Britain (with the long-term unemployed becoming a progressively larger proportion of those without work: Phillips, 1992), must now be considered alongside other international correlates of global recession (Pixley, 1993). The cross-border movement of 'economic migrants' and asylum seekers has increased, particularly after the fall of eastern European communist states, and in parts of western Europe there has been a related resurgence of neo-fascist activity which governments' have condemned while, at the same time, tightening rules on residency and citizenship rights. Freedom of movement and the opportunity to seek work within the area of the European Union are rights of citizenship that have some bearing on re-shaping social policy issues like unemployment. However, as with all systems based on criteria of eligibility, there are also those who are excluded. In the history of citizenship rights, those falling (or pushed) into the excluded category have been those with little power, those at the margins of society or those who should be seen (and seen to labour) but not heard. One view of this history is that 'citizenship' has been defined quite distinctly as a device for implementing a racist policy of immigration rules.

> In a legal sense, citizenship was and essentially still is a device for the administration of immigration control, an aspect of policy whose princi-pal aim has been to keep as many black people as possible, whether Asians or Afro-Caribbeans, out of the country. (Gordon,1991, p. 77)

More broadly, as Cook (1993, p. 137) has recently observed in a discus-sion of racism, citizenship and exclusion,

> the important issue here is that full and equal citizenship (involving the elimination of social inequality) appears incompatible with the opera-tion of free market economics. It is therefore deeply ironic that the leading proponents of the free market (New Right politicians) were to 'rediscover' and re-work the theme of citizenship throughout the 1980s and subsequently add it to their own political lexicon.

These themes of exclusion and citizenship, particularly in relation to new considerations about 'race' (for example, Brah, 1994) and gender (for example, Walby, 1994), currently stimulate much debate about the past and future of social policy: for example, whether the ethical socialists are correct that it is not bad housing and poverty but the lone-parent family that best explains a post-war increase in delinquency among youth (Dennis and Erdos, 1992); or whether the concept of the 'underclass' is valid or misleading (Gallie, 1994); or whether class analysis remains useful to our understanding of a socially stratified society far removed from that of the immediate post-war years (Crompton, 1993). As Cahill (1994, p. 3) remarks 'The era in which the Beveridge consensus was born – the 1940s – was very different from the present.' The essays that follow illuminate some of the ways in which social policy questions have been transformed in recent years and will continue to change into the next century.

## CRITIQUES OF THE POLICY RESEARCH PROCESS

The collection opens with some reflections on the promise and failures of social policy research. In a more optimistic climate, earlier social administration research was conducted with something of a natural presumption that it would be useful to and possibly influential upon social policy decision-making. Whether this was actually the case or not cannot be debated here. However, the papers by Bartley, and by Pawson and Tilley, comment on the relationship between social research and social policy making today. Bartley is concerned with the intriguing question of 'whatever happened to the debate about the health effects of unemployment that was so lively from 1979 to 1987?'; Pawson and Tilley pose and answer a similarly intriguing question: 'why "rigorous" social science evaluations fail'.

Bartley argues that research and policy debates are thoroughly and constantly entwined, but that it is not the simple existence or validity of research findings that mean they get taken on board in public and policy thinking. Rather, they are driven onto the stage of policy relevance by a form of entrepreneurialism. Such pushing of new knowledge claims has, of course, always been a necessary part of challenging orthodoxies, shifting paradigms or just making simple suggestions; however, it is also important to note that in a social climate where the entrepreneur rules then it is the entrepreneur of social policy research whose voice will carry over the heads of quieter colleagues. The paper presents a quite complex analysis of the policy-making process and the contribution (and varied fates) of research debates. It presents a social history of recent social policy research as 'fragile knowledge' and asks questions that we should note well.

Pawson and Tilley also have some questions. For those exasperated by the failures of both social policy implementation and social policy research their practical questions will ring bells. 'Why', the authors ask, 'do the supposedly most rigorous social science evaluations often produce such desperately disappointing results?' and 'can evaluation play a progressive part in taking policy and understanding forward?' From a critique of quasi-experimental models of evaluation (in this case taking crime prevention initiatives as an example), the authors move to 'show how a generative account of causality, contained in scientific realism, can be built into social scientific evaluation'. Their conclusions consider why policy making should have more regard for evaluation, and why evaluators should have more regard for new ways of thinking about methodology.

## RACISM, HEALTH AND POLICY THINKING

Over the past fifteen years, Conservative reform of the National Health Service has focused attention on change in the organisation and funding of the service. The 'internal market' that has been created emphasises the rationalisation of health resources by new smaller units of service delivery, 'Trusts'. As many have pointed out (Strong and Robinson, 1990; Flynn, 1992) this represents a shift in decision-making power away from physicians and to the newly empowered and highly remunerated class of professional managers. It also signifies a most dramatic change in the ethos of the NHS, away from its open availability as part of the entitlements of citizenship encompassed in the British welfare system, and towards a more overtly commercially regulated and clinically rationed set of operations, which are geographically highly variable.

These changes however, should not blind us to various problems which persist and which a cultural analysis of the health service can illuminate. Among other deleterious outcomes, these changes have served to reinforce particular 'common sense' assumptions about the nature of welfare 'clients' and the distribution of health and disease inherited from positivist biomedicine and British imperial sensibilities. In opening this section of the book, Bob Carter and Marci Green argue that both social policy implementation and academic sociology have been heirs to 'race-ist' thinking. Sociological writing, especially certain prominent British texts, as well as social policies, have assumed that 'races' are real in either the sense of biologically or culturally bounded groups of individuals (for a review of the changing terms of the debate see Solomos and Back, 1994).

While the biological definition of 'race' may have attenuated in recent years, Carter and Green argue that cultural racism, flagged in the literature by Hall (1991) among others, has persisted in theoretical writings and flourished in practice. Although we often think of the idea that 'races' constitute culturally homogenous groups with particular pathologies as a relic of colonialism, there are obvious continuities in the present. This is quite evident, for example, in the New Right discourse on the 'underclass' (Morris, 1994), but persists in more avowedly liberal policy discussions around issues of inequalities and difference among client groups.

The chapters by Waqar Ahmad and Charles Watters testify to the continuity of racist thinking in the conceptualisation of health problems and the delivery of services. Partly as a result of the emphasis on the changes in the structure of health services, discourses which influence disgraceful medical practices have been largely ignored in British medical sociology. As an example of such discourses, Ahmad points to the overwhelming tendency in the medical and health research communities to explain the high rates of perinatal mortality, congenital malformations and stillbirths in sections of the Asian community in terms of the consanguinity hypothesis. Even in the absence of any reliable evidence on the relationship between consanguinity and obstetric outcome, the tendency has been to link the two. This, argues Ahmad, is related to a number of fears having to do with 'incest', 'arranged marriages', the diseases of foreigners, the resilience of biological 'stock' and wider British concerns about the practices of Muslims in particular. The temptation in such a discourse is to create and conflate images of diseased or disabled bodies and diseased or disabled cultures. Such a discourse firmly fixes the health problem in the nature of the 'alien' culture and the individuals who comprise it, and ignores both the environment of racism in which many ethnic minorities live and the racist practices of the health service delivery system itself.

The prevalence of racial stereotyping among health professionals and researchers is also the theme of Watters' paper. As with the consanguinity hypothesis, Watters shows that particular stereotypes of 'Asians' (often depicted as a homogenous group) are brought forward to explain epidemiological findings concerning psychiatric differences between those represented as Asian and those in other categories. This has serious implications. For example, Watters argues that stereotypes of the 'somatising' Asian patient and social representations of the 'supportive' Asian community have a knock-on effect on the kinds of services that are provided for these patients and communities. Once such targeted services are in place, they merely serve to reaffirm the racist assumptions as to the peculiar nature of the health of the group.

What these three chapters indicate is that social policy analysis needs to recognise taken-for-granted racist assumptions. Perhaps more than anything else, they show that the *culture* of British social policy analysis and welfare service delivery should be investigated when looking at questions of difference and inequality.

## CITIZENSHIP, RIGHTS AND INEQUALITIES

In this section (as in the volume as a whole) the authors and their case studies reflect a wide geographical spread of social policy issues across Britain. Evans and Fraser discuss the differential use of public space in the cities of Manchester and Sheffield, Jones describes inequalities and problems in young people's access to housing in Scotland, and Foster reports on the recent history of community conflict and racism in the battle over public housing on the Isle of Dogs in London.

Evans and Fraser are concerned to 'uncover some of the ways in which the different populations in the city are forced by economic necessity, inaccessibility or lack of well-being in public spaces, amongst other reasons, into a marginalised use of public space'. They are concerned then with what Sayer (1994) has referred to as 'the aetiology of urban change', where 'flows of people, commodities, money and capital loop in and out of different parts of the city, which of course is merely a corner of a wider, global matrix'. The flows of people described here fall into four case studies, on youth, gays, shoppers and women. This paper points to new and important areas for social policy to do with the meanings that public spaces and their use have for people. Interestingly, Cahill's (1994) *New Social Policy*, described as a 'social life analysis of social policy', organises its discussions around the identification of some similar 'new' themes 'from the perspective of everyday life', including travelling, shopping, working and playing. In the next paper, Gill Jones focuses on one of the groups from above – the problems youth face in getting some space of their own. In a detailed analysis, drawing on two sets of survey data as well as qualitative interviews, the author examines the accessibility of the Scottish housing market for young people and concludes that most of the latter find themselves either on the margins of the market, or excluded altogether. Jones demonstrates the unequal nature of housing access (Sullivan, 1994) and that this is not merely age-related, but that most young people are in what can be described as a 'youth housing market' (Pickvance and Pickvance, 1994). Lack of housing provision, or even possibilities, for young people extends their dependency and removes their claim to direct citizenship rights, which instead are assumed to be indirectly transmitted to them through their parents. Families which may not be able or willing to support their young for an extended period of their transition to the adult world face further pressures. At the same time, current policy reflects an expectation that the family will always be a 'safe haven' for the young, a belief which has been proven dangerously wrong many times in recent years. The issues Jones raises in the Scottish context are, of course, paralleled south of the border.

The next paper brings to mind the closing observations of the earlier paper by Evans and Fraser: 'we are mindful' they note, 'of the fact that *spaces* can take on different appearances and atmosphere as they become *places* in which different groups interact. This may involve an element of conflict.' As Janet Foster found in her study of housing allocation and housing need on the Isle of Dogs, in London's Docklands, the 'urban neighbourhood' can easily lose its neighbourly qualities amid competition, conflict and racism. Here again, the changes that shape social policies and social practices are not limited to parochial matters: 'International, national and local factors all had an impact on events in Docklands.' Foster primarily considers the interweaving and cross-influencing of micro-level, community factors within the prevailing social policy context. And this is quite enough, for at work here is an unaccountable, large-scale Development Corporation selling property for middle-class residential use that was previously earmarked for rental by local people, constraints on local authority expenditure, the impact of the 'right to buy' policy on council housing stocks, and the pressures for conflict between the traditional 'locals' – a white, working-class community and the resented 'newcomers', Bengalis, being re-housed in the area. The recent news coverage of neo-fascist political activity in this area of London illustrates the highly sensitive and worrying tone of community relations here.

## ENVIRONMENT, PLANNING AND BUREAUCRACY

The need to care for the natural and physical environment represents one of the major impediments and limits to the maintenance of the free-market ethos nurtured by the Conservative Government. In relation to most national and international matters of environmental importance, the Government has deferred such concerns in favour of the more important economic imperatives of business. That is, economic growth has been seen as the only viable engine for national recovery and demands from opposition parties and environmental organisations for more regulation of business on issues such as pollution and recycling have been depicted as foolish, 'trendy' and counterproductive. With the exception of some concern for the 'English landscape' in some shire counties, the market has been considered the best arbiter of what is good for the environment.

It is interesting in view of this that sociological knowledge, which could potentially adjudicate between the competing interests by looking into public attitudes and utilisation of less wasteful forms of consumption, has also been subordinated to short-term needs. This circumvents the main environmentalist argument that long-term planning of the use of resources must hold priority over any short-term goals, including economic revitalisation. This is one of the conclusions to flow from Elizabeth Shove's detailed chapter on the sociology of sociological research into energy-saving strategies in buildings. Like the reform of public services generally, environmental research has been made to conform to the model of competitive tendering and the demands of financial stringency. This process has held out less and less funding for more and more contractors, resulting in fragmentary, 'bite-sized' contracts emphasising 'deliverables' to the management structures which are responsible for overseeing the contracting. Under such procedures, any kind of sociology which is about understanding complex processes gets diluted and reduced. Shove pinpoints a general feature of contemporary state-funded research – that it is becoming increasingly unsociological or asocial and that it is linked to the political and ideological goals of the current Government.

While the cards are being stacked against both the environment and sociology, perhaps all is not lost. Individuals and groups often resist autocratic power, and perhaps no better example has presented itself in this country than popular opposition to the Government's road-building schemes. In her chapter, Kate Burningham focuses on the language used by those opposing more roads in their fight against the 'expert knowledge' of the bureaucrats employed to participate in public inquiries and planning disputes. Finally, Carlo Ruzza investigates the supra-national level of bureaucratic decision-making on the environment. Britain under the Conservatives has been a reluctant partner to European initiatives in all matters pertaining to 'social' planning. However, it is perhaps increasingly difficult for the governments of individual countries to escape the embrace of European programmes. Ruzza's study of decision-making among European Community bureaucrats in Brussels examines environmental regulation as the outcome of complex bureaucratic dynamics. While, as Ruzza points out, these do not exactly conform to Weber's 'iron cage' imagery, the agenda is loaded towards somewhat conservative policies since it depends on balancing the lobbying of business and the environmentalist movement, as well as the influence of governments and public opinion.

CONCLUDING COMMENTS

The papers presented here are not examples of traditional, ameliorative social policy analysis that 'take for granted' what 'the problem' is. All the contributors question the nature of the problems and policies they address, and their contributions are the stronger for this. Several recurring themes bind the collection together and, in particular, the authors identify a general process of erosion – of citizenship and rights, and of opportunities for independent, sociological social policy research. Finally, the papers emphasise the difference and diversity of (late-) modern society and find current social policies to be sadly misconceived, inappropriate and inadequate.

### Notes

1.    This is a process begun in the early 1980s with the setting up of the DHSS Specialist Claims Control Teams (Scraton and South, 1983), continuing recently with the establishment of an entire organisation, the Child Support Agency, devoted to 'saving taxpayers money' (not, as one might suppose, to improving the financial lot of single mothers or the welfare of children).

2.    We are grateful to the contributors for the efforts they have made in revising their original conference papers. We should also note that there were several other papers which we would have liked to include here if space had permitted.

3.    A useful article on poverty in Britain, by Michael Durham (1993), looks at how 'the canard of the "deserving" and "undeserving" poor has returned from the mists of the last century'.

### References

Brah, A. (1994) 'Time, Place, and Others: Discourses of Race, Nation, and Ethnicity' (review essay), *Sociology*, 28: 3, pp. 805–13.

Cahill, M. (1994) *The New Social Policy* (Oxford: Blackwell).

Cook, D. (1993) 'Racism, Citizenship and Exclusion', in D. Cook and B. Hudson (eds), *Racism and Criminology* (London: Sage).

Crompton, R. (1993) *Class and Stratification* (Cambridge: Polity Press).

Dennis, N. and Erdos, G. (1992) *Families without Fatherhood* (London: Institute for Economic Affairs, Health and Welfare Unit).

Downes, D. and Morgan, R. (1994) 'Hostages to fortune'? The Politics of Law and Order in Post-war Britain' in Maguire, M., Morgan, R. and Reiner, R. (eds), *The Oxford Handbook of Criminology* (Oxford: Clarendon Press).

Durham, M. (1993) 'Benefits of Tory Morality', *The Observer*, 14 November, p. 14.

Edelman, M. (1987) *Constructing the Political Spectacle* (Chicago: University of Chicago Press).

Esping-Andersen, G. (1990) *The Three Worlds of Welfare Capitalism* (Princeton, NJ: Princeton University Press).

Flynn, R. (1992) *Structures of Control in Health Management* (London: Routledge).

Gallie, D. (1994) 'Are the Unemployed an Underclass? Some Evidence from the Social Change and Economic Life Initiative', *Sociology*, 28: 3, pp. 737–57.

Gordon, P. (1991) 'Forms of Exclusion: Citizenship, Race and Poverty', in Becker, S. (ed.), *Windows of Opportunity* (London: Child Poverty Action Group).

Gregory, J. (1987) *Sex, Race and the Law: Legislating for Equality* (London: Sage).

Hall, S. (1991) 'The Local and the Global: Globalisation and Ethnicity', in King, A. (ed.), *Culture, Globalisation and the World System* (London: Macmillan).

Lowe, R. (1993) *The Welfare State in Britain since 1945* (London: Macmillan).

Marshall, T. H. (1950) *Citizenship and Social Class* (Cambridge: Cambridge University Press).

Morris, L. (1994) *Dangerous Classes* (London: Routledge).

Phillips, M. (1992) 'The New Road to Wigan Pier', *The Guardian*, Outlook Section, 21 November, p. 25.

Pickvance, C. and Pickvance, K. (1994) 'Towards a Strategic Approach to Housing Behaviour: A Study of Young People's Housing Strategies in South-east England, *Sociology*, 28: 3, pp. 757–77.

Pixley, J. (1993) *Citizenship and Unemployment: Investigating Post-Industrial Options* (Cambridge: Cambridge University Press).

Samson, C. (1994) 'The Three Faces of Privatisation', *Sociology*, 28: 1, pp. 79–97.

Sayer, A. (1994) 'The Aetiology of Urban Change', *Sociology*, 28: 2, pp. 559–66.

Scott, J. (1994) *Poverty and Wealth* (London: Longman).

Scraton, P. and South, N. (1983) 'In the Shadow of the Welfare Police', *Bulletin on Social Policy*, 13: pp. 45–53.

South, N. (1994) 'Privatizing Policing in the European Market: Some Issues for Theory, Policy and Research', *European Sociological Review*, 10: 3, pp. 219–233.

Solomos, J. (1987) 'Anti-Discrimination Legislation: Symbolic Policies?' in Jenkins, R. and Solomos, J. (eds), *Racism and Equal Opportunities Policies in the 1980s* (Cambridge: Cambridge University Press), pp. 30–53.

Solomos, J. and Back, L. (1994) 'Conceptualising Racisms: Social Theory, Politics and Research', *Sociology*, 28: 1, pp. 143–62.

Strong, P. M. and Robinson, J. (1990) *The NHS: Under New Management* (Milton Keynes: Open University Press).

Sullivan, O. (1994) 'Processes of Housing Access: A Dynamic Approach to Housing Consumption', *Sociology*, 28: 3, pp. 679–97.

Titmuss, R. (1958) *Essays on 'The Welfare State'* (London: Allen & Unwin).

Walby, S. (1994) 'Is Citizenship Gendered?', *Sociology*, 28: 2, pp. 379–95.

Young, J. (1992) *The Rise in Crime in England and Wales 1979–1990* (Middlesex Polytechnic/University: Centre for Criminology).

# Part I
# Critiques of the Policy Research Process

# 2 'Probably, Minister …': the 'Strong Programme' Approach to the Relationship between Research and Policy

Mel Bartley

This paper is based on a study of the ways in which research and policy debates concerning the health effects of unemployment were related to each other in the UK over the period 1979–87. Briefly, what happened in the debate? An American study by Professor M. H. Brenner (1979), indicating that the usual downward trend in death rates levelled out when unemployment was high, was published in the UK. These findings were used to exert political pressure. In turn, the work of Brenner also came under pressure: several problems concerning his methods were pointed out. A British government study then produced findings suggesting that unemployment had no effect on health. Several British research groups then entered the debate, using methods which were less open to the methodological criticisms aimed at the American research. However, when the largest and most sophisticated British study was published, in 1987, there was hardly any response, either academic or political (Moses et al., 1987). This work, which suggested that there was an independent effect of unemployment on mortality risk, has never been explicitly refuted. But academic papers continue to appear which are written as if these findings had never been reported. Discussion of policy issues such as the level of unemployment benefits, or the availability of re-training, make no reference to health. Now that unemployment is once again high in the UK, there has been no revival of the debate.

This paper will argue that the question 'Does research affect policy debate and, if so, how?' is not an appropriate one. The two processes are thoroughly entwined. My study of the unemployment and health debate has indicated that it is not the mere existence of research findings, or even the opinion of the academic community as to their quality, which ensures

17

the entry of the results of scientific studies into the public sphere and policy debate. This finding is in agreement with recent advances in the sociology of science and technology in France and Britain using the so-called 'strong programme' in the sociology of knowledge. These approaches imply that a form of *entrepreneurialism* is required before findings become facts. First, findings must be promoted as 'knowledge-claims'. In order to become either 'scientific fact' or 'policy-relevant', knowledge-claims must then attract the assent of a number of groups, a network, which will pick up and pass on the claims intact to a wider audience. In technical terminology, the findings of research must become 'obligatory points of passage'. Understanding the relationship between research and policy is the same problem as understanding the construction of knowledge in general. Policy questions themselves give rise to a 'demand for facts'. How this demand is satisfied is a question concerning the organisation of disciplines and professions, and their relationship to the modern state.

The debate on the health effects of unemployment may be regarded as a 'social problem process'. For the exponents of this idea, social problems are not in themselves self-evident states of affairs, but rather the outcome of activities, which Spector and Kitsuse term (1977, pp. 72–3) 'claims-making'. A primary task of the researcher, therefore, is to examine how some situation or condition is asserted to be a 'social problem', and how collective activity is organised around these definitions and assertions.

The social-problem analyst is not concerned with whether or not 'condition *x*' even exists, let alone with whether it is in some final sense 'truly' morally objectionable. Rather, she or he must analyse the discourse on the existence of the problem as 'factual claims-making' and the moral discourse as 'value-claims-making'. Factual and value-claims are inter-woven throughout the career of the problem, and Spector and Kitsuse propose four 'phases' in which this career can be divided:

(1)   Stage One is that in which a group or groups point to the existence of some condition (a factual claim), indicate that it is undesirable in some way (a value-claim), and attempt to promote it to a higher position on the agenda of public and political debate.

(2)   In Stage Two, some official organisation or institution recognises the 'truth' of the knowledge-claim, or at least begins an official investigation to clarify these claims, and begins to formulate an official 'policy response'.

(3) In Stage Three, the original groups declare themselves unsatisfied with official response, and the 'policy failure' or 'cover-up' becomes a new problem claim.

(4) In Stage Four, claims-making groups abandon their attempt to satisfy their grievances and/or to resolve the asserted problem through official channels and begin to develop 'alternative, parallel, or counter-institutions'.

This 'stages model' is not put forward by Spector and Kitsuse as anything more than a working hypothesis. The research procedure which they advocate is to investigate the claims-making strategies of all the groups engaged in a social-problem process, which may include a wide variety of professions, pressure groups, 'moral crusaders', official agencies and the media.

A critical elaboration of this approach, as it can be applied to the British policy process, is offered by Manning (1985). Like Spector and Kitsuse, he takes a 'developmental' approach, and focuses on the process of claims-making rather than on the question of 'whether the problem really exists'. This is not a 'natural' but rather a 'social history'. To Spector and Kitsuse's stages he adds a possible 'loop' back from the third to the second stages (an example is the setting up of a Royal Commission) and observes that 'Group claims can get stuck in this loop and disappear' (pp. 9–10). He also adds the concepts of 'individualisation' of social problems, which I will call 'moral fragmentation', and (following Nelkin, 1975) of defining certain problem areas as exclusively the domain of 'experts' which I will call 'technical fragmentation', as processes which accompany the progress of problem-claims through these stages.

Manning devotes more attention than Spector and Kitsuse to the nature of 'the State'. He sees the State as a 'site of conflicts and struggle' over the allocation of goods and services. Claims upon the State for goods and services are made by pressure groups of various kinds, and here the analysis of Richardson and Jordan (1979) is a useful addition to the social-problem model. Richardson and Jordan go so far as to argue that, in the course of social-problem processes,

> There is a breaking-down of conceptual distinctions between government, agencies and pressure groups; an interpenetration of departmental and client groups. (p. 44)

They contend that officials and pressure groups are, to some extent, symbiotic. One reason for this, which is not spelt out explicitly by Richardson and Jordan, but which was spoken of by participants in the debate described here, is the need for an official wishing to carve out a 'career', to be seen to initiate and/or promote a successful programme or innovation. Contact with pressure groups and 'dissident' academics can be a good source of 'bright ideas' which, when used with skill and discretion, benefit officials' careers.

Richardson and Jordan offer their own version of the 'stages model' of a social problem process, based on that of Downs (1973). In this model, more prominence (than that accorded in Spector and Kitsuse's version) is given to two additional 'stages':

(1)  The 'dramatic event' which alerts the public to the issue.

(2)  The 'decline of public interest' which sets in once the high cost of 'solving' the problem has been realised.   (p. 90)

They dismiss the idea that the policy agenda is set by pressure groups and interest groups openly lobbying the legislature: 'Campaigns are the currency of unsuccessful groups; permanent relationships are the mode of the successful' (p. 123).

What have been called here 'social-problem processes' are central to policy-making, and usually involve the making of both knowledge-claims and value-claims by various groups pursuing a range of interests. Each process may go on to give rise to either new facts, or new policies, or both or neither. But in many cases, it is the success of value-claims in changing policy which leads to the acceptance of knowledge-claims as fact, rather than the other way round. The investigator needs, therefore, to keep an open mind about the direction of influence.

In recent approaches to the social study of science, keeping such an open mind is one of the basic methodological principles. Following this principle will produce a model of the relationship between research and policy which goes a step beyond the conventional approaches. The differences between the two can be explored starting from two recent accounts of the conventional model of the relationship between research and policy, provided by Booth (1988) and Tizard (1990).

## ALTERNATIVE MODELS OF THE RESEARCH/POLICY RELATIONSHIP

Tizard (1990) has written a comprehensive and up-to-date summary of opinions on how research influences policy, from the perspective of a distinguished research career. Drawing on the work of Carol Weiss, Tizard lists four alternative models of the relationships: linear, problem-solving, political and enlightenment. The linear model, according to Weiss (for example, in Weiss, 1979), best describes the relationship between basic research in the natural sciences and technological development. Most commentators agree that this is not an appropriate model for social research. The model which sees knowledge as produced in response to policy-makers' specific needs is also dismissed: policy-makers do not, in fact, await the outcomes of studies before taking action (or deciding not to). The third model discussed by Tizard is the political model (which she points out may masquerade as a 'problem-solving' one), in which the policy-maker or customer commissions research which they know will support a decision to do what they had already decided upon. Under this heading falls the type of 'cosmetic' research held to be commissioned by government departments when it is expedient to be able to say 'research is being done' (as part of the 'loop' phases in the social problem process). Lastly, Tizard chooses for discussion Weiss's notion of an 'Enlightenment' model:

> That is, the new conceptualisations of an issue that emerge from research trickle and percolate through to both policy makers and the general public, challenging taken for granted assumptions and creating an 'agenda for concern'.   (Tizard, 1990)

Finding none of these fully satisfactory, Tizard moves on to discuss why it is that some studies have impact on policy, however this impact may be conceptualised. Her experience also renders the idea that studies have impact because of their technical quality 'very implausible'. She ends up proposing a model in which a series of 'gateways' are involved. This is regarded as a far more specific process that the rather 'vague concept of "dissemination"' currently in vogue with research councils. Examples of gateways include the quality press, and professional advisers to politicians. They also include 'ideological gateways'. She concludes:

> there has to be some degree of match between the ideology of the researcher and the guardians of the gateways.

Booth (1988) also contrasts a linear, or as he puts it, 'purist' model and a 'problem-solving' model. The first, in his view

> holds simply that research generates knowledge that impels action . . . [and is] firmly grounded in a rational view of the policy-making process.

in the second:

> it is policy rather than theory that disciplines the research.   (p. 239)

Readers may recognise in both these authors' 'problem-solving' types the principles of the customer devising the research needs and the research practitioner carrying out the necessary studies. Booth draws parallels with engineering research and development. He goes on to list the standard criticisms of these rationalistic models: that research is often used to legitimate policies which would have been implemented in any case; that policy-makers use research selectively to vindicate existing states of affairs; that research is merely decorative; that it is used to head off the need for action of any kind (p. 240). The policy-making process is, in any case, he argues, not sufficiently clear-cut for anyone to be able to isolate an individual who makes a final decision, and therefore it is futile to search for definitive signs of 'the research influence'.

Booth contrasts to the rationalist and problem-solving models of the relationship between research and policy his own version of the *political model* in which:

> The policy process comprises different groups, with different interests, in pursuit of different ends [and] research becomes entangled in the political debate between these constituencies. [ p. 244] . . . For policy research to exert any influence it must inevitably be embedded in political struggle. . . . In this process researchers act as *partisans for the value of their research.*   (p. 245, my emphasis)

Thus adding to the picture of ideological compatibility drawn by Tizard a notion that researchers who influence policy debate are those who set out to do so.

Rein (1980, 1983) has called for a study of the 'interplay' between social science and social policy, rejecting notions of 'utilisation' as a one-way process. Rein proposes that

> there are no facts [for example] about unemployment . . . that are independent of the policy considerations that inform them . . . the analytic concepts are themselves policy concepts . . . the challenge is not linking research to policy but uncovering the latent policies which organize the empirical research.   (Rein, 1980)

Here, Rein does not perhaps go far enough along the road he has indicated to us, in that the above suggests that 'latent policies' are not themselves shifting and open to negotiation. Several participants in the debate were well aware that the interaction between researcher and policy-maker did not necessarily take the form of the policy-maker presenting clear questions for research. On the contrary, it was as likely that researchers would skilfully 'sell' questions to policy-makers who had not clearly defined their needs in advance.

Lindblom (1979) writes of the *'partisan mutual adjustment'* which takes place between experts and the parties in policy debates to arrive at both a satisfactory account of 'the facts' and a solution which will eventually be implemented. The interactive relationship discussed by Rein (1980) and Lindblom (1979), and the 'partisan' approach recommended by both Booth (1988) and Tizard (1990) have implications for understanding research itself as tied-in with policy debates: the very 'facts' themselves may be the outcome of the overall processes of mutual accommodation between all parties, scientists included.

What these approaches all somewhat underemphasise is the micropolitical activism undertaken by many scientists, regardless of their policy orientations at the macro level. This additional step is most fully analysed by 'translation' theorists in the 'strong programme' of the sociology of science. Latour (1987) sums up the relationship between science and its applications:

> every time you hear about a successful application of science, look for the progressive extension of a network. Every time you hear about a failure of science, look for what part of which network has been punctured.   (p. 242)

And furthermore:

> We know that these networks are not built with homogeneous material but, on the contrary, necessitate the weaving together of a multitude of different elements which renders the question of whether they are 'scientific' or 'technical' or 'economic' or 'political' or 'managerial' meaningless.   (p. 232)

And, for sociologists of science, the network in question includes all the parties to what are thought of as the 'issue communities' of a modern polity: political parties, professions, and bureaucracies of both State and private industry.

But Latour demonstrates, by a rich collection of case studies, that this possibility of alignment is a fragile one, an 'accident prone process'. In my study I attempted to go behind the public statements of the controversy on unemployment and health to look at this process.

Firstly, I looked at the map which lay before potential participants in the early days of the debate, in order to see what were the aims and objectives of the most active participants, and the kinds of alliances and enrolments which could have appeared possible. Then I concentrated on the scientists rather more closely, to see them engaged in ongoing processes of knowledge construction, and how 'the health of the unemployed' fitted into these. Then the debate was re-examined as a series of attempts by the different individuals and groups involved to advance their own positions by creating and holding together networks of allies, and the ways in which the fate of these attempts affected ideas about both 'knowledge' and 'policy'.

The aim was not to make judgement on the 'correctness' or 'incorrectness' of the claims, but to trace the ways in which groups in the scientific and trans-scientific environment of the researchers adopted or opposed knowledge-claims, or took up a 'wait and see' position, all as part of their own occupational and micro-political strategies.

In order to see how this process developed into the 'UK unemployment and health debate', it is necessary to examine three sets of circumstances: the changes in the position of public health medicine, changes in the funding of research in social medicine, and the way in which government departments commissioned and carried out research on social questions in the UK in the late 1970s and 1980s. In a short paper, these matters can only be dealt with in a very superficial way. But without some idea of these matters, it is very difficult to understand the British debate on the health of the unemployed. My hope is that this account may draw attention to the ways in which political administration deeply influences the very questions which scientists are drawn to ask, and the data and methods which they have available to answer them.

## PROFESSIONS, ADMINISTRATORS AND SCIENTISTS

In the 1970s and 1980s, a series of profound changes was taking place in what was at the beginning of the period called 'community medicine' and is now (once again) called public-health medicine. Some of these were intended to rationalise public expenditure on health, and others produced a form of knowledge appropriate to this rationalisation. During the early 1970s, there was an increasing emphasis on the need for planning, evaluation, efficiency and cost-effectiveness, both in health and in other areas of public administration, in an attempt to control what had come to be seen as runaway growth in government expenditure. The emphasis on planning, in turn, gave rise to perceived needs for different kinds of information about the health and welfare of the population and the provision of services, and for new kinds of experts to collect and analyse this information. In particular, there was increasing dissatisfaction with the individual doctor's clinical judgement as the determinant of spending on health care. This opened an opportunity for other professional or disciplinary groups to make claims to a different, non-clinical form of expertise in the health field. Practitioners of public-health medicine could seek an important role by developing links with the planning and administration of health services as part of the drive toward rationalisation of the State sector which took place in the late 1960s and early 1970s. However, there was another powerful disciplinary group with ambition to fill this position. This was health economics. Although not a 'profession' in the same way as medicine, and in some ways less powerful, the position of economics in the UK is strengthened by the dominance of economists as advisers to governments.

The first stage of the debate, in terms of the model of social problem process, was initiated by 'community medicine'. The work of Brenner was brought to public attention by a group of 'radicals' within this professional group. They were reacting to profound changes in the role of public-health medicine after the 1970 reorganisation of local authority health and social services and the 1974 reorganisation of the NHS. These two changes effectively stripped public-health medicine of its 'empire', and reduced its status considerably. Some regarded the work of community physicians as in danger of becoming little else but administration, far removed from a concern with 'the health of the community' in any real sense. They hoped to regain a position of greater importance by pointing out that policies adopted by governments could have hidden costs – health costs – which only public-health doctors could understand and deal with. On a more international level, we can see a similar idea in the notion of 'intersectoral' health work advocated by the World Health Organisation. The effect of unemployment on health was a good vehicle for this kind of claim.

Brenner's work was, therefore, promoted by a group of public-health doctors and picked up by the media. This gave rise to considerable political concern, and to a search for scientific backing for a counter-balancing view. It was striking that in the debate on unemployment and health, all of the major papers which claimed that there was no danger to health were written by economists. In terms of the 'social problem stages model' described above, the economists provided the 'official response'. It become clear that the economists were not centrally interested in community-health issues, this debate was rather a 'sideline' for them. At the same time, they were making a series of advances into the territory of health planning, with some degree of success (this process still goes on; at the time of writing, Professor of Health Policy at the London School of Hygiene, the 'top' institution for training in public health and policy, is an economist).

In some ways, then, the major players in the debate were public-health doctors and health economists. Members of these groups, however, carried out little original research on the question. This was done mostly by social scientists and statisticians working in independent research units funded by the UK Medical Research Council. And the most rigorous research was carried out by a group of demographers and social statisticians with close links to government, using official government data, taken from censuses and death registration records. These data were obtained from the Longitudinal Study based at the Office of Population Censuses and Surveys (OPCS). In order to see why this research group become involved in the debate, we need to have a brief look at what was happening to government research at this time.

## GOVERNMENT AND RESEARCH

During the period of the unemployment and health debate, the position of statisticians within government departments appeared to many to be becoming weaker. This was partly due to the so-called Rayner Review of the Government Statistical Services (GSS). The atmosphere in 1979–80 can be contrasted to that of the mild and late 1960s, the period of growth in employment of professional staff by government when it had been assumed that more information led to better planning. The emphasis by 1980 was on the burden to businesses of having to collect so many statis- tics. The review concentrated on the cost of statistics and the management of this work within individual departments. As a result of the review, the GSS was to be cut by some 25 per cent between May 1979 and April 1984. Efficiency reviews deeply affected the statisticians working inside government departments, particularly the OPCS (the government body which carries out censuses and also the registration of deaths and births in England and Wales). Such pressures led to a perceived need to demon- strate more vigorously the value of the kind of information-linkage studies made possible by a combination of the way the OPCS was organised and new computing and information handling technology. Examining links between employment and mortality was a perfect example of this. Why then were the statisticians so happy to report findings which ran against government policy?

The Rayner Review had raised the issue of 'professional integrity' high on the agenda of debate inside and outside of Whitehall. As well as being civil servants, government statisticians have undergone specialist training which encompasses not only the transfer of skills but also of values. Accuracy and objectivity are part of their professional ideology. In addition, there is more general notion of 'public service' which is common to many professions. In this way, the statisticians shared an ideology with medicine, rather than economics.

So there were three groups seeking a more prominent role in the health-planning process, at a time when health-planning questions were high on government agendas. Those disciplines whose members claimed that unemployment did affect health were the more threatened ones (social/medical statistics) and the professional group with whom they allied (community medicine) was similarly threatened, in its turn, by successive rounds of National Health Service reorganisation. Economists, in contrast, had relatively well-established alliances with policy-makers in government departments. Some were also quietly pursuing a long-term strategy of enrolling factions within the medical profession, by offering economics as the key discipline for management of the reorganised health service.

## INDEPENDENT SCIENTISTS

But what accounts for the involvement of 'pure researchers' in the debate? This was simply a matter of opportunity. And once again, we need to look at changes in the relationship between government and researchers. The late 1970s had also seen a reorientation towards efficiency and customer-relevance in research (the so-called 'Rothschild principles'). Medical research units came under pressure to do work less dominated by internal criteria ('curiosity-driven research') and more influenced by the needs of customers, of which government was becoming a more important one. It was, therefore, not too difficult to get funding for such a policy-relevant topic as the health of the unemployed. This did not mean that outside researchers, any more than the statisticians, produced answers which they thought government wanted to hear. They did not: all research carried out in independent units suggested that unemployment did affect health (particularly heart disease and suicidal behaviour). It did, however, mean that the research was done in a hurry, using data from studies which had not been designed to investigate this question.

Where independent researchers differed from economists and from government statisticians was in their relationship to pressure groups. Some researchers did participate in pressure-group activity, as did some public-health professionals. In fact it was the participation of, especially, the public-health doctors in political pressure-group activity which placed 'the health of the unemployed' on the political agenda, and thereby gave rise to a demand for research. For the public-health professionals, the unemployment and health debate was far more important than an attempt to discover more facts about the determinants of community health. They intended to use the issue (amongst others) to show that wider social policies should not be decided without an input from medical experts. They argued that only if this was done would policy-makers know the full cost of their decisions.

During the long period of time needed to produce credible research results, however, the situation of the public-health profession changed. Its status was further changed by reorganisation of the National Health Service in 1982, and the 'Griffiths' managerial reforms, during which public-health doctors began to develop a new empire based around health education, health promotion ('Healthy Cities'), measurement of health need and resource allocation. The appearance of AIDS may also have played a part in this. New posts of Director of Public Health became available, more similar to the role of the Medical Officer in the inter-war period. Once the pressure groups had lost interest in the question of the health of the unemployed (which they did for a variety of reasons), the impact of research commissioned during the period of high political activity was almost completely lost.

This process had (and still has) consequences for what we think we can show from existing data on the relationships between health and social position. A striking example can be drawn by looking at what it is technically possible to do in secondary analysis of large cohort studies which track mortality. The major technical advance which was made during the unemployment and health debate was the development of a way to distinguish high mortality due to selection of a group into a social condition (such as unemployment) from high mortality due to the effects of that condition itself. This discovery was, in turn, more or less a by-product of the method used to calculate death rates in longitudinal studies.

If you want to measure the death rate of a certain group in a given year, the number of deaths during that year in the group is the numerator and the

number of people in the group at the *beginning* of the year is the denominator. But what is the appropriate denominator in a cohort which is being
followed over many years? If you take as your denominator the population
at the beginning of a long period of follow-up, this takes no account of the
fact that as people die the population shrinks. As a consequence, the death
rate by the end of the period will be too low. So mortality in cohorts is
conventionally analysed in terms not of persons but of 'person years at
risk'. This is a method of subtracting persons from the rate denominator at
the time of death while still allowing them to 'contribute' to the denominator for the period of time they were alive. Say, for example, that
someone dies half way through 1989. If the death rate for that year is cal-
culated at the end of the year, they will be made to 'count', but only as
'half a person year'.

As more or less a by-product of this method, it can be noticed that in
some groups (such as people enumerated at census in institutions such as
hospitals) there is often a 'clump' of deaths early on in follow-up, and that
once these deaths have taken place, the mortality rate for the remainder of
the group falls. In other words, these were a particularly 'sick' group
within the cohort. In the groups of persons enumerated in hospitals at
census there is high mortality soon afterwards, and then the rate falls
sharply, because those who were in hospital for serious diseases die, and
eventually we are left with those who were in hospital for things like vari-
cose veins whose risk of mortality is no greater than that for the rest of the
population. If a social group, say the unemployed, contains a larger than
average number of 'sick' people, then in the same way the mortality of the
group of unemployed would be inflated at the beginning of follow-up, then
fall. By contrast, there are other social groups in which mortality starts
out at an average sort of level and then rises and continues at a higher than
average level. In these groups, it can be concluded that high mortality is
not due to the presence of members who were sick in the first place; they
do not have high mortality because they were 'health-selected'. So there
must be something about being in that group which itself increases the
risk of mortality.

This is not an easy concept to grasp. The fieldwork for the research
reported here entailed long periods of 'participant observation' in public-
health and medical-statistics settings, towards the end of which the
dawning of my own comprehension took the form of the sort of 'gestalt
switch' (or perhaps 'conversion experience') frequently reported by ethno-
graphers. In addition, the process of computing person years at risk is
rather a complex one. Statistical packages are only just beginning to
become available. 'Person years analysis' of the OPCS Longitudinal Study

is not offered by the team which supports outside secondary analysts of the data set. A large amount of skilled person-power is required for this, and resources are not sufficient. It is the contention of this paper that because the discovery of the difference between the 'selective' and 'causal' patterns of mortality was made during a heated debate with apparently political implications at the time, the method has not been widely disseminated. This makes it seem even more difficult to understand, and may result in its disappearance as a tool of analysis.

A similar point was made some twenty years earlier by Sir Donald Acheson concerning 'record linkage' techniques, developed by his group in Oxford in the 1960s, which allow patients to be followed through the health care system. The aim was to

> trace [patients'] course wherever they are re-admitted . . . [and] rates of return to work, according to conditions and type of treatment. (Acheson, 1968)

This proved to be infeasible, not for any technical reason but because, as he saw it, of 'departmental boundaries' and a 'defensive negative view . . . at the moment, alas, the departmental barriers are up and the trenches are manned' (Acheson, 1968). Work on record linkage does continue in Oxford, but even at a time of increasing emphasis on the need for greater attention to effectiveness and efficiency of medical care, and of enormously greater power and sophistication in data-handling hardware and software, the technique is not in general use.

CONCLUSION: FRAGILE KNOWLEDGE

The fragility of many claims and techniques arising from research may be seen as the *consequence* of the strategic re-grouping of those involved in policy-related scientific debates. Certainly there is no evidence to support the opposite case. The claims made by the most prominent researchers in the unemployment and health debate were dropped by the rest of the policy community, and their techniques not widely adopted. But this was not because conclusive evidence against these claims had been accumulating. The new techniques which emerged were not discredited. They were merely abandoned, left in the twilight world or 'limbo' phase which some have regarded as typical of the social-problem process.

McCarthy (1986) suggests that one reason why social-problem processes enter the 'fourth stage' of a 'twilight world of lesser attention and spasmodic recurrences of interest' is what he calls

The 'dilettantism' of 'those who simply become bored and disenchanted by the issue and passively await the arrival of a new . . . issue'.

In this context 'those' include Ministers, civil servants, academics and journalists, as well as 'middle class do-gooders' who 'flippantly desert' issues, leaving them 'largely unresolved' (pp. 100–4)

We can perhaps go beyond a concept of 'dilettantism' in explaining why expert groups abandon social problems. Academics, for example, must enrol resource holders if they wish to acquire the funds to do research of any kind. Secondly, although necessary discretion exercised by both academics funded by government departments and by civil servants created considerable problems in interpreting some of what was said, questions about the degree of 'pressure' applied to unruly experts have to be addressed. Only a fine line divides the ability to 'see what the customer wants' from 'government suppression of research', and some material in my study did indicate that certain researchers felt under considerable pressure to abandon work on the effects of social inequality and unemployment on health. Dilettantism would be rather a simplified picture of the way in which unemployment and health faded as an issue of interest to researchers. If there is dilettantism or opportunism, it appears to be institutional rather than individual.

Be that as it may, once the public-health doctors (and some ancillary groups such as health educators, health promoters, etc.) lost interest in the question of the health of the unemployed, there were no other groups waiting to take it up. There was no one to write press releases putting complex research into language more accessible to the popular media, or to explain that research to government officials or parliamentarians. And once it was no longer a political hot potato, 'unemployment and health' no longer motivated government departments to persuade scientifically respectable groups to devote resources to such a messy topic (Bartley, 1992).

I think that this analysis has some rather serious implications. This is because the type of process which my study described does not only go on in cases where the topic of inquiry is so obviously 'political'. The mechanism by which unemployment may damage health and increase mortality risk has been even now not been fully investigated (Bartley, 1994). Many people had great sympathy with the move to make medical research more relevant to policy questions. But questions for whom? If it appears that the scientific agenda is itself deeply affected by policy debate (and really it would be surprising if it were not so) then the question of public involvement, of the 'democratisation' of science policy is raised. There is a lot of research in medical sociology showing the value of the 'lay knowledge' of people who suffer from long-term chronic diseases to the understanding of disease processes. Similarly in epidemiology, communities possess an understanding of their own conditions and situations which research ignores at its peril. The attempt to make research more 'customer-friendly' could indeed represent an opportunity to improve both its relevance and its explanatory power in the field of public health and medical care. The notion that there is a 'pure science' with no allies – no 'customers' – needed to be questioned. An understanding of how this market works may also lead to ideas for change.

Who are the effective 'customers' for knowledge about health and illness? In the case of research on the health effects of unemployment, government departments were predominant. But there are others such as the pharmaceutical, food and tobacco industries whose interests are not necessarily in prevention, but whose 'market power' far outweighs that of the consumer. In putting forward knowledge-claims against such opposition, techniques in epidemiology become more and more complex. This in itself may result in a further alienation of consumers from the ideas, and a feeling that it is easy to lie with statistics, that no-one can be trusted. If money truly 'followed patients' under the reformed NHS, we would see an explosion in care for the elderly, in attempts to understand psychological illness and to overcome the problems of disability. For this to happen in practice, an institutional form needs to be found which makes those with the greatest health needs effective members of the knowledge-creating community.

### References

Acheson, D. (1968) 'Social and Medical Statistics: Some Remarks on Contemporary British Medical Statistics', *Journal of the Royal Statistical Society* (Series 4) 131: pp. 10–28.

Barnes, B. (1982) 'The Science-Technology Relationship: A Model and a Query', *Social Studies of Science*, 12: pp. 166–72.

Bartley, M. J. (1992) *Authorities and Partisans: The Debate on Unemployment and Health* (Edinburgh: Edinburgh University Press).

Bartley, M. J. (1994) 'The Relationship between Unemployment and Health: What are the Mechanisms?', *Journal of Epidemiology and Community Health*, 48: pp. 333–7.

Booth, T. (1988) *Developing Policy Research* (Aldershot: Avebury).

Brenner, M. H. (1979) 'Mortality and the National Economy', *The Lancet*, 15 September, pp. 568–73.

Downs, D. (1973) 'Up and Down with Ecology', in Bains J. (ed.), *Environmental Decay* (Boston, Mass.: Little, Brown).

Latour, B. (1987) *Science in Action* (Milton Keynes: Open University Press).

Lindblom, C. (1979) 'Still Muddling, not yet Through', *Public Administration Review*, 39: pp. 517–26.

McCarthy, M. (1986) *Campaigning for the Poor* (London: Croom Helm).

Manning, N. (ed.) (1985) *Social Problems and Welfare Ideology* (London: Gower).

Moser, K. A., Goldblatt, P., Fox, A. J. and Jones, D. R. (1987) 'Unemployment and Mortality: Comparison of the 1971 and 1981 Longitudinal Study Samples', *British Medical Journal*, 294: pp. 86–90.

Nelkin, D. (1975) 'The Political Impact of Technical Expertise', *Social Studies of Science*, 5: pp. 35–54.

Richardson, J. J. and Jordan, A. G. (1979) *Governing under Pressure* (Oxford: Martin Robertson).

Rein, M. (1980) 'Interplay between Social Science and Social Policy', *International Social Science Journal*, 32: pp. 361–8

Rein, M. (1980) *From Policy to Practice* (New York: M. E. Sharpe).

Spector, M. and Kitsuse J. I. (1977) *Constructing Social Problems* (Menlo Park, CA: Cummings).

Tizard, B. (1990) 'Research and Policy: Is there a Link?' *The Psychologist*, 10: pp. 435–40.

Weiss, C. (1979) 'The Many Meanings of Research Utilisation', *Public Administration Review*, 39: pp. 426–32.

# 3 How (and How Not) to Design Research to Inform Policy-making

Ray Pawson and Nicholas Tilley

Imagine, if you will, a senior police officer or policy adviser reading the following conclusion to a review of some twenty publicly funded professional evaluations of the effectiveness of community policing experiments:

> The question is, is it (community policing) more than rhetoric? There are ample examples of failed experiments, and huge American cities where the whole concept has gone awry. On the other hand, there is evidence in many evaluations that a public hungry for attention has a great deal to tell the police and are grateful for the opportunity to do so. (Skogan, 1992).

What is the likely reaction to this? What is to be made of it? What has been learnt so far? There are failed experiments and non-failed experiments. So what? Why should a series of evaluation studies be funded at the taxpayer's expense if this is the conclusion? Is the police officer or policy adviser any wit the wiser following a series of studies ending up here?

Our sympathies are entirely with any exasperation felt and robustly expressed. They are emphatically *not* with the social scientists whinnying on with excuses about the technical difficulties and uncertainties of the work. *Nor* are they with the more-research-is-needed chorus, if more research will merely mean more of the same.

Those commissioning evaluations want them so that their policy-making can be better informed. Presumably the reason for bringing in social scientists is to avoid overblown self-serving assessments, which committed practitioners are apt to construct, accounts which are all too liable to collapse at the first critical prod.

We ask three questions in this chapter. First, why do the supposedly most rigorous social science evaluations often produce such desperately disappointing results? Second, is there any alternative to endless

34

uncertainty and equivocation on the one hand and spurious success stories on the other? Third, can evaluation play a progressive part in taking policy and understanding forward?

We start with the bad news and then move on, in due course, to what we hope is the good.

## WHY 'RIGOROUS' SOCIAL SCIENCE EVALUATIONS FAIL

Quasi-experimentation marks the current orthodoxy over high-grade social scientific evaluation. It is shown diagrammatically in Figure 3.1. Its basic logic is desperately simple, and disarmingly familiar to us all. Take two more or less matched groups (if they are really matched through random allocation, you can call it real experimentation; 'quasi-ness' following from the impracticality of this in many cases). Treat one group but not the other. Measure both groups before and after the treatment of the one. Compare the changes in the treated and untreated groups, and, hey presto!, you have a measure of impact. The senior police officer, policy adviser and social scientist are at one in appreciating the beauty of the design. We all are. At one level, it has become an icon of the scientific way of evaluation (Cook and Campbell, 1979), at another it embodies the common-sense reasoning wrapped into advertising campaigns telling us that Washo is superior to Sudz.

It will be necessary to take a brief excursion into the philosophy of the social sciences to explain why quasi-experimentation cannot deliver on its initial promise. However, the point to be made has immediate practical consequences, and to illustrate the argument one of those community policing studies included in the overview, whose conclusion we have

| | Pre-test | Treatment applied | Post-test |
|---|---|---|---|
| Experimental group | $O_1$ | $X$ | $O_2$ |
| Control group | $O_1$ | | $O_2$ |

FIGURE 3.1  *The classic experimental design*

quoted, will be looked at in some detail. We examine Trevor Bennett's British study (Bennett, 1989, 1991), because it is, as we shall see, a masterpiece of its kind.[1]

There are two ways of looking at causation: the successionist and the generative (Harré 1972). The *successionist* looks at causation 'externally'. Cause simply describes constant conjunctions between events. The action of billiard balls is archetypally describable in these terms. We can observe regularity of cause and effect as one ball collides with another and forces it to move. The *generative* conception of causation, or, as it is sometimes called, the *realist* notion, sees the matter of causation 'internally'. Cause describes the *transformative potential* of phenomena. Gunpowder can serve as a standard example here. Its potential to explode describes powers which inhere in its chemical composition.

Quasi-experimentation is uncompromisingly successionist. Its aim is to establish the causal conjunction between events by so organising observation and measurement that we can find whether $X$, our intervention, is really followed by $Y$, its effect.

The quasi-experimentalist tries to cancel out differences between subjects by coming as close as possible to their random allocation to 'treatment' and 'non-treatment' conditions. This supposedly ensures that the programme, and only the programme, could impact on the outcome. In field experiments this can be done only approximately since often entire localities are taken as experimental and control groups. In Bennett's study of community policing, in fact, two experimental areas, one in London and the other in Birmingham, were adopted, and then a number of non-treatment control locations were selected. All the areas chosen were expected to show high levels of fear of crime on the basis of high recorded crime rates and 'visual indicators' of disorder such as graffiti, broken windows, criminal damage and litter. Cleverly, Bennett created 'composite control areas' for each of his experimental ones, to try to make certain that particular, chance local events did not determine the comparison between changes in them and in the experimental areas.

Once experimental and control areas have been identified, the procedure is straightforward. Make measurements from both before and after intervention and compare. Bennett surveyed a sample of residents from the experimental and control areas, asking questions about fear of crime, experience of crime and encounters with the police.

Following the best standard practice, Bennett also checked that the programme had been properly implemented. He did so by arranging measurements of 'contact rate'. Half the eligible London households had been contacted within 6 months, whilst the same proportion was contacted within 8 months in Birmingham. Ultimately, over the 12 months of the experiment, 88 per cent of the Birmingham and 87 per cent of the London households were contacted. On average, at least one police officer was in the area for 10.6 hours each day in Birmingham and for 10.4 hours in London. There were no police officers present for only 2 days in the Birmingham, and 11 in the London experimental area. On the basis of this it is concluded that 'the main programme elements were implemented effectively and constitute a programme capable of being evaluated in terms of its outcome effectiveness' (Bennett, 1991, p. 6).

Bennett came up with a mixed bag of conclusions. His major concern was with *fear of crime*, since some American studies had arrived at results suggesting that police patrols could reduce this. In fact, it had *not* gone down in Bennett's experimental areas. Secondary findings included the following:

(1)  The programme was noticed. Thus, the percentage of residents who 'know some police officer by name or sight' increased by 35 percentage points (from 15 to 50) in the Birmingham and by 20 (from 12 to 32) in the London experimental area. This contrasts with an increase by only 3 percentage points (from 10 to 13) in the Birmingham control and a decrease of four (from 21 to 17) in the London control area. There was an increase by 34 percentage points of those in the Birmingham experimental area who had 'seen a police officer in the past two weeks', though no change in this in the experimental area in London.   (Bennett, 1991, p. 6)

(2)  Actual changes in 'rates of criminal victimisation', as Bennett expected, did not vary between experimental and control areas. (Bennett, 1991, p. 7)

(3)  One aspect of 'perceptions of the area', namely 'satisfaction with area', showed statistically significant improvement in the Birmingham experimental area, and another aspect, 'sense of community', did so in London.   (Bennett, 1991, pp. 9–10)

(4)  With regard to 'informal social control practices', the Birmingham experimental group evidenced positive change in 'control of crime' through 'taking action in response to burglary' and 'asking neighbours to watch property when away', whilst the London experimental sample registered improvement only in the latter.   (Bennett, 1991, p. 10)

(5)   'Satisfaction' and 'contact' with the police improved substantially in both experimental areas.   (Bennett, 1991, p. 11)

So, there we have it, a rigorous design, followed painstakingly, producing, as far as we are concerned, some trustworthy results. What is wrong with this? From the policy-maker's perspective quite a lot. Nothing much follows at all so far as policing practices go. We are left in the dark about whether, where or how we might take community policing forward. Especially in the light of the results of other studies surveyed by Skogan, the action implications are a blur. No generalisable conclusions are forthcoming. No progression is evident. It is hard to see that previous uncertainties have been lessened or that a future programme to reduce remaining uncertainties is suggested. What we have are the typically mixed results from a one-off experiment, produced, it should be added, by a technically astute and experienced researcher at an elite academic institution. There is nothing cumulative about the study's achievements.

Thus we come to our first key question: *What is it about quasi-experimental evaluation which leads even the very best of it to yield so little?* The central problem lies in the deficient and defective conception of the programme which is built into the methodology. By this we mean that the quasi-experimental method itself smuggles in a particular set of understandings about what programmes are and how they work. We look first at programme deliverers and then at programme recipients.

From the point of view of those delivering the programme, it is reduced to a set of mechanical operations – contacts with the public, and days and average hours on the estate. This is a stark description of what is likely to be rather more complex and multifaceted. In practice, the programme, it transpires, was indeed rather more than what is suggested in the minimal measured features. A range of activities other than mere contact were encouraged, including leafleting, counselling, problem identification, monitoring actions taken, offering security advice and so on. Most significantly, 'beat officers were encouraged to manage their daily schedules as much as possible and to devise methods of achieving their own and team objectives' (Bennett, 1989, p. 30). This is highly suggestive of implementation differences which may well explain some of the London/Birmingham variations in outcome patterns noted earlier.

Our complaint here, however, is not merely the technical one that we have uncovered a mite of unconsidered variation within the design. Our point is that programmes are the products of skilled action by human agents, not reducible to the 'facticity' of a given event. It is not programmes that 'work' as such, but the practitioners' attempt to change the reasoning processes of their subjects. It is not contact patrols that 'work' as such, but something about the *character* of the contact. Quasi-experimentation gazes past these vital issues, since the experimental/control comparison, which is at the heart of the logic, demands we see the programme as a kind of binary dosage which is simply 'present' or 'absent'.

Let us turn to the other side of the equation, switching attention from the deliverers of the programme to its recipients. The quasi-experimental conception is again deficient. Communities clearly differ. They also have attributes that are not reducible to those of the individual members. These include cultures (for example religious beliefs), structures (for example employment patterns), and relationships (for example contacts between ethnic groups). A particular programme will only 'work' if the community conditions into which it is inserted are conducive to its operation, as it is implemented. Quasi-experimentation's method of random allocation, or efforts to mimic it as closely as possible, represent an endeavour to cancel out difference, to find out whether a programme will work without the added advantage of special conditions liable to enable it to do so. This is absurd. It is an effort to write out what is essential to a programme – social conditions favourable to its success. These are of critical importance to sensible evaluation, and the policy-maker (and for that matter the academic, though perhaps for other reasons) needs to know about them. Making no attempt to identify especially conducive conditions and in fact ensuring that the general and, therefore, the unconducive are fully written into the programme almost guarantees the mixed results we characteristically find.

In the case of Bennett's study, we learn virtually nothing of the communities acting either as experimental sites or as controls. Hence, the issue of what might operate to facilitate or impede effectiveness of the programmes is not addressed. The design makes it irrelevant, so its exclusion is neither surprising nor culpable. All we know is that the experimental 'estates' are small (of about 2000 households), well-bounded, that they had high crime rates and that there were similar amounts of graffiti and litter. We know nothing of the character of the community into which the community policing experiment was introduced. Variations in levels of interaction, internal divisions on the basis of age or race, class relations, rates of unemployment, isolation or otherwise from the city centre, population turnover and so on are not considered, but in a fairly obvious way mark differences in community which may inform how a social programme is received. We know even less of the 'control' estates. Indeed, whilst the device of using unreal 'composite' groups is excellent in quasi-experimental terms, by our lights it reveals a crucial weakness since particular communities and events in them will make a difference.

*Our argument is that precisely what needs to be understood is what it is about given communities which will facilitate the effectiveness of a programme!* And this is what is written out.

Moreover, the one community feature we do learn of in regard to the experimental communities is overlooked in the analysis. Initial 'level of satisfaction' with area rates 1.84 in Birmingham, but only 1.54 in London. 'Sense of community' rates 1.96 in Birmingham, but 1.71 in London. These 10–20 per cent differences are indicative of real differences in the estates and presumably stem from such collective factors as social and ethnic divisions, amounts of community and street activity, levels of friendship and kinship ties, turnover and tradition and so on. Bennett, however, views these scores as input variables with an eye to whether they change. But it is just these sorts of differences, combined perhaps with implementation differences, which may explain whether a programme works. For instance, looking back at the basic results, we note the apparently higher rate at which the programme was 'experienced' in Birmingham than in London (Bennett, 1991, p. 6 ). The extent to which an officer is 'seen' on the streets depends, somewhat self-evidently, on the amount of street activity in the community. This is one of several such matters neither commented on nor considered in Bennett's own study, since his method directs him away from it.

There is little doubt that quasi-experimentation attends to many problems in 'lay' evaluation. In the latter, self-interest, combined with an uncritical or very selectively critical attention to evidence, has undermined the value of much evaluation work. The aspiration to set up sophisticated experiments enabling the evidence to speak for itself was, in its way, quite admirable. It promised policy-makers more reliable judgements on the effectiveness of programmes, on the basis of which decisions could be made not on prejudice but on facts. A very great deal of money flowed into the coffers of the quasi-experimental evaluator as a consequence of this promise.

We certainly share the quasi-experimentalist's aspiration to rescue evaluation from prejudice and to set it on as secure as possible a social scientific basis. The previous arguments should not be understood as yet another round of the tiresome 'critiques of positivism'. What we have argued does not require the leap into supposing that the fate of social programmes is merely part of the 'power play', or simply 'constituted in discourse', or otherwise rendered incapable of empirical research. We wish to be attentive to the policy-maker's concerns for messages which are useful for rational decision-making. The next and more positive part of the paper will try to show how a generative account of causality, contained in scientific realism, can be built into social-scientific evaluation. We shall argue that this can produce much more useful results than those found in quasi-experimentation with its incorporation of successionist thinking.


## AN ALTERNATIVE TO QUASI-EXPERIMENTATION: SCIENTIFIC REALISM TO THE RESCUE

At the heart of the alternative approach to evaluation we wish to promote here is attention to precisely those points at which the quasi-experimentalist fails (see also Pawson, 1989; Pawson and Tilley, 1992). There are three interlinked ingredients to the scientific realist evaluation methodology we are advocating: 'mechanism', 'context' and 'outcome pattern'.

### Mechanism

Mechanism questions ask what it is about a social programme which is expected to have an effect. Whereas quasi-experimentation treats what is done as an independent variable which may (or may not) be followed by a dependent variable, scientific realism treats what is done as a vehicle to release a causal power which can change a situation. On first hearing, this may sound a bit abstract. Let us take an example to clarify what is being said. Consider property marking. Property marking does not physically prevent anything from being stolen. An item is not directly protected by it. The scientific realist question is 'what is it about property marking which might lead it to cause a reduction in theft?', and this produces hypotheses like Laycock's (1992) that what property marking does is to alert prospective burglars to the increased risks attendant to their 'working' in a particular area. With regard to community policing, exactly the same sort of question arises: what is it about community patrols which might lead them to cause a reduction in fear of crime, in crime rates, improved community spirit and so on? It is precisely this question which is not asked in Bennett's piece, except as an afterthought. It is not built into the evaluation proper. Bennett (1991, p. 2) thus refers in passing to Maxfield's (1987) suggestion that the police may have a role in reducing fear by better apprising the public of the real risks of victimisation. This mechanism of 'improved understanding', which might have been built into both the community patrols and their evaluation, is disregarded. A second potential mechanism referred to in passing by Bennett relates to ways in which a community's confidence that it can resist crime might be enhanced, but again this receives no attention in the method-driven evaluation. By contrast, the account of the patrols incorporated into the evaluation proper is, as we have seen, stark and mechanical. It is poorly textured and fails to consider explicitly how what was planned and done might impact on the problems supposedly addressed by the programme.

## Context

Context questions ask about the conditions needed for a mechanism to operate. The context may either inhibit the working of mechanisms or facilitate them. It does not make sense to ask whether something works without specifying the conditions for its doing so. Consider our earlier example of gunpowder. Gunpowder has the casual potential to explode. It only does so, however, if the conditions are right. It needs to be dry, in a confined space, etc. In just the same way the causal mechanisms potentially released in social programmes can only function in conditions conducive to their operation. Think again of the example of property marking. Supposing that its deterrent effect does indeed work through the burglars' recalculation of risk, in order for this potential to be released in a particular community Laycock (1992) suggests that there needs to be extensive publicity (to be received by prospective offenders) and there must also be a very high take-up rate (some 70 per cent were property marked in her study area). Only in these conditions will the burglar effectively be deterred. Moreover, periodic injections of publicity will be needed if the effect is to be maintained. In the case of community policing, we cannot specify context without first understanding mechanisms which may be released. Take Bennett's reference to increased community confidence. We can speculate that contextual needs for such a mechanism to operate might include the present lack of such confidence, a sufficiently stable population for community institutions to crystallise, the absence of powerful oppositional groups with credible alternative messages, a community not already so divided that a new police initiative could itself become a source of friction, and so on. In the event, as we showed above, we learn very little of the nature of the community contexts into which the community policing programme was inserted and, furthermore, this was not related to what was done there and how it might impact on the potential operation of mechanisms and their ultimate effects.

It needs to be stressed that context and mechanism are but two sides of the same coin. No mechanism operates in a vacuum. Any mechanism is always contextually conditioned. In attempting to achieve a given end, in deciding what mechanism to attempt to trigger, the policy-maker and practitioner clearly cannot sensibly disregard context.

## Outcome Pattern

The term 'outcome pattern' means exactly what it says. The outcomes of a programme are generally more complex than simply a matter of a tick or a cross, indicating success or failure. Instead, there will be a range of outcomes, often following from both internal contextual variation and the releasing of several mechanisms. In the case of the policing patrol experiment, Bennett notes a range of outcomes. Consider, in particular, the variation between the apparent experience of the programme in London and Birmingham, especially the differing rates of change in levels of 'police officer recognition' (which receives no discussion in Bennett). What we need is to relate such outcome-pattern variations to the contextually determined operation of causal mechanisms released by the programme. Explanations are incomplete unless they connect 'mechanism' to 'context' to 'outcome'. We might hazard a 'guess', for example, that the potential for change accruing from community contact is structured according to different work/travel patterns in the capital and regional urban areas. Such speculation is not possible in the case of Bennett's study. We simply lack the data to do so.

Let us take instead another recent example, where a very sensitive study of context and mechanism makes sense of a quite complex outcome pattern. This piece of work was not construed in scientific realist terms, indeed it includes some quasi-experimental aspects. Nevertheless, it possesses all the ingredients of a realist explanation and constitutes, we submit, a superior form of evaluation.

Hope and Foster (1991) examined patterns of change in an English public housing estate. The 'mechanisms' identified in their study relate to social control, physical vulnerability and social mix. They were 'fired' though management changes, a programme of refurbishment and housing allocation practices. The 'context' was one of an unpopular estate with a poor reputation, with a housing stock comprising a mix of two-storey terraced housing, high-rise and medium-rise blocks of flats with a given age and household structure distribution within the estate. The 'patterned outcomes' included increased overall levels of criminality, a changed geographic distribution of crime within the estate, and higher overall levels of social control and decreased fear of crime. The 'model' developed shows how the causal forces identified combined and interacted to produce the complex and contradictory outcomes described. Refurbished houses became more popular, reducing turnover of tenants, increasing desirability, reducing physical vulnerability and increasing confidence of residents. There, crime went down. Gradual reallocation of elderly residents from tower blocks (where they had comprised 42 per cent of the residents) to sheltered smaller blocks led to a changed composition of the tower blocks. More poor, non-family, formerly homeless young people moved in, including 'some recently released from prison or institutional care'. Criminally inclined newcomers provided a route into more serious crime for local young gang members. Crime and predation of the weak and recently arrived increased, especially within the tower blocks. Amongst residents of the area of terraced housing which had not yet been refurbished, morale increased, with management more responsive to residents and plans for physical improvements. Hope and Foster summarised their explanation as follows, 'In this particular configuration of events, environmental design modifications and improvement in management quality (including tenant involvement) interacted with changes in tenant turnover and allocation to the estate. Their combined effect was to alter the internal "culture" of the estate to produce an intensification both of social control and criminality which found expression in differences between parts of the estate and various groups of tenants' (p. 24).

Figure 3.2 shows diagrammatically how we 'deconstruct' the notion of an 'external programme' into a relationship between mechanism, context and outcome pattern. What produces the outcome pattern is not the intervention itself, but the way it releases causal powers effecting change.

It should be noted here that at its most general what is being examined in *all* evaluation studies is planned social change. What the researcher is trying to work through are the ways in which by doing $X$, the intervention, in context, $C$, causal mechanisms, $M$, are fired, which lead to a

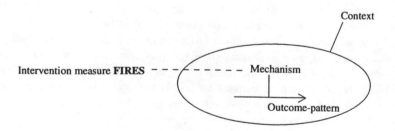

FIGURE 3.2    *Scientific-realist evaluation*

pattern of intended (and unintended) outcomes, *O*. The crime prevention evaluation discussed here is merely one special case of this universal evaluation task.

Before pulling together lessons of the arguments for evaluation and policy development, let us turn to one more example, this time a study in which a tentative effort has been made to undertake an evaluation in the scientific realist terms outlined here. We also draw out the way in which scientific-realist evaluation has direction and can lead to progressively more refined policy and understanding. The study (Tilley, 1993) was an evaluation of the seemingly banal and obvious matter of closed circuit television (CCTV) in car parks.

## THE PROGRESSIVE CHARACTER OF SCIENTIFIC REALIST EVALUATION: A CASE STUDY OF CCTV IN CAR PARKS

Just as there is nothing about police patrols which intrinsically reduces fear of crime, so too there is nothing about CCTV in car parks which intrinsically inhibits car crime. It certainly does not create a physical barrier making cars impenetrable. The scientific realist begins by pondering the rather different mechanisms through which CCTV may, nevertheless, lead to a reduction of car crimes and the contexts needed if these potentials are to be realised. We begin with *mechanisms*:

(1) *The 'caught-in-the act' mechanism.* CCTV could reduce car crime by making it more likely that *present offenders* will be caught, stopped, removed, punished and deterred.

(2) *The 'you've been framed' mechanism.* CCTV could reduce car crime by deterring *potential offenders* who will not wish to risk apprehension and conviction by the evidence captured on videotape or observed by an operator on a screen on which their behaviour is shown.

(3) *The 'nosey parker' mechanism.* The presence of CCTV may lead to increases in usage of car parks, as drivers feel less at risk of victimisation. Increased usage could then enhance natural surveillance which may deter potential offenders, who feel they are at increased risk of apprehension in the course of criminal behaviour.

(4) *The 'effective deployment' mechanism.* CCTV may facilitate the effective deployment of security staff/police officers towards areas where suspicious behaviour is occurring. They then act as a visible presence which might deter potential offenders. They may also apprehend actual offenders red-handed and muzzle their criminal behaviour.

(5) *The 'publicity (general)' mechanism.* Publicity given to CCTV and to its usage in catching offenders may be received by potential offenders, who are then led to avoid the increased risk they believe to be associated with committing car crimes in CCTV-covered car parks. The perceived risks of offending exceed the perceived benefits, and offending either ceases or is displaced by place or offence.

(6) *The 'publicity (specific)' mechanism.* CCTV, and signs indicating that it is in operation could symbolise efforts to take crime seriously and to reduce it. The potential offender may then perceive crime to be more difficult or risky and is deterred.

(7) *The 'time for crime' mechanism.* Those car crimes which can be completed in a very short space of time may decline less than those which take more time, as the offender calculates the time taken for police or security officers to come or the probability that panning cameras will focus in on him/her.

(8) *The 'memory jogging' mechanism.* CCTV and notices indicating that it is in operation may remind drivers that their cars are vulnerable, and they may thereby be prompted to take greater care to lock them, to operate any security devices, and to remove easily stolen items from view.

(9) *The 'appeal to the cautious' mechanism.* It might be that cautious drivers, who are sensitive to the possibility that their cars may be vulnerable and are habitual users of various security devices, use and fill those car parks with CCTV and thereby drive out those who are more careless, whose vulnerable cars are stolen from elsewhere.

It is clearly possible that more than one of these mechanisms may operate simultaneously. Which (if any) mechanisms are fired turns on the context in which CCTV is installed, and this varies widely. Consider the following:

(i) *The 'criminal clustering' context.* A given rate of car crime may result from widely differing prevalences of offending. For example if there are 1000 incidents per annum, this may be by anything from a single (very busy) offender to as many as 1000 offenders (or still more if they operate in groups). A mechanism leading to disablement of the offender (as in (1) above) holds potential promise according to the offender–offence ratio.

(ii) *The 'style of usage' context.* A long-stay car park may have an enormous influx of vehicles early in the morning when it becomes full up. It may then empty between five and six in the evening. If the dominant CCTV-fired mechanism turns out to be increased confidence and usage (as in (3) above) then this will have little impact, because the pattern of usage is already high with little movement, dictated by working hours not fear of crime. If, however, the car park is little used, but with a very high per-user car-crime rate then the increased usage mechanism may lead to an overall increase in numbers of crimes but a decreased rate per user.

(iii) *The 'lie of the land' context.* Cars parked in the CCTV blind spots in car parks will be more vulnerable if the mechanism is increased chances of apprehension through evidence on videotape (as in (2) above), but not if it is through changed attributes/security behaviour of customers (as in (8) or (9) above).

(iv) *The 'alternative targets' context.* The local patterns of motivation of offenders, together with the availability of alternative targets of car crime, furnish aspects of the wider context for displacement to car crimes elsewhere, whatever crime reduction mechanisms may be fired by CCTV in the specific context of a given car park.

(v) *The 'resources' context.* In an isolated car park with no security staff and the police at some distance away, the deployment of security staff/police as a mobile and flexible resource to deter car crime (as in (4) above) is not possible.

Actual outcome patterns will follow from the working through of the range of potential mechanisms whose functioning is rendered possible by contexts conducive to their operation. The ideal empirical evaluation would collect 'before' and 'after' data to give an overall picture of outcomes as in the standard quasi-experimental approach. Thereafter, much more attention would be paid to gaining data which tapped mechanism and contextual variation. Thus the standard scientific-realist data matrix would make comparisons of variation in outcome patterns across groups, but those groups would not be the standard experimental-versus-control-group comparison. Instead they would be defined by the mechanism/ context framework. One would need to run a systematic range of comparisons across a series of studies to understand which combination of context and mechanism in the above model works best.

In the work described here this was not possible. The evaluation was conducted *post hoc*. The schemes were already in place, they were installed in an uncoordinated fashion and thus only routinely collected data were at hand. In these circumstances, the best that could be done was to reconstruct certain items of data which cast doubt on the probability of some mechanisms and furnished some support for the possibility that others were operating.

In the six sites for the research, reductions in car crime were generally found following installation of CCTV, though where data were available for a number of years the impact was found to fade over time. It was also found that convictions attributable to CCTV operation were negligible. In only one car park were claims made that this had occurred at all, and even then it was infrequent. Screens showing what the cameras could pick up were watched conscientiously; operators of the system appeared competent at manipulating the cameras; videotapes with time and date superimposed were kept; and good, supportive relations with the police were maintained. In all but one car park, CCTV had been installed alongside other complementary measures. For example, in one, uniformed security guards were deployed on the basis of suspicious activity observed on the screen. In another, the local beat police officer suggested to the children at a school adjacent to the car park that they could be seen and individually identified using the CCTV system. In a third, the system was given substantial publicity in the local press. Visits to the sites and to the control rooms revealed that the cameras were relatively unresponsive. At wide angle very little detail could be discerned, certainly not sufficient to be sure in most cases that an offence was being committed. Homing in on what might be a criminal act took more time then would be needed for the skilled car criminal to enter a car. Even then, the image was rarely sharp enough to make the perpetrator recognisable. In one car park, where the camera was turned at night to the roof of the leisure centre attached to the car park in response to break-ins through it, the number and proportion of car crimes during those hours increased.

This is a highly summarised version of what, in the first place, had to be a rough and ready overview. However, even data collected on such a piecemeal basis begin to suggest a few judgements about mechanisms and contexts which make good sense of the outcome patterns described, though it leaves more than one possibility open.

To put it starkly, CCTV does not remove offenders by catching them. It does not need to have that degree of technical sophistication to make offenders recognisable to have an effect. It does seem that prospective offenders are (at least for a while) deterred by the (mistaken) notion that risk is increased by the operation of CCTV. Most else remains unclear. It does so, so to speak, because the scientific realism entered too late. That which would need to be measured could not be reconstructed after the event with the data available. Consider, for example, the possibility that the 'appeal to the cautious' mechanism may play a part in certain contexts. In relation to this, a survey of cars parked before and after installation of CCTV, together with signs indicating its operation, could ascertain changes in numbers left locked and in the extent to which attractive goods were left on display. This could be complemented with data on changing patterns of thefts from cars, including the sorts of items stolen from them and where they were in the car.

One step beyond what is achieved in the study briefly summarised here would thus be simply to think through potential mechanisms, contexts and outcome patterns in advance and to put in place those necessary measurement arrangements ahead of scheme implementation, to enable appropriate 'before' measures. It is by no means transparent at first sight that looking inside parked cars would comprise part of the evaluation process. That needs early thought and pre-planning. The same would go for measures of the sites of car crimes suggested by the *you've been framed* mechanism in the *lie of the land* context.

It is not necessary, of course, that a single set of mechanism/context relations be postulated. Enough has been said to show that such an aspiration would be misplaced both for CCTV in car parks and, we would suggest, for most other programmes also. There is scope for more refined arbitration between alternative mechanisms, for measurement of respective contributions where more than one is operative, and for developing more sophisticated understandings of the contexts needed for the operation of mechanisms. The study described here is, thus, very much a first step. It can be conceived as a precursor to a series of iterated studies. The remaining empirical uncertainties will not be disposed of at a stroke. They can, though, be reduced and at the same time, the relationship between the mechanisms and their contextual conditions begin to be formalised.

There is, we can see, a direction to the initial scientific-realist evaluation of CCTV and car crime. It also helps bring out the potential of the method more generally. What we have so far are essentially *ad hoc* lists of mechanisms and contexts. These we see as useful as a starting point for further research. What is needed is *movement towards a theoretically specified set of mechanisms and their required contexts which would enable* (ceteris paribus) *predictions to be made about outcome patterns.*

Tilley (1993) can be seen, then, as a first step in what could be a progressive research programme, where we move from crudely articulated and partially evaluated models toward more fully articulated, more thoroughly tested ones. Our understanding of CCTV and car park crime in this way can be improved through a *series* of evaluation studies. Rather than the set of inconsistent and mysterious results of repeated quasi-experimental evaluations (found in regard to community policing) the scene is set for cumulative understanding of how and where CCTV can play a part (and for how long) in reducing crime in car parks. This should not only be of interest to the academic evaluator, but also to the practitioner wishing to learn how to effect a particular piece of social change.

## CONCLUSIONS AND IMPLICATIONS

This has been a tale of two evaluation methods: the quasi-experimentalist and the scientific realist. Why should those concerned with policy care about methodology? The policy-maker needs to be clear about the rationale for evaluation. The questions we assume the polity are interested in when commissioning evaluation are more or less as follows:

(a) Has a given problem at a specific time and place been cracked? For example, 'Has the problem of burglary on Beebop Estate been solved?'

(b) Is it worth continuing to devote resources to a particular programme? For example, 'Should we continue to pay £100 000 per annum into this programme to contain burglary on Beebop Estate?

(c) What lessons for future policy and practice can be picked up from this programme? For example, 'Should the programme on Beebop Estate be extended to other estates, indeed, should it be incorporated (as a cost-effective problem solution) into national policy?'

(d)   What political pay-off is there from publicising this programme? For example, 'Can the minister or councillor plausibly boast about the burglary reduction work on Beebop Estate as a major achievement of the programme?'

Scientific realism is helpful in informing answers to all these questions (yes, even the fourth!). It should be clear that we are sceptical of the power of quasi-experimental evaluations, though some of their basic facets, such as before-and-after comparison, will provide materials useful in answering (a). As an aside, we note that quasi-experimental evaluations are an advance on lay evaluations since the latter may be superficially attractive in feeding welcome news for question (d), but are liable to be very misleading on (a), (b) and (c). Scientific realist evaluation outstrips all rivals in being helpful in regard to answers to all these questions. Its central focus is on question (c). It should help clarify what we do and do not yet know of a field of action, and a series of studies should widen and deepen understanding. It should allow plausible answers to policy questions, giving suggestions that in specified context *C*, programme *P* will trigger causal mechanisms *M*, to produce outcome patterns *O*. It refuses to accept that panaceas are available. Social programmes operate in social contexts shaping their effects. This refusal to provide simple yes/no answers to policy questions may be unpalatable to some, but that is the price of realism. In the end, it promises more cost-effective and more appropriately targeted programmes. In answering (c), questions, (a), (b) and (d) are of course also addressed, for the scientific-realist approach homes in on what it is about what precisely is being done which has an effect in a given context: it gives answers thus to the question of whether the problem has been solved and the role of the programme (a), (b). In doing this it gives firmer grounds for claims made for credit (d). Finally, scientific-realist evaluation also meets Rosenbaum's (1988) famous requirement for us to 'open up the "black box" of community crime prevention' (or any other black box for that matter) by showing *how* programmes work.

There can, of course, be better and worse scientific-realist evaluations. The evaluator needs ideally to be in on the programme at the start. This is, in part, to help in the programme development, but above all to make sure that there is a *programme theory*, a notion that by doing *X* in the situation being confronted (context, *C*) causal mechanisms, $M_1 \ldots n$ may be fired with consequences including outcome patterns $O_1 \ldots n$. In our experience, practitioners tend to hold these ideas implicitly if sketchily. Most importantly from the point of view of the evaluation, this theory needs to be made explicit and to be built into the evaluation from the start in order to pinpoint appropriate 'before' measures. The evaluator needs to remain close to the programme to note changes in practice theory and in context to remain true to the programme.[2] The case study of CCTV in public car parks was, admittedly, limited by its *post hoc* character, though this was far from fatal to the enterprise. It illustrated also that there is no need to work with only one theory, and it would certainly not be necessary for the evaluator to be restricted to the practioners' theories, useful though these are likely to be in most cases.

It should be clear that whilst the examples used in this paper are all taken from the field of crime prevention, this is only because that is familiar territory to the authors. Our basic claim *that social initiatives only work if they fire the appropriate mechanism in the appropriate context* will apply, however, in all of the policy domains explored in this volume. This little epigram, after all, is but one instance of what is more commonly known in sociology as 'the duality of structure and agency'. In governmental and, perhaps more surprisingly, in academic circles, there is sometimes a bland acceptance that evaluators are mere technical underlabourers. As soon as one incorporates the notion that programmes are, in fact, attempts to engage in socially constrained choice-making, then the need for a sociologically informed, theory-driven approach becomes evident.

It is our view, if our arguments are correct, first that there are intrinsic weaknesses in quasi-experimental evaluation methods which will reveal themselves in whatever field a social programme is being evaluated and, second, that the strengths of the scientific-realist approach will be found generally to allow evaluations more progressively to inform policy development. Though, in Lakatos's terms (Lakatos, 1978), the quasi-experimental programme for evaluation may once have been progressive (over lay-participant evaluations), it has become degenerative, failing to yield new insights. We would like to think that there is something progressive about the scientific-realist approach sketched out here, which can better serve both the interests of the social scientist and those of the policy-maker.

### Notes

1.    We do not do full justice to all the subtleties in Bennett's study. We focus only on its overall logic and the way in which, despite sophistication in implementation, it cannot but fail. A more extensive critique is contained in the original conference paper 'OXO, Tide, Brand X, and New Improved Evaluation', available from the authors.

2.  The evaluator also needs ideally to retain some distance to avoid collusion with wishful thinking which may infect practitioners, though that, as they say, is another story.

# References

Bennett, T. (1989) 'Contact Patrols in Birmingham and London: An Evaluation of a Fear Reducing Strategy', report to the Home Office Research and Planning Unit.

Bennett, T. (1991) 'The Effectiveness of a Police-initiated Fear-reducing Strategy', *British Journal of Criminology*, 31: 1, pp. 1–14.

Cook, T. D. and Campbell, D. T. (1979) *Quasi-Experimentation* (Chicago: Rand McNally).

Harré, R. (1972) *The Philosophies of Science* (Oxford: Oxford University Press).

Hope, T. and Foster, J. (1991) 'Conflicting Forces: Changing the Dynamics of Crime and Community on a Problem Estate', presented at the British Criminology Conference, York.

Lakatos, I. (1978) *The Methodology of Scientific Research Programmes* (Cambridge: Cambridge University Press).

Laycock, G. (1992) 'Operation Identification, or The Power of Publicity', in Clarke, R. (ed.), *Situational Crime Prevention: Successful Case Studies* (New York: Harrow and Heston), pp. 230–8.

Maxfield, M. (1987) *Explaining Fear of Crime: Evidence from the 1984 British Crime Survey*, Research and Planning Unit Paper 34 (London: Home Office).

Pawson, R. (1989) *A Measure for Measures: A Manifesto for an Empirical Sociology* (London: Routledge).

Pawson, R. and Tilley, N. (1992) 'Re-evaluation: Rethinking Research on Corrections and Crime', *Yearbook of Correctional Education*, pp. 1–30.

Skogan, W. (1992) 'Community Policing in the United States', presented at the Paris Crime Reduction Conference.

Tilley, N. (1993) *Understanding Car Parks, Crime and CCTV: Evaluation Lessons from Safer Cities*, Crime Prevention Unit Paper 42 (London: Home Office).

# Part II
# Racism, Health and Policy Thinking

# 4 Naming Difference: Race-thinking, Common Sense and Sociology

## Bob Carter and Marci Green

The classification of people, events and experiences by 'race' remains something of an orthodoxy in sociology and social policy.[1] The belief in the value of 'race' categories is still ingrained in the approaches, content and methods of academic research, making comprehension of social actions and relations outside of a 'race' discourse difficult to develop. For decades, sociologists have proclaimed the importance of 'racial' matters in shaping institutional life and structuring social interaction: in our work we have recorded the nuances of 'racial' conciousness, the race-ist policies of governments and politicians, and the 'race' principles by which labour markets, housing markets and other distributive mechanisms of social resources have operated.

However, while sociologists have looked at this thing called 'race', less often have we questioned what has made 'race' a category for describing and analysing persons, events and social relations; rarely do we address a logic of classification whose terms, we contend, have limited the imagination. In this paper we argue that central to the process which maintains a 'race' discourse in sociology is the elision of common sense and sociological sense, that in matters of race-thinking sociologists have retreated from the precepts of the sociological project. To make this case, we first examine race thinking and suggest an alternative vocabulary. We then consider some of the processes, theoretical and practical, which keep race thinking in place, give it its common-sensibility, its persistent, taken-for-granted weight. Thirdly, we raise some methodological issues for sociology and social policy, particularly in an era witnessing the militant resurgence of a racialised politics of identity.

Race-thinking takes numerous forms. Its crudest version is expressed in the assumption that 'races' exist as biologically distinct phenotypical or genotypical groups, and that each 'race' has its own, exclusive, modes of being, conduct and consciousness. Once designated in this way, 'races' are then hierarchically valued.

Various writers (Barker, 1981; Gould, 1981; Fryer, 1984; Rich, 1986; Miles, 1989) have identified this version of race-thinking with 'scientific racism', a discourse popular in the eighteenth and nineteenth centuries, but one to which few, if any, contemporary sociologists would subscribe. This has not meant the abandonment of race-thinking by social researchers though, or the reliquishing of 'race' as a central category of sociological analysis. On the contrary, sociologists have been able to draw on a more compelling formulation, one that has allowed race-thinking to flourish and prosper. This is the version of race-thinking with a strong interactionist pedigree: to paraphrase W. I. Thomas, if we believe 'races' are real then they are real in their consequences; 'races' do not really exist but are real none the less. Absent from this conception are the explicit hierarchical valuations characteristic of 'scientific racism', but carried over from earlier versions of race-thinking are the habits of classification and representation of the Other in 'race' terms. 'Race' continues to be conceived as a social fact with the same explanatory and descriptive import as, for instance, social class.

A glance at some of the standard contemporary undergraduate sociology texts confirms this largely taken-for-granted nature of 'race' categories. These texts are significant because it is through them that students begin to think sociologically. Abercrombie *et al.* (1992), for example, use the language of 'race relations' in their discussion of changing patterns of immigration and they invoke the term 'racial' in their account of class and racism. These terms only make sense if one both attributes some ontological status to 'races' and assumes that 'race' classifications serve some explanatory function.

Bilton *et al.* (1991) have a section on 'race relations'. Their descriptions of 'racial' prejudice – 'the subordination of racial groups' – 'interracial' conflict and the larger theoretical question of the relationship between 'race' and social stratification consolidate the veiw that 'race' is a useful category of analysis. They do address some sociological perspectives on 'race' and inequality, but the processes by which 'race' has become a category of classification are not considered. Neither, for that matter, do they – or Abercrombie *et al.* – query the meaning of this thing called 'race' or what comprises the 'racial'. Even when critical of the biological bases of 'race' sociologists continue to talk of the problematic relationship between 'race' and class, relying on common-sense thinking around these concepts and so reaffirming the epistemological status of 'race' (see, for example, Lee and Newby, 1989, pp. 158–9).

Further, these introductory texts become an element in the race-making or racialising process, that 'dialectical process of signification'

(Miles, 1989, p. 75) whereby any human attribute, such as language, country of origin, religion, skin colour, is used to define and construct differentiated social collectivities (see also Husband, 1982 pp. 11–13). The attributes so signified vary historically, but all racialising instances share common features: as a representational process of defining an Other, they are essentially processes of boundary formation, accomplishing a key ideological inversion, the *naturalisation* of *social* relations.

Another contemporary variant buries its race-thinking within the vocabulary of culture and ethnicity; what, following Hall (1991), we might describe as cultural racism. Populations are distinguished from one another by virtue of their culture; each culture – or ethnic group – is claimed to have its own history and modes of conduct. The preference for cultural or 'ethnic' categories seems, in some ways, to signal an advance on race-thinking, since the commitment to biologically grounded theories of social behaviour can be abandoned. However, while sociologists acknowledge that cultural boundaries are elusive and non-discrete, the treatment of ethnic groups often implies a fixity present in 'race' discourses. Secondly, there is a sociological fashion for distinguishing between 'races' and 'ethnic' groups;[2] this is done on the grounds that colour signifies 'race' whilst linguistic, religious and national attributes are the principles of a constructed community and identity. The problem here is that since colour is 'physical', 'race' reappears once more rooted in nature; the social process by which colour comes to bear a self-evident visibility is obscured, allowing it to stand *naturally* as a signifier of 'race'. The production of colour as a regime of visibility (Foucault, 1979), as an apodictic basis for the study of social behaviour, is hidden, yet it is precisely this productive process that needs to be explored. In this sense 'race' operates at dual ideological levels, as a representation of social relations as 'race relations' and as a signifier that conceals its source in the social production of particular knowledges.

How are such knowledges reproduced? Essentially they are realised through specific practices: administrative, political and ideological. Let us give some examples. In Britain during the late 1940s and the 1950s, successive governments found themselves having to wrestle with what they defined, in the words of a 1950 Cabinet Working Party, as 'the problem of coloured Colonial immigration', the migration of black British subjects from Colonies and former Colonies to Britain (Carter *et al.* 1987). Why should this constitute a problem? After all, governments had been busily recruiting workers from Europe in sponsored schemes since 1947; by the end of 1950 over 73 000 European Voluntary Workers, as those recruited under these schemes were called, had settled in Britain (Kay and Miles,

1992). The issue, as Cabinet documents bluntly stated, was colour, and the essential Other-ness this was taken to signify, an Other-ness whose central axis was the unassimilability of black people to a British 'way of life'. Colour and the 'colour problem' came to form a particular regime of truth about black immigration, a discourse richly productive of 'knowledge' about black people.

This knowledge was constantly tested, refined, given greater coherence, by the numerous interdepartmental committees and working parties established to gather and orchestrate information about the 'colour problem'. The sources of this information were the continuous reports submitted by Employment Exchanges on the 'racial' employability of black workers and their suitability for menial and dirty jobs; by the Assistance Boards on the 'racial' proclivity of black people for scrounging; by the Ministry of Health on the various diseases likely to be visited upon the British people by 'coloured colonial' immigrants; by the Home Office and innumerable constabularies on the 'law and order' problem lurking beneath the skin of the internal Other. Together these reports not only provided the truth propositions – about black people and unemployment, about black people and slum housing, about black people and criminality – deemed necessary by politicians seeking to build a case for the legislative restriction of black immigration, but also gave 'race' a greater ontological weight and, in so doing, embedded its policy recommendation – keep them out – in a secure foundation of commonsensical and social scientific 'truth'. In such ways politicians and governments play a central part in racialising social relations, creating events as 'racial', constructing relations as 'race relations', and making policy on the basis of these. Social scientists occupy a key position in this process, advising governments about 'race relations' and generating 'race relations' research (which is different from research into racisms and their effects).

The connection between governments' racialisation of human subjects and social scientific practice is perhaps more visible in the United States. Research into the Americanization movement (Green, 1993) – a nation-building project around the turn of the century – sharply revealed the production of race-thinking and its use by social science. Working collectively, politicians, educators, civic and social reformers and early sociologists constructed official versions of the 'race' composition of America. One form in which this appeared was the 1911 Government Commission Reports on Immigration (US Commission on Immigration, 1911, Abstracts vols I and II),[3] in which a taxonomy of 64 'races' appeared. No single criterion designated 'race' membership but this did not deter the government or social scientists from the process of classification or from the larger project of proving that a 'race' presence threatened the survival of the nation. Survival, they argued, required pro- grammes of enforced assimilation of immigrants, particularly from south- ern and eastern Europe, and if they failed, then deportation and immigration controls were to be more vigorously pursued. While the Americanization movement dissipated in the early 1920s, it left a pro- found legacy: the construction of new 'race' identities, volumes of data on 'race' and employment, 'race' and crime, 'race' and education, 'race' and urban life – volumes consulted by subsequent generations of social scien- tists, historians, politicians, educationalists and 'race' activists in writing their histories of 'race relations' and founding their specialisms on 'race' and 'ethnicity' (see, particularly, Webster, 1992; Fields, 1990).

These examples are instructive. First, the repeated use by sociologists of official government statistics which use 'race' categories, maintains the value of 'race' classification in sociological research. Sociologists have continued to accept the analytical constituents of a 'race' discourse, using them to produce and re-produce accounts of 'race relations' in matters of housing, employment, health, education and identity formation. In other words, sociologists often use data derived from political decisions about what to record and in what terms.[4] These politically generated categories then appear as neutral, demographic variables and serve as the working tools rather than the subjects of sociological analysis.

These practices in turn are linked to an immediacy, an urgency, about race-problem-solving, which has induced sociologists to collude with the state in the formation of a 'race' discourse. Problem-solving has its place in sociology, and certainly the development of the discipline in the United States owes much to this approach. But a distinction has to be made between 'the problems', as social subjects understand and act on them, and 'the problems' as sociologists see them. Our evidence from the US and the UK suggests that the distinction has been ignored.

However, the relation between policy-makers and sociologists is not sufficient to explain the reproduction of race-thinking. Conceptual confu- sion about the social facticity of 'race' carries its own responsibilities. For example, sociologists have claimed that 'race' identities and relations are powerful agents in structuring consciousness and conduct. Since human subjects experience these identities and relations as real, such 'facts', it is argued, cannot be ignored and are, therefore, the proper subject matter of sociology.

The belief that 'races' exist has obvious consequences for social action: for instance, physical violence towards those perceived to be of another 'race', to keep them in their place, to compel them to go somewhere else or even to eliminate them; legislation to prevent 'races' mixing or to prevent 'members' of one 'race' from discriminating against those of another; patterns of discrimination and exclusion. Further, these are real, material consequences, part of the world as it is, shaping our perceptions of social reality as it is experienced at the level of everyday life. In contemporary Britain, it *is* frequently black people who occupy low-paid, low-status jobs, who form the longest queues at the airport passport control, who are overwhelmingly the target of racist attacks. It does not follow from any of this, though, either that 'races' exist, as opposed to a belief in their existence carrying consequences for social action, or that 'race' is a useful analytical category, as opposed to an ideological construct.

Recognising that the idea of 'race' is a constituent element in everyday common sense, then, does not entail importing 'race' as an analytical concept into sociology and according it a *sui generis* reality. On the contrary, any account of the social processes of discrimination and exclusion using the transhistorical, asocial, common sense category 'race' must forfeit any claim to be regarded as sociological.

Bauman (1992) has commented on the relationship between sociological sense and common sense. Sociologists, he points out, have to start with daily life (the life world) and so are always bound to remain on both sides of the experience they try to interpret, inside and outside at the same time. However, Bauman suggests that there are seminal differences between common sense and sociology, two of which are pertinent to our argument in this paper.

First, sociologists are obliged to use responsible speech, that is define rigorously and with precision the terms and concepts they employ to make sense of society; it would be our contention that race-thinking avoids responsible speech because 'race' has no real world referent.

Second, since the power of common sense partly depends on the self-evident power of its precepts, sociologists are obliged to defamiliarise the familiar, to develop a critique of everyday life and the ways in which its routine nature informs our common sense while being informed by it; race-thinking, transhistorical and a-sociological, is the reinstatement of the familiar in sociology. Working within the vocabulary of the 'race' familiar, we would be hard put to comment sociologically upon, for instance, the recent news that after 28 years of 'being a Jew', Ian Rosenthal became Jonathan Bradley, an Arab (*Guardian*, 15 March 1993, pp. 10–11); or to make sociological sense of the adoption advert asking for foster parents for two young boys – Mark and Michael – 'who are African Caribbean and white English' and who 'need a permanent new Black family who reflect their background' (*Guardian*, 22 March 1993, 'Lambeth Family Finders'). How would we conceptualise the resurgence, in Europe, in

India, in the USA and much of the rest of the world, of a numerous politics of racialised identities, volk racism and ethnic cleansing? Sociological sense requires that we distance ourselves from the taken-for-granted constructs, however compelling or politically judicious they may be for social actors or the state.

Abandoning race-thinking suggests a fruitful redirection of sociological concern, away from a superficial obsession with the phenomenal forms of 'race' difference to an examination of those social and political processes whereby 'race' comes to be a constitutive category of human action. Thus Miles (1989) and others (for example, Lunn, 1985; Green and Carter, 1988; Fields, 1990; Holmes, 1991; Carter *et al.*, 1987; Cross and Keith, 1993; Green, 1993; Solomos, 1993) have employed the concept of racialisation to explore how 'race' discourses are generated and maintained, particularly through the enactment of discriminatory immigration and nationality legislation, as well as the ways in which an international capitalist division of labour has utilised these discourses for assessing the labouring capacities of different human beings according to their 'race-ial' characteristics.

This critical stance towards 'race' has received added impetus from those theorists who have addressed wider issues of identity and difference. Significant here is the work of Foucault (1979). His emphasis on the discursive formation of subjectivity acts as a powerful liquefier of all fixity, corroding the basis of identity politics. Other writers, such as Hall (in Hall *et al.*, 1992),[5] have developed these insights more specifically in the context of debates about modernity and the imaginary communities of national cultures. This radical historicising of identities carries important consequences for understanding 'race': identities become profoundly relative, can be made and unmade, shift and alter. Being a Bosnian or a Serb, a Christian or a Muslim, Aryan or non-Aryan, is always and unavoidably an act of social imagining and so always and inevitably an unstable and fissiparous state, sometimes even a murderous one. Rattansi and Donald (1992), Goldberg (1990) and Bhabha (1990) have developed this approach into a systematic exploration of racist discourses.[6]

CONCLUSION

We have argued that sociologists have employed 'race' categories through our routine practices of teaching, researching and advising. In doing so they have consolidated and extended the status of race-thinking. Sociologists might, instead, reflect on the production of those regimes of

truth which take 'race' as given: what they look like, how they are produced and sustained, especially through academic and social-policy discourse. This is not simply an issue of epistemology, of sociologists
cleaning up concepts. It is about shedding the categories which reinstate
the problems we may see out to solve.

Our contention is that social science has resisted the interrogation of the
concepts 'race', 'racial' and 'race relations', a charity rarely extended to
other common-sense concepts. This resistance derives from several
sources, not least of which are the profound ideological potency of racialising theories of social action, the urgency of political problem solving
and the 'race relations' remit within which much social-policy research is
funded. Certainly, sociologists are not the sole agents of racialisation, but
they continue to play their part.

Insofar as we can intervene in the public process of meaning-making
and social-policy formulation, clear thinking on the causes and character
of race-thinking is essential. We believe that problem solving is limited
whenever sociological studies posit as real and independent those categories which are themselves the product of other social processes. Thus
studies of 'mixed race' relationships, of 'mixed race' children, of 'trans-
racial' adoption of 'race' and education, 'race' and housing, 'race' and
health provision, assume the very object which must be explained and
treat 'race' as an active, *a priori* subject in social relations. Instead, we
need to enquire how it is that social relations appear as 'race relations'
and government agencies come to employ 'race' categories as key organising principles for the distribution of social and economic resources.

The use of 'race' as an analytical concept has implications beyond the
sphere of racialised relations. Social theory, for instance, is often troubled
by 'race' categories and the effort involved in trying to employ an
untheorised, common-sense concept for sociological purposes. To take
one example: Lee and Newby (1989), whose excellent text is used widely
to introduce students to key themes and issues in sociological analysis,
attempt to explore the relationship between 'race' and class (pp. 158–9),
regarded by them and many other writers as a 'stumbling block' for
Marxist theory. Yet nowhere in their account do they provide a definition
of 'race' or of what constitutes 'racial' phenomena, or 'racial' conflict or
'racial' disadvantage. Instead, common sense is allowed to fill the silence:
if there is 'racial' conflict there must be 'races' to conflict; if there is
'racial' disadvantage there must be 'races' to be disadvantaged. Marxism
may have difficulties in developing analyses of racisms and racialisation
(although we would argue that these have been exaggerated) but it does
not have a problem understanding 'race' and class. There cannot be a

problem of 'race' and class since 'races' do not exist. Reformulating the issue as one of racialisation and class formation is altogether more promising (see Miles, 1993).

We are not arguing, let us repeat, that racisms and discriminatory behaviour do not exist, nor are we denying that many people continue to believe and act as if 'races' are real. Evidence for this is not limited to Britain or the United States, as recent global events make plain. The challenge to sociologists is to understand and make sense of these beliefs and practices, tasks for which a race-free sociological vocabulary is indispensable.

## Notes

1. This is not to overlook some more recent texts, for example Gilroy (1987), Cross and Keith (1993) and Solomos (1993), which are critical of the orthodoxy of race-thinking.
2. See, amongst others, Jones (1991, pp. 166–8) and Johnson (1990, Index). More to the point here is the confusion about the referents for the concepts 'race' and ethnic minorities.
3. These reports were published in 42 volumes under the Directorship of Senator William P. Dillingham. See especially vol. V for the system of 'race' classification devised by the Commission. Dillingham was a vociferous exponent of immigration controls and he campaigned successfully for their passage through Congress in 1917, 1921 and 1924.
4. See Gordon (1992) for an interesting account of the racialization of census data.
5. The exploration of racism and identity is, it should be noted, not exclusively a consequence of post-Foucauldian work. The work of Fanon (1986) is an outstanding and obvious exception, whilst Sartre also investigated similar themes in his *Anti-Semite and Jew* (1960).
6. Racism, it might be noted, is also often conceived as transhistorical, a-sociological form, for example in many forms of Racism Awareness Training; see Sivanandan (1982) and Webster (1992) for a critique. There are difficulties with these 'postmodernist' perspectives. None the less they offer new ideas, especially on racism as discourse and its relation to other discourses of, say, nation and gender (see, for instance, Carter, 1993; Norris, 1992).

## References

Abercrombie, N. and Warde, A., with K. Soothill, J. Urry and S. Walby (1992) *Contemporary British Society* (London: Polity Press).
Barker, M. (1981) *The New Racism* (London: Junction Books).

Bauman, Z. (1992) *Thinking Sociologically* (Oxford: Basil Blackwell).

Bhabha, H. (ed.) (1990) *Narrating the Nation* (London: Routledge).

Bilton, T., Bennett, K., Jones, P., Stanworth, M., Sheard, K. and Webster, A. (1981) *Introductory Sociology* (London: Macmillan).

Carter, B (1993) 'Naming Difference: Recent Social Theory and the Teaching of "Race"', *Social Science Teacher*, 22:1, Autumn, pp. 19–21.

Carter, B., Harris, C. and Joshi, S. (1987) 'The Racialisation of Black Immigration: The Conservative Government of 1951–55', *Immigrants and Minorities*, 6: 3, November, pp. 335–347.

Cross, M. and Keith, M. (eds) (1993) *Racism, the City and the State* (London: Routledge).

Fanon, F. (1986) *Black Skin, White Masks* (New York: Grove Press).

Fields, B. (1990) 'Racism in America', *New Left Review*, 181: May/June, pp. 95–118.

Foucault, M. (1979) *Discipline and Punish: The Birth of the Prison* (Harmondsworth: Penguin).

Fryer, P. (1984) *Staying Power: The History of Black People in Britain* (London: Pluto Press).

Gilroy, P. (1987) *There Ain't No Black in the Union Jack* (London: Hutchinson).

Gould, S. J. (1981) *The Mismeasure of Man* (London: Norton).

Goldberg, T. (ed.) (1990) *Anatomy of Racism* (Minneapolis: University of Minnesota (Press).

Gordon, P. (1992) 'The Racialization of Statistics', in Skellington, R. with P. Morris, *'Race' in Britain Today* (London: Sage and Open University Press).

Green, M. and Carter B. (1988) '"Races" and "Race makers": The Politics of Racialization', *Sage Abstracts*, 13: 2, May, pp. 4–29.

Green, M. (1993) 'The Americanization Movement: A Case Study in the Politics of Production', PhD dissertation, University of Wolverhampton.

Hall, S. (1991) 'The Local and the Global: Globalization and Ethnicity', in King, A. (ed.), *Culture, Globalization and the World System* (London: Macmillan).

Hall, S., Held, D., and McGrew, T. (1992) *Modernity and its Futures* (Cambridge: Polity Press/Open University).

Holmes, C. (1991) *A Tolerant Country? Immigrants, Refugees and Minorities in Britain* (London: Faber).

Husband, C. (ed.) (1982) *'Race' in Britain: Continuity and Change* (London: Hutchinson).

Johnson, N. (1990) *Reconstructuring the Welfare State* (Hemel Hempstead: Harvester Wheatsheaf).

Jones, K. (1991) *The Making of Social Policy 1830–1990* (London: Athlone).

Kay, D. and Miles, R. (1992) *Refugees or Migrant Workers? European Volunteer Workers in Britain 1946–1951* (London: Routledge).

Lee, D. and Newby, H. (1983) *The Problem of Sociology: An Introduction to the Discipline* (London: Hutchison).

Lunn, K. (ed.) (1985) *Race and Labour in Twentieth Century Britain* (London: Frank Cass).

Miles, R. (1989) *Racism* (London: Routledge).

Miles, R. (1993) *Racism after Race Relations* (London: Routledge).

Norris, C. (1992) *Uncritical Theory: Postmodernism, Intellectuals and the Gulf War* (London: Lawrence & Wishart).

Rattansi, A. and Donald, J. (eds) (1992) *'Race', Culture and Difference* (London: Sage/Open University).

Rich, P. (1986) *Race and Empire in British Politics* (Cambridge: Cambridge University Press).

Sartre, J. P. (1960) *Anti-Semite and Jew* (New York: Grove Press).

Sivanandan, A. (1982) *A Different Hunger: Writings on Black Resistance* (London: Pluto Press).

Solomos, J. (1993) *Race and Racism in Contemporary Britain*, 2nd edn (London: Macmillan).

US Commission on Immigration (1911) *Abstract of Reports of the Immigration Commission in 2 Volumes*, Senate Document no. 747, 61st Congress 3rd Session (Washington: Government Printing Office).

Webster, Y. O. (1992) *The Racialization of America* (New York: St Martin's Press).

# 5 Consanguinity and Related Demons: Science and Racism in the Debate on Consanguinity and Birth Outcome

Waqar Ahmad

## INTRODUCTION

The tendency to locate health inequalities in cultural or genetic differences between groups is not new (Crawford, 1977). It is particularly true in 'explaining' ethnic health inequalities ranging from tuberculosis to rickets, and from syphilis to obstetric outcome. In the West, black people have often been aligned with depravity, disease and death. Recently in Britain a new discourse, focused largely on the Pakistani-origin population, has emerged which combines notions of presumed genetic pathology with pathological cultures in the guise of clinical concerns about 'unnaturally' high rates of consanguineous marriages (i.e. marriages with blood relatives, often first cousins). As argued by Proctor and Smith (1992), consanguinity is increasingly indicted as the major explanatory factor for the higher rates of perinatal deaths and congenital malformations among the Pakistani population. That the informal culture within British obstetrics maintains a strong belief in the 'truthfulness' of the consanguinity hypothesis (with the rate of consanguineous marriages among Pakistanis reported to be higher than 50 per cent) (Darr and Modell, 1988; Bundey et al., 1989), in explaining their poor obstetric experience is not in doubt.[1]

This chapter offers an assessment of the 'consanguinity hypothesis' in relation to the obstetric experience of Britain's Pakistani-origin population and concludes that the fascination with consanguinity within the NHS owes more to racism than to science. Although the focus is on birth outcome in the Pakistani-origin population, of necessity it refers also to the general Asian (and other black) populations and other health issues.

68

Britain's black minorities suffer health inequalities in terms of high perinatal mortality rates (defined as deaths of the foetus or new-born between 28 weeks of pregnancy and first week of life) and other indices of birth outcome. In particular, the Pakistani-origin population shows consistently the highest perinatal mortality rates and highest rates of congenital malformations (Gillies *et al.*, 1984; Chitty and Winter, 1989; Balarajan and Raleigh, 1989). For example, Balarajan and Raleigh's (1989) analysis of figures for England and Wales for years 1982–5 show that women born in Pakistan had perinatal mortality rates of 19/1000 compared to the rate for UK-born mothers at 10/1000. Parsons *et al.*'s (1993) analysis of Office of Population Censuses and Surveys (OPCS) data for England and Wales shows that in 1990 babies of mothers born in Pakistan had the highest rates of stillbirth at 9.1/1000 total births compared with the UK-born mothers' rates of 4.4/1000.

The high rate of consanguineous marriages among the Pakistani population has been noted as a critical factor (Bundey *et al.*, 1989; Chitty and Winter, 1989). This factor has been argued to account for high perinatal mortality rates and high congenital malformations and stillbirth rates, supposedly related to genetically inherited disorders. Although other personal (e.g. age of mother, parity), service-related and environmental factors have been mentioned in research, consanguinity is fast gaining popularity as the primary explanatory factor within medical discourse.

As will be argued, it is far from easy to disentangle the relative contribution of consanguinity in relation to a variety of other influences on obstetric outcome (Pearson, 1991). The subsequent discussion is organised under four broad headings, focusing on an assessment of the epidemiological evidence, problems related to uncritical conceptualisation and use of ethnic and social class classifications, racism and discrimination in maternity services and wider life, and the demonology constructed around consanguinity and located in the 'deviant and alien' culture of Muslims of Pakistani origin.

## INCONSISTENCY AND CONFUSION: THE EPIDEMIOLOGICAL EVIDENCE

Although seen as 'abnormal' in contemporary Britain, kinship patterns based on consanguineous marriages are common in many parts of the world, including the Muslim world and the Indian sub-continent (Fox, 1967). However, as Bittles *et al.* (1992) note:

In contemporary western societies consanguineous marriages are often regarded with suspicion and anecdotes as to their unfavourable biological effects abound. . . . [In] the past there has been over-estimation of the contribution of recessively inherited disorders to pre-productive mortality in the population as a whole. At family level the large scale Karnataka study illustrated that excess mortality associated with consanguinity is observed in the progeny of only a minority of couples. (p. 113)

In assessing the likely impact of consanguinity on congenital malformations, there are numerous 'technical' problems. In an authoritative review, Little and Nicoll (1988) note a number of pertinent points. First, most studies are based on *overt* congenital anomalies. However, as most embryos with major anomalies abort spontaneously at an early stage, the new-born babies with anomalies therefore represent a highly selective sample of all affected conceptuees. Secondly, not all anomalies are detectable at birth and some neurodegenerative and metabolic disorders which are determined congenitally are excluded from the definition without good cause. Thirdly, they note that some of the variation may be due to differences in consultation patterns, service conditions, availability and acceptance of genetic counselling and attitudes to and acceptance of post mortems (to ascertain cause of death).

Little and Nicoll also note inconsistencies in the results of British studies. For example, Terry *et al.* (1985) found high rates of congenital malformations in the Indian group, while the Pakistani group in their study had the highest rates of consanguineous marriages. Subsequent studies from the same centre in Birmingham have failed to produce convincing evidence of a link between consanguinity and anthropometric measurements of babies (Honeyman *et al.*, 1987), a finding consistent with studies from Saudi Arabia (Saedi-Wong and al-Frayh, 1989) and elsewhere (Schull and Neel, 1965).

Chitty and Winter (1989), among others (for example, Gillies *et al.*, 1984), report the highest incidence of neural tube defects in Pakistani babies. However, this may be explained by late bookings resulting in non-detection during antenatal care and therefore termination not being offered or accepted. The generalisability of these findings is also in doubt. Little and Nicoll (1988) cite studies suggesting that high rates of neural tube defects is a common phenomenon in Northern India and Pakistan and is not associated with any particular group (p. 170). Indeed, in reviewing possible explanations of infant mortality in Pakistan, Sathar (1987) and

Zaidi (1989), although holding opposing theoretical perspectives, make no mention of consanguinity as an explanatory factor.

A further serious problem with some major British studies of birth outcome is the incomplete and/or inaccurate information on consanguineous status. For example, data on consanguinity were missing for 82 per cent of 'European', 70 per cent of Pakistani and 77 per cent of Indian mothers in the study by Chitty and Winter (1989). Darr and Modell (1988), in an analysis of 100 randomly selected maternity records of Pakistani women in Bradford, reported that only 59 had information on consanguinity; they also noted errors in recording consanguinity in 16 cases.

In the methodologically commendable classic studies conducted by Schull, Neel and colleagues in Japan, no evidence was found for an association between inbreeding and stillbirth (1965). Subsequent work in Hiroshima and Nagasaki remained inconclusive; while in Hiroshima there was a positive association, in Nagasaki the non-consanguineous marriages had the highest rates of stillbirth (quoted in Macluer, 1980). Macluer (1980) in a major review of evidence notes that:

> None of the several large and well-designed studies summarised above showed consistent inbreeding (or outcrossing) effects on human fetal deaths. There seems little point in collecting and analysing more and bigger data sets. (p. 258)

It was noted by Schull and colleagues that variations in socio-economic conditions confounded the study of effects of consanguinity (quoted in Macluer, 1980). This is supported by contemporary experiences in Southern India. Consanguinity is common in Karnataka, Andhra Pradesh, Tamil Nadu and Kerala, the southern states of India. However, Kerala boasts the best health indices in the whole of India, probably accounted for by an extremely high literacy rate for women as well as for men (around 90 per cent), universal provision of health care and access to meaningful participation by women in all walks of life. Paradoxically, Kerala is also among the poorest states in India.

Interestingly, a radical re-assessment of the consanguinity debate appears to be taking place among geneticists. In the well-publicised meeting of the American Association for the Advancement of Science in 1993, presenters suggested that the fears about cousin marriages are over-exaggerated and based on crude assumptions (see reports in *The Independent*, 1993 and *The Observer*, 1993). Indeed, some researchers emphasised the potential genetic benefits of inbreeding in 'flushing out' the deleterious genes from the human genome. It has been argued that the current concerns about consanguinity in Britain relate to the Victorian fears about interbreeding as a threat to the future of the 'British race'. Bittles, a leading researcher from King's College, London, was quoted as saying:

> In Victorian times, first cousin marriages were regarded as being a threat to the entire structure of civilisation, and our current attitudes stem from these days. Even today, in America, 30 states prohibit such marriages and, in nine, they constitute criminal offences. (*The Observer*, 1993)

## Social Class and Ethnic Classifications

That social class has an impact on birth outcome and early years of life is beyond doubt. Pharoah and Alberman's (1990) analyses of OPCS data for England and Wales for 1979–80 and 1982–3 show stark social class differences for both males and females. The social classes I : V ratio of excess deaths for females was 1 : 1.92 for stillbirths, 1 : 1.71 for neonatal deaths, 1 : 2.31 for postneonatal deaths, 1 : 2.58 for mortality in years 1–4, 1 : 1.85 in years 5–9 and 1 : 1.58 for years 10–14. That for males was 1 : 1.9 for stillbirths, 1 : 1.9 for neonatal deaths, 1 : 2.45 for postneonatal deaths, 1 : 3.38 for mortality in years 1–4, 1 : 2.07 for years 5–9 and 1 : 1.77 for years 10–14. It is inconceivable that material deprivation is not a significant factor in explaining at least some of the excess mortality and congenital malformations in Pakistani babies. However, why there seems to be a lesser impact on Bangladeshi babies in the neonatal and postneonatal period requires explanation (Balarajan and Raleigh, 1989; Andrews and Jewson, 1993).

For the minority ethnic communities too, Balarajan and Botting (1989) show clear social class gradients in birth outcome. However, the poorer birth outcome experience of the Pakistani population is apparent even after controlling for social class (based on the Registrar General's occupational classifications), apparently lending support to the suggestion that the higher rates of consanguinity among the Pakistani-origin population may have clinical significance.

However, there are a number of problems in both ethnic and social class categorisation in this area which make interpretation of findings difficult. Health services data variously define 'ethnicity' on the basis of 'mothers' country of birth', and often at such broad levels as 'mothers of Indian subcontinent origin' or 'New Commonwealth origin'. Even some well-meaning community surveys have categorised ethnicity at the level of 'Asian', 'European' and 'African' (including Caribbeans and Africans) (Nzegwu, 1993). With over 50 per cent of Asian and other black populations being British-born, such classifications are fast becoming meaningless. However, I start with questions about the utility of and the uncritical use of 'social class' in some studies of ethnic differences in health and health care (Balarajan *et al.*, 1989; Balarajan and Raleigh, 1989). These categorisations in themselves influence how social/medical facts are constructed.

*Social class*
Social class defined on the basis of the Registrar General's occupational groups has been criticised from a number of quarters in recent years (Jones and Cameron, 1984; Arber, 1990). In particular, feminist critiques have focused on the appropriateness of defining married women's social class on the basis of their husbands' occupation. Arber (1990) argues:

> Relationship between class and health for women should be considered in their own right. Occupational class analysis should use classifications which more adequately reflect meaningful distinctions between women's occupations. However, if the primary concern is to understand how material circumstances influence women's health it may be more appropriate to leave the strait-jacket of class, and more directly measure women's material circumstances. (p. 39)

Two types of problems arise in using traditional measures of social class to assess the impact of material circumstances on ethnic minority health, particularly birth outcome. First, at a general level, when there is a two-fold disparity in unemployment rates between the white and some ethnic minority, namely Pakistani and Bangladeshi, populations (Skellington and Morris, 1992), the use of social class based on current or last occupation has questionable validity. Unemployment is related to both psychological and physical ill-health, although the exact mechanisms of this relationship remain contested (Smith, 1987). Within occupational categories, there is consistent evidence of minority ethnic populations earning less income, more likely to occupy the lowest job categories, more likely to be on shift work and on night shifts (Brown, 1984; Skellington and Morris, 1992). Certain categories of 'self-employed' people – owners of small family businesses with family members under-employed in these and other 'ethnic' businesses such as taxis and restaurants – also do not fit neatly into the occupational classifications. Andrews and Jewson (1993) note that apart from problems of the questionable utility and validity of social class, a greater proportion of ethnic minority populations live in inner-city areas and 'will suffer disadvantages associated with inner-city dereliction, environmental pollution and poor quality public services (including health services)' (p. 146).

They also note the fallacy of some cumulative indices of social deprivation. For example, the Jarman Index is tautological: it uses the proportion of ethnic minority population in an area as a factor in reaching a deprivation score. Thus areas with high minority populations, by definition, will have high deprivation scores (Jarman, 1983). Townsend *et al.* (1988) and Scott-Samuel (1984) include owner-occupation as a local area index of material status. Numerous studies show that the high owner-occupation among Pakistani and Indian origin populations is not indicative of high quality of housing (Bhat *et al.*, 1988; Skellington and Morris, 1992), and can perhaps best be seen as indicative of, and a reaction to, institutional racism in local government housing policies. Much of this housing is confined to the older, cheaper and low-amenities segments of the private sector (Bhat *et al.*, 1988; Smith, 1989; Skellington and Morris, 1992).

The second type of problem in using social class categorisation relates to its use in defining the material circumstances of Asian women. There are two main strands of the feminist critiques of social class: that because of the increasing number of women in paid employment their own occupational status should form the basis of their class position; and that the husband's occupation does not adequately reflect the socio-material circumstances of woman within the household economy. The second element of this critique is particularly true here. With large proportions of Asian, particularly Pakistani and Bangladesh, women being outside the labour market, for a variety of reasons (and not necessarily to do with 'culture'), classifying them with reference to husband's social class (itself a dubious exercise) borders on the absurd (Skellington and Morris, 1992). Even when they are employed, the health-enhancing impact of paid employment may be diminished because of racism at work.

*Ethnic classifications*
One of the problems in considering ethnic minority health issues is that there is a tendency to 'racialise' health inequalities and thus present them as located in 'ethnicity' or 'race' rather than socio-economic status (Sheldon and Parker, 1992; Ahmad, 1993). For example, Bowler (1993) notes that midwives she studied used ethnicity as a 'master definition' – that 'they are not the same as us' was a more important categorisation than

the women's background, class or education. To some extent the notion of 'ethnicity' ('good'), almost invariably undefined, in epidemiological research is used in opposition to the notion of 'race' ('bad') – for example, see the introduction to Cruickshank and Beevers (1980). The supposedly inherent neutrality of the concept 'ethnicity' itself appears to be the justification or excuse for the lack of consideration of racism – the discourse on 'ethnicity' or 'culture' occupies the centre stage in the politics of 'new racism', as discussed later (Solomos, 1993).

Sheldon and Parker (1992) highlight some of the dangers in uncritically using 'ethnic' categorisations. First, they note that there is a tendency to represent effects as causes: 'Rather than observed ethnic variation prompting the search for underlying causes, it *becomes* the explanation; effect is converted into cause' (p. 64). Thus the higher perinatal mortality and congenital mortality rates in the Pakistani population can somehow be 'explained' with reference to their Pakistani 'ethnicity'. They also note that such uncritical use of ethnic categories can lead to cultural stereotyping, the tendency to view ethnic difference as deviance, and neglecting or at best reducing the importance of racism and social structures in determining inequalities in health and health care choices.

Ethnic categorisation in health service data has been problematic, particularly so now when some much-used categories such as 'mothers' country of birth' and 'Commonwealth citizen' are meaningless. Ahmad and Sheldon (1993) have criticised the categorisation used in the 1991 Census and its incorporation into the NHS minimum data sets, for both the possibility of potential misuse of data leading to further racialisation of health differences between ethnic groups and for the limited utility of such categories as either explanatory variables or as tools for planning and delivery of services. As Andrews and Jewson (1993) note, the ethnic categorisation itself is, to some extent, responsible for the construction of ethnic differences in birth outcome and infant health. For example, the differences in birth outcome between the 'Pakistan' and 'Bangladeshi' groups in this country only became apparent following the formation of Bangladesh (formerly 'East Pakistan'). Otherwise we would still be considering the combined figures under the category 'Pakistani', and some of the differences between the Pakistani group and other groups would thus have been masked. Likewise, one needs to ask how meaningful is a heterogeneous category like 'Indian', which encompasses differences of religion, caste and class, regional background, diet and custom. Indeed, studies which have focused on the sub-Indian groups show as great differences (Chetcuti *et al.*, 1985) as those focusing on difference between the Indian and other groups. What health differences lie hidden under the blanket of 'Indian-ness' in the same way as the differences between the Pakistani and the Bangladeshi populations were hidden under the overall figures for the 'Pakistani' population?

In summary then, one needs critically to consider the taken-for-granted ethnic and social class categorisations in relation to an assessment of ethnic differences in health, including birth outcome and infant health. The level at which 'ethnicity' is categorised in studies of perinatal epidemiology makes interpretation of results problematic. Also, as highlighted, social class categorisations cannot be accepted as unproblematic. As they are, the explanatory value of ethnic and social class classifications is at best dubious and it is likely that these categories hide more than they reveal.

## RACISM AND SERVICE DELIVERY

It is widely acknowledged that the quality of care and its availability varies inversely with the needs of the population, so that the best-trained doctors and nurses and the best-equipped hospitals are in areas where there is least morbidity and mortality (Tudor Hart, 1971). Whereas this fact is widely recognised, relatively little research has focused on ethnic minorities' access to health services. In particular, racism as a barrier to equity in service delivery has received scant attention, whilst much research has focused on personal and cultural 'deficiencies' of Asian women in using maternity services (Rocheron, 1988; Ahmad and Husband, 1993).

The wider literature on 'race' and racism suggests two broad levels at which racism operates, individual and institutional, although the newer manifestations in the guise of 'cultural' or 'new racism' are particularly pertinent here (Solomos, 1993). Many writers have argued that the structures of health care, and state welfare more generally, discriminate against the minority ethnic communities at an institutional level (Mama, 1992; Ahmad and Husband, 1993) so that the underlying assumptions and the structures and procedures employed, themselves disadvantage black people, irrespective of whether the intention to discriminate is present. Health needs located in the racially iniquitous structures of society are thus represented as personal or cultural failings and the disadvantageous institutional arrangements remain intact. The resistance of health authorities to adapting to the needs of a changing population was highlighted in a report by the National Association of Health Authorities (NAHA, 1988; see also Johnson, 1993). Although the report encouraged a flurry of high-profile public relations activity by health authorities across the country in the few months after its publication, five years later there is little evidence of any substantive improvement. The situation is little changed from that described in the survey by Donaldson and Odell (1984), where action by district health authorities consisted largely of translated materials and interpreters.

Racism in health service delivery and the construction of ethnic-minority health problems has received little attention from sociologists of health (Ahmad, 1993), whilst some argue that the epidemiological researchers as yet lack both the willpower and the conceptual sophistication to tackle it (Sheldon and Parker, 1992). The need to fill this gap is emphasised by Andrews and Jewson (1993) who, in a recent assessment of explanations of ethnic differences in infant mortality, argue:

> Some issues remain under-investigated. Individual and institutionalised racism in service delivery, or in British society more generally, have rarely been the overt focus of study. Little attention has been directed towards the probability that racial or ethnic stereotyping may shape diagnosis or recorded causes of death. (p. 142)

This issue has attracted much attention in psychiatry, in terms of both the categorisation of mental illness and the delivery of mental health services to ethnic minorities (Sashidharan and Francis, 1993), but deserves consideration in all aspects of welfare provision. As I will argue, it is an important factor in considering the likely explanations of differentials in birth outcome.

*Racist stereotypes*
Many writers have reported on health professionals holding negative stereotypes of Asian patients. Indeed, the Jarman Index of social deprivation, based on general practitioners' perceptions of their workloads and favoured by the Department of Health in the assessment of deprivation payment to GPs, assumes that ethnic minority patients are necessarily a burden on health care resources (Jarman, 1993). Wright's (1983) study of general practitioners' showed that in addition to holding other negative stereotypes, they thought Asian patients abused services. This also was the finding of a more recent study by Ahmad *et al.* (1991) who stated:

> the clear picture to emerge was that GPs held less positive attitudes towards Asian patients. Consultations with Asians were felt to be less satisfying, they were thought to require longer consultations, to be less compliant, and perceived to make excessive use of health care, including visits for 'trivial' and 'minor' reasons. (p. 54)

In a recently published qualitative study of midwives' perceptions of Asian (largely Pakistani) women, Bowler (1993) notes remarkably similar negative perceptions:

> The midwives' stereotypes contained four main themes: the difficulty of communicating with the women; the women's lack of compliance with care and abuse of service; their tendency to 'make a fuss about nothing'; and their lack of 'normal maternal instinct'.   (p. 157)

Such stereotypes impact on the quality of care offered to Asian women. Kushnick (1988) gives an example of how the widely held notion of Asian women 'making a fuss about nothing' led to an Asian woman being denied emergency attention in a labour ward despite suffering severe pain and repeatedly requesting help: her baby was dead upon birth. As Littlewood and Lipsedge (1989) and others (for example, Centre for Contemporary Cultural Studies (CCCS), 1992) show, such stereotypes have a long history. Black people were at times said to have too low a threshold for pain and at other times thought to be unnaturally resistant to pain. This apparent inconsistency is not problematic, in that both these stereotypes served the same purpose of defining the 'normal' 'us' in opposition to the 'deviant', 'dangerous' and 'abnormal' 'others'.

*Quality of care*
The operation of the inverse care law against Asian women also means they have access to poor-quality general-practitioner and maternity care. Clarke and Clayton (1983) showed how this poor quality of care was an independent risk factor in terms of higher perinatal mortality rates for Asian women in Leicestershire. Asian women were more likely to be registered with general practitioners who did not possess post-graduate qualifications and who were not on the obstetric list; 'Asian and non-Asian mothers with general practitioners who were not on the obstetric list had more than twice the risk of a perinatal death.'

Clarke and Clayton (1983), among others (Jain, 1985; Firdous and Bhopal, 1989) have reported that Asian women start attending antenatal clinics later than white women. Jain reported that a major reason for Asian women's late bookings was the late referral from their general practitioner (Jain, 1985). In a Bradford study based on interviews with 74 Asian (mainly Pakistani) and 74 white women in the city's two maternity units, the Asian women were less likely to get any choice in pain relief, delivery position and mobility during labour (Theodore-Gandi and Shaikh, 1988). Eighty-two per cent of Asian and 12 per cent of white women would have preferred a female doctor – the maternity units are still unable to provide the choice of female doctor, with only one of the consultant obstetricians, and very few junior doctors in maternity ward, being female (in 1993).

It is reasonable to assume that effective use of services requires access to appropriate information, in addition to a relationship between service users and providers which is based on mutual respect and trust. The lack of interpreters and information in accessible form (translated material is often of poor quality and because of assumptions about literacy is still inaccessible to many women) hampers the informed use of services by Asian women. Firdous and Bhopal (1989) reported that Asian women were less knowledgeable about such procedures as amniocentesis. Provision of sensitive services to minority ethnic groups is often seen to be inimical to the interests of the white service users (Braham *et al.*, 1992; Bowler, 1993). Bowler quotes the response of a consultant obstetrician to the question of whether the hospital was considering appointing interpreters to ease communication difficulties with Asian women:

> Of course not. We haven't even got enough nurses. If you ask me they shouldn't be allowed into the country until they can pass an English exam. (p. 161)

One reason for the high perinatal mortality rates and high rates of lethal and non-lethal congenital malformations is likely to be the poor quality of general-practitioner and maternity care available to Pakistani women. It is assumed that terminations will not be acceptable to Pakistani women for religious reasons, and therefore this choice may not be offered (Darr, 1990). Many congenital malformations are detected by tests early in the pregnancy. The later bookings by Pakistani women, coupled with the lower knowledge of available procedures and the prevalent racial stereotypes, may result in fewer such detections and fewer offers of termination. It is also possible that termination at an advanced stage of pregnancy will be less acceptable, and therefore more likely to be rejected.

Darr's work with Asian parents of thalassaemic children shows that commonly held stereotypes of Pakistani women constructed the choices offered to them (Darr, 1990). Elsewhere Darr and colleagues note that:

> assumptions about their low utilisation of prenatal diagnosis were based on social prejudice and influenced by language difficulties. Typical comments from health workers were 'Muslim families have a fatalistic attitude and do not take any initiatives, they are not interested in prenatal diagnosis, as it is against their religion – there is no point discussing it, they marry their cousins, if they didn't they wouldn't have genetic problems.' (quoted in Anionwu, 1993)

Sensitive genetic counselling can be effective, and acceptable (Modell *et al.*, 1980; Constantinides, 1986; Darr, 1990; Anionwu, 1993). However, counselling services remain inadequate, with many authorities with sizeable Asian populations providing minimal or no genetic counselling services (Anionwu, 1993).

*Empowerment*

It can be argued that a central issue in both the fight for appropriate services of an acceptable standard and the effective use of available maternity services is the empowerment of women generally (Pizzini, 1989), in this case these Asian women. The Department of Health-funded Asian Mother and Baby Campaign, through the provision of linkworkers, attempted to aid women in communicating more effectively, though to consider language as the only or sufficient criterion for effective communication is itself simplistic. Although there is some evidence that the scheme was effective in easing communication problems and challenging racism at the individual level, it failed to make any impact on such issues as institutional practices and choice of female doctor (Rocheron, 1988). In the Bradford-based study by Theodore-Gandi and Shaikh (1988), only a minority of women relied on linkworkers: most depended on help from friends and relatives or on crude sign language. An alternative approach aimed at providing advocacy support to ethnic minority women, where the 'advocates' are located and accountable to managers outside the health services, has worked well in Hackney and has been suggested as a progressive model of empowering women in their relationship with maternity services (Parsons and Day, 1992). There is evidence that the scheme had a beneficial impact on birth outcome.

A consideration of racism in health service delivery, at both institutional and individual levels, is important. Through racially discriminatory institutional practices and racial stereotypes, Pakistani and other Asian women are denied equality of access to maternity care. This is likely to be a significant factor in observed inequalities in perinatal mortality and congenital malformations between ethnic groups.

## CONSTRUCTING DEMONS: BIOLOGY, CULTURE AND RACISM

The focus on consanguinity in preference to socio-economic or service factors in explaining the poor obstetric experience of Pakistanis is not surprising. There is a long history of using ideas about the 'inherent' and 'stable' racial and cultural traits which are supposedly shared by members of a 'racial stock' to define, explain and shape responses to the perceived needs of 'black' or minority communities. Thus there have appeared discourses on black, oriental and colonised people's intelligence, educational performance and intellectual achievements, sexuality, and proneness to particular diseases due to supposed genetic or cultural deficits. In the health services, and in the literature on health and health care of Britain's minority populations and particularly Pakistani Muslims, the ideology of 'race' and notions of cultural and biological difference combine to result in a particular racialised construction of minority populations' health needs. The official responses to issues thus defined have reflected these racialised constructions (Rocheron, 1988; Ahmad, 1989). Thus, for example, the problem of high perinatal mortality in 'Asians' was addressed through *cultural* interventions under the Asian Mother and Baby Campaign; higher rates of rickets were 'related' to perceived culturally inappropriate practices which were to be resolved by a move towards British style of diet and dress; and the higher prevalence of tuberculosis among Asians was seen as a result of the communities 'importing' the disease into Britain, rather than it being a consequence of life experience in Britain (Rocheron, 1988; Ahmad, 1989; Smith, 1989).

Muslim family forms, and particularly the 'arranged marriage', have always been seen to be problematic in the West. For example, with reference to the colonisation of India, the British colonial administration claimed that they were a liberalising force, especially for the women, who were seen to be socially, economically and sexually oppressed: in Avtar Brah's words (1992) 'ruthlessly oppressed creatures who must be saved from their degradation'. Thus the media now carry stories of British-born and 'liberated' Asian girls being forced into arranged marriages; the arranged marriage is posed as a threat to individual freedom and the British way of life. It is also seen as necessary for the reproduction of the related 'evil' of consanguineous marriage, as most arranged marriages tend to be with blood relatives. The white liberal professionals often act as champions of the 'oppressed' young person, often a woman, against 'outdated' and oppressive practices imported from the 'Third World'. Yasmin Alibhai-Brown (1993) considers these popular concerns as expressed in the British media:

> Here we are, so the stories go, pathetic Asian women, hurled into hellish pits by our vicious fathers and many brothers, there to dwell with our even more beastly husbands. . . . Look at the recently publicised cases of women who kill their partners after years of abuse.

Inevitably, when it involved an Asian woman – Karanjeet Alluwalia [in this case not Muslim] – the focus was on the accursed arranged marriage. Just a few weeks after Alluwalia's trial, there were two equally horrific stories of white women driven to murder, one of whom had suffered hideous mutilation for ten years. I do not recall headlines screaming 'Love marriage Horror for White British Women'.   (p. 28)

If one couples these ideological constructions with further 'monstrous' acts such as marriage with consanguines, blood relatives, you have the making of a highly-charged discourse which combines notions of cultural pathology with genetic pathology and illicit sexual relationships verging on incest which complement the notion of Asian, particularly Muslim women as helpless, passive, oppressed and in need of being saved. The discourse on consanguinity bears all the hallmarks of the historically incestuous relationship between professional medicine and racism and the cultural manifestations of contemporary racism. As Solomos (1993) notes:

contemporary manifestations of race are coded in a language which aims to circumvent accusations of racism. In the case of new racism race is coded as culture. However, the central feature of these processes is that the qualities of social groups are fixed, made natural, confined within a pseudo-biologically defined culturalism.   (p. 190)

The fusion of biological and cultural determinisms in the guise of consanguinity provides a discourse which locates the poor birth outcome of the Pakistani populations in their own genetic and cultural deficits, so that they become dangerous to their own health.

CONCLUSION

Pearson (1991) in her review of ethnic differences in child health concludes:

There is no simple explanation of these complex differences in the health of ethnic minority babies throughout their infancy. The relative significance of genetic, environmental or therapeutic factors will not be easily disentangled.   (p. 89)

This, indeed, is the message of this chapter.

However, consanguinity is fast becoming the 'cause' of a variety of health problems of the Pakistani and Muslim minorities. That the research literature on consanguinity remains inconclusive, as discussed, is conveniently side-stepped. The fact that in studies of effects of consanguinity, it is nearly impossible to control for numerous confounding variables – including socio-economic status, education and quality of health care – is easily ignored. The consanguinity hypothesis provides an excellent means of blaming the victim and absolving health services and wider racial inequalities from responsibility. Better still, by not doing anything health professionals can claim to be adopting a progressive 'anti racist' stance and to be on the side of the Pakistani population, as the only action you could recommend, they would argue, would be for communities to abandon this alien and deleterious habit.

Attempts to link consanguinity with the Pakistani population's health are likely to gain momentum over the years to come. Combining notions of diseased genes with diseased cultures, consanguinity as an hypothesis to 'explain' higher perinatal deaths and congenital malformations in Pakistanis is too attractive to be discarded just because it fails to stand up to scrutiny. The emphasis on consanguinity in isolation from a consideration of important social factors represents an example of medicine serving racism.

## Acknowledgements

Embryonic versions of this chapter were presented at the National Perinatal Epidemiology Unit, Oxford, and later at the Annual Conference of the British Sociological Association at the University of Essex, in April 1993. I am grateful to colleagues there and to M. A. Kalam, Russell Murray, Reg Walker and Colin Samson for comments.

## Notes

1.  This is no longer confined to obstetrics. At various professional and social meetings, I have met consultants in haematology, ophthalmology and oncology who believed consanguinity to be the major cause of, respectively, 'strange bleeding disorders', 'peculiar eye diseases', and 'exciting tumours'. 'What else could it be?', one of them asked me.
2.  This perception is widespread. In my professional dealings with health practitioners it has also been referred to as 'the plenty pain syndrome' and is located in the widely held belief among British health professionals that Asian people have a lower pain threshold than white people.

84     *The Social Construction of Social Policy*

## References

Ahmad, W. I. U. (1989) 'Policies, Pills and Political Will: A Critique of Policies to Improve the Health of Ethnic Minorities', *Lancet*, i: pp. 148–50.

Ahmad, W. I. U. (1993) 'Making Black People Sick: 'Race', Ideology and Health Research', in Ahmad, W. I. U. (ed.), *'Race' and Health in Contemporary Britain* (Milton Keynes: Open University Press).

Ahmad, W. I. U. and Sheldon, T. (1993) ''Race' and Statistics', in Hammersley, M. (ed.), *Social Research: Philosophy, Politics and Practice* (London: Sage).

Ahmad, W. I. U. and Husband, C. (1993) 'Religious Identity, Citizenship and Welfare: The Case of Muslims in Britain', *International Journal of Islamic Social Science*, 10: 2, pp. 217–33.

Ahmad, W. I. U., Baker, M. R. and Kernohan, E. E. M. (1991) 'General Practitioners' Perceptions of Asian Patients', *Family Practice*, 8: 1, pp. 52–6.

Alibhai-Brown, Y. (1993) 'Marriage of Minds not Hearts', *New Statesman & Society*, 12 February, pp. 28–9.

Andrews, A. and Jewson, N. (1993) 'Ethnicity and Infant Deaths: The Implications of Recent Statistical Evidence', *Sociology of Health and Illness*, 15: 2, pp. 137–56.

Anionwu, E. (1993) 'Sickle Cell and Thalassaemia: Community Experiences and Official Response', in Ahmad, W. I. U. (ed.), *'Race' and Health in Contemporary Britain* (Milton Keynes: Open University Press).

Arber, S. (1990) 'Opening the Black Box: Inequalities in Women's Health', in Abbott, P. and Payne, G. (ed.), *New Directions in the Sociology of Health* (London: Falmer Press).

Balarajan, R. and Botting, B. (1989) 'Perinatal Mortality in England and Wales: Variations by Mothers' Country of Birth (1982–1985)', *Health Trends*, 21: pp. 79–84.

Balarajan, R. and Raleigh, S. V. (1989) 'Variation in Perinatal, Neonatal, Post-neonatal and Infant Mortality in England and Wales by Mothers' Country of Birth, 1982–85' in Britton, M. (ed.), *Mortality and Geography*, OPCS, Series DS no. 9 (London: OPCS).

Balarajan, R., Yuen, N. and Raleigh, S. V. (1989) 'Ethnic Differences in General Practitioner Consultations', *British Medical Journal*, 299: pp. 958–60.

Bhat, A., Carr-Hill, R. and Ohri, S. (1988) *Britain's Black Population* (Aldershot: Gower).

Bittles, A. H., Shami, S. A. and Rao, N. A. (1992) 'Consanguineous Marriage in Southern Asia: Incidence, Causes and Effects', in Bittles, A. H. and Roberts, D. F. (eds), *Minority Populations: Genetics, Demography and Health* (Basingstoke: Macmillan/Galton Institute).

Bowler, I. (1993) ''They're Not the Same as Us'': Midwives' Stereotypes of South Asian Maternity Patients', *Sociology of Health and Illness*, 15: 2, pp. 157–78.

Brah, A. (1992) 'Women of South Asian Origin in Britain: Issues and Concerns', in Braham, P., Rattansi, A. and Skellington, R. (eds), *Racism and Antiracism: Inequalities, Opportunities and Policies* (London: Sage).

Braham, P., Rattansi, A. and Skellington, R. (eds) (1992) *Racism and Antiracism: Inequalities, Opportunities and Policies* (London: Sage).

Brown, C. (1984) *Black and White Britain* (London: PSI).

Bundey, S., Alam, S., Kaur, A., Mir, S. and Lancashire, R. J. (1989) 'Race, Consanguinity and Social Features in Birmingham Babies: A Basis for Prospective Study', *Journal of Epidemiology and Community Health*, 44: pp. 130–5.

Centre for Contemporary Cultural Studies (CCCS) (1982) *The Empire Strikes Back* (London: Hutchinson).

Chetcuti, R., Sinha, S. H. and Levene, M. I. (1985) 'Birth Size in Indian Ethnic Subgroups Born in Britain', *Archives of Disease in Childhood*, 60: pp. 868–70

Chitty, L. and Winter, R. M. (1980) 'Perinatal Mortality in Different Ethnic Groups', *Archives of Disease in Childhood*, 64: pp. 1036–41.

Clarke, M. and Clayton, D. (1983) 'Quality of Obstetric Care Provided to Asian Immigrants in Leicestershire', *British Medical Journal*, 60: pp. 866–9.

Constantinides, P. (1986) 'Health Care Services for Populations at Risk for Genetically Inherited Disease', paper presented at British Association for the Advancement of Science Conference, 3 September.

Crawford, R. (1977) 'You are Dangerous to your Health: The Ideology and Politics of Victim Blaming', *International Journal of Health Services*, 7: 4, pp. 663–80.

Cruickshank, J. K. and Beevers, D. G. (1989) *Ethnic Factors in Health and Disease* (London: Wright).

Darr, A. (1990) 'The Social Implications of Thalassaemia Among Muslims of Pakistani Origin in England', PhD thesis, University of London.

Darr, A. and Modell, B. (1988) 'The Frequency of Consanguineous Marriages among British Pakistanis', *Journal of Medical Genetics*, 25: pp. 186–90.

Donaldson, L. and Odell, A. (1984) 'Planning and Providing Services for the Asian Population: A Survey of District Health Authorities', *Journal of the Royal Society of Health*, 104: pp. 199–202.

Firdous, R. and Bhopal, R. S. (1989) 'Reproductive Health of Asian Women: A Comparative Study with Hospital and Community Perspectives', *Public Health*, 103: pp. 307–15.

Fox, R. (1967) *Kinship and Marriages* (Harmondsworth: Penguin).

Gillies, D. R. N., Lealman, G. T., Lumb, K. M. and Langdon, P. (1984) 'Analysis of Ethnic Influence on Stillbirths and Infant Mortality in Bradford 1975–81', *Journal of Epidemiology and Community Health*, 38: pp. 214–7.

Honeyman, M. M., Bahl, L., Marshall, T. and Wharton, B. A. (1987) 'Consanguinity and Fetal Growth in Pakistani Moslems', *Archives of Disease in Childhood*, 62: pp. 231–5.

*The Independent* (1993) 15 February.

Jain, C. (1985) *Attitudes of Pregnant Asian Women to Antenatal Care* (Birmingham: West Midlands Regional Health Authority).

Jarman, B. (1983) 'Identification of Underprivileged Areas', *British Medical Journal*, 286: pp. 1705–9.

Johnson, M. R. D. (1993) 'Equal Opportunities in Service Delivery: Responses to a Changing Population', in Ahmad, W. I. U. (ed.), *'Race' and Health in Contemporary Britain* (Milton Keynes: Open University Press).

Jones, I. D. and Cameron, D. (1984) 'Social Class Analysis: An Embarrassment to Epidemiology', *Community Medicine*, 6: pp. 37–46.

Kushnick, L. (1988) 'Racism, the National Health Service and the Health of Black People', *International Journal of Health Services*, 18: 3, pp. 457–70.

86     *The Social Construction of Social Policy*

Little, J. and Nicoll, A. (1988) 'The Epidemiology and Service Implications of Congenital and Constitutional Anomalies in Ethnic Minorities in the UK', *Paediatric and Perinatal Epidemiology*, 2: pp. 161–84.
Littlewood, R. and Lipsedge, M. (1989) *Aliens and Alienists: Ethnic Minorities and Psychiatry*, 2nd edn (London: Unwin Hyman).
Macluer, J. W. (1980) 'Inbreeding and Human Fetal Death' in Porter, I. H. and Hook, E. B. (eds), *Human Embryonic and Fetal Death* (New York: Academic Press).
Mama, A. (1992) 'Black Women and British State: Race, Class and Gender Analysis for the 1990s', in Braham, P., Rattansi, A. and Skellington, R. (eds), *Racism and Antiracism: Inequalities, Opportunities and Policies* (London: Sage).
Modell, B., Ward, R. H. T. and Fairweather, D. T. (1980) 'Effects of Introducing Antenatal Diagnosis on Reproductive Behaviour of Families at Risk for Thalassaemia Major', *British Medical Journal*, 280: pp. 1347–50.
National Association of Health Authorities (NAHA) (1988) *Action Not Words: A Strategy to Improve Services for Ethnic Minority Groups* (Birmingham: NAHA).
Nzegwu, F. (1993) *Black People and Health Care in Contemporary Britain* (Reading, Berks: International Institute for Black Research).
*The Observer* (1993) 21 February.
Parsons, L. and Day, S. (1992) 'Improving Obstetric Outcome in Ethnic Minorities', *Journal of Public Health Medicine*, 14: pp. 183–92.
Parsons, L., Macfarlane, A. J. and Golding, J. (1993) 'Pregnancy, Birth and Maternity Care', in Ahmad, W. I. U. (ed.), *'Race' and Health in Contemporary Britain'* (Milton Keynes: Open University Press).
Pearson, M. (1991) 'Ethnic Differences in Infant Health', *Archives of Disease in Childhood*, 66: pp. 88–90.
Pharoah, P. O. D. and Alberman, E. D. (1990) 'Annual Statistical Review', *Archives of Disease in Childhood*, 65: pp. 147–51.
Pizzini, F. (1989) The Expectant Mother as Patient: A Research Study in Italian Maternity Wards', *Health Promotion*, 4: 1, pp. 1–10.
Proctor, S. R. and Smith, I. J. (1992) 'A Reconsideration of the Factors Affecting Birth Outcome in Pakistani Muslim Families in Britain', *Midwifery*, 8: pp. 76–81.
Rocheron, Y. (1988) 'The Asian Mother and Baby Campaign', *Critical Social Policy*, 22: pp. 4–23.
Saedi-Wong, S. and al-Frayh, A. R. (1989) 'Effects of Consanguineous Matings on Anthropometric Measurements of Saudi Newborn Infants', *Family Practice*, 6: pp. 217–20.
Sashidharan, S. and Francis, E. (1993) 'Epidemiology, Ethnicity and Schizophrenia' in Ahmad, W. I. U. (ed.), *'Race' and Health in Contemporary Britain* (Milton Keynes: Open University Press).
Sathar, Z. A. (1987) 'Seeking Explanations for High Levels of Infant Mortality in Pakistan', *The Pakistan Development Review*, 26: 1, pp. 55–70.
Schull, W. J. and Neel, J. V. (1965) *The Effects of Inbreeding on Japanese Children* (New York: Harper & Row).
Scott-Samuel, A. (1984) 'Need for Primary Health Care: An Objective Indicator', *British Medical Journal*, 288: pp. 457–8.

Sheldon, T. and Parker, H. (1992) 'Use of "Ethnicity" and "Race" in Health Research: A Cautionary Note', in Ahmad, W. I. U. (ed.), *The Politics of 'Race' and Health* (Bradford: Race Relations Research Unit, Bradford University).

Skellington, R. and Morris, P. (1992) *'Race' in Britain Today* (London: Sage).

Smith, R. (1987) *Unemployment and Health* (Oxford: Oxford University Press).

Smith, S. J. (1989) *The Politics of 'Race' and Residence* (Oxford: Polity/ Blackwell).

Solomos, J. (1993) 'Race and Ethnic Relations in Contemporary Social Theory', paper presented at the Annual Conference of the British Sociological Association, University of Essex, 5–8 April.

Terry, P. B., Bissenden, J. G., Condie, R. G. and Mathew, P. M. (1985) 'Ethnic Differences in Congenital Malformations', *Archives of Disease in Childhood*, 60: pp. 866–79.

Theodore-Gandi, B. and Shaikh, K. (1988) *Maternity Services Consumer Survey Report* (Bradford: Bradford Health Authority).

Townsend, P., Phillimore, P. and Beattie, A. (1988) *Health and Deprivation: Inequality and the North* (London: Croom Helm).

Tudor Hart, J. (1971) 'The Inverse Care Law', *Lancet*, i: pp. 405–12.

Wright, C. (1983) 'Language and Communication Problems in an Asian Community', *Journal of the Royal College of General Practitioners*, 33: pp. 101–14.

Zaidi, A. (1989) 'Explanations for High Levels of Infant Mortality in Pakistan: A Dissenting View' (comment on Sathar, 1987), *The Pakistan Development Review*, 28: 3, pp. 251–8.

# 6 Representations of Asians' Mental Health in British Psychiatry

## Charles Watters

The purpose of this paper is to explore representations of people of South Asian origin in British psychiatry and, furthermore, to examine the implications which specific representations may have on the mental health services which Asians receive. I argue that studies of the mental health of Asians in Britain are essentially of two kinds. Firstly they are those conducted in the main by psychiatrists and psychologists, which seek to establish levels of psychiatric morbidity among Asians as compared with the indigenous white population. The focus of these studies has frequently been an analysis of psychiatric hospital admissions. The second type of study can be described as being more anthropological in character and has been oriented towards identifying concepts of mental health and illness among Asians and the impact of what are construed as culturally specific forms of symptom presentation on interaction with psychiatrists and other professionals involved in the delivery of mental health services.

In both instances, I argue, studies of the mental health of Asians in Britain have tended to support and promote particular views of Asian people's problems which have had a significant impact on the services which they receive. A feature of such representations is that they are underpinned by essentialist notions of the characteristics of Asian people and Asian culture suggesting that Asian populations have certain fundamental features which transcend historical and cultural variables. Not only do representations implicitly homogenise Asian populations in Britain, but they also have what Hall (1992, p. 254) has identified as a 'constitutive' role. As such, they have a 'formative, not merely an expressive place in the constitution of social and political life'. Within the context of British mental health services, representations do not merely occur in certain prescribed institutional settings, but may have a role in defining and creating contexts in which Asians receive treatment for mental health problems.

In the context of literature aimed at offering clinical advice on the treatment of Asians, a selective range of 'cultural' factors are highlighted at the expense of consideration of the impact of a range of socio-economic variables which may have a significant impact on Asians' mental health. Asian women, for example, are frequently characterised as being 'passive' or 'isolated' as a result of their culture. Deficiencies in Asian languages are cited as a reason why Asians allegedly are disposed towards somatising their psychiatric problems. While epidemiological studies have been oriented towards answering broad questions regarding the psychiatric morbidity of Asians as an apparently homogeneous group, evidence from anthropological studies which have focused on specific Asian groups is cited in psychiatric literature as providing evidence which can be generally applied. This latter tendency is of particular concern in view of Sperber's (1975, p. 3) observation that anthropologists may be predisposed towards focusing on what they perceive to be the more exotic and symbolic aspects of cultures. In a British context, Currer's (1986) research on concepts of mental health and illness among Pathan women can be seen as an example of an orientation towards investigating the most traditional Asian communities. Here I examine representations of Asians in a number of key texts concerned with the mental health of black people and focus on the way in which Asian people are viewed as utilising psychiatric services, including their alleged tendency to present with a range of somatic complaints.

In a range of quantitatively orientated studies, evidence has been sought to determine whether Asians are more or less likely than whites or other sections of the population to suffer from mental health problems. On the basis of the above, a range of conflicting and often contradictory evidence with respect to the mental health status of Asians in Britain has been produced. In an extensive survey of admissions in England and Wales, Cochrane (1977) suggests that people of Indian or Pakistani origin are less likely than white British to be admitted to psychiatric hospital. In presenting his findings on Asians, Cochrane distinguishes those who were born in India and Pakistan, and males and females. While all Asian groups were less likely than white British to be admitted, his findings suggested that those born in India were more likely to be admitted than those of Pakistani origin, with Indian males most likely to enter psychiatric hospital. These findings, however, should be treated with a degree of caution. These results were not judged to be statistically significant and, furthermore, Cochrane's survey included all admissions and, as such, it is not possible to ascertain the proportion of admissions which were re-admissions. A study conducted by Hitch (1975) in Bradford between 1968 and 1970 presented a very different picture, in which people of Pakistani origin were more likely than white British to be admitted. In the case of Pakistani females, Hitch's findings suggest that they were almost twice as likely to enter psychiatric hospital than were whites. By contrast, he did not find significantly high rates among those born in India. On the basis of a study undertaken in South-east England, Dean and his colleagues reported the reverse, with significantly high rates for Indians but low rates for Pakistanis (Dean *et al.*, 1981). A further study undertaken in Manchester between 1973 and 1975 and based only on first admissions, suggested that all Asian groups were significantly more likely than whites to be admitted to psychiatric hospital (Carpenter and Brockington, 1980).

## MIGRATION AND MENTAL HEALTH

In seeking to explain these apparently contradictory results, a variety of theories have been developed with respect to the relationship between migration and mental health, with high rates of admission being associated with the 'stress of migration' while low rates are explained by reference to a process of 'selection'. According to Cochrane, the latter process takes place in the sending society and ensures that only those who are 'well adjusted' are allowed to migrate. In seeking to explain why this theory does not appear to apply to other migrant groups included in Cochrane's study who appear to have high psychiatric morbidity, he argues that there are special features associated with the selection of Asian migrants which ensure that the latter are 'well adjusted'. According to Cochrane,

> Where poverty, lack of contact with Western culture, poor communication and distance present great obstacles to migration, and where failure to achieve acceptable living standards in the country of origin cannot be attributed to personal failure, it may be that only the most stable members of the population can overcome these obstacles and become immigrants. This would account for the low rates of mental illness among Asians.   (Cochrane, 1977)

Put crudely, Cochrane's argument is that where migration is difficult to achieve, only those who are particularly well adjusted are likely to succeed. The theory of 'selection' is even used to explain differences in psychiatric morbidity between Pakistanis and Indians. In a community study concluded in Birmingham (Cochrane and Stopes-Roe, 1977), Indian- and Pakistani-born people were interviewed to ascertain the extent to which they displayed symptoms associated with mental ill-health. On the basis of this study it was concluded that Pakistani-born people displayed less psychiatric symptoms than did Indian-born people. Cochrane and Stopes-Roe suggest that this difference is due to the fact that as the Indian sample were better educated (most had had secondary education), they may have found the process of migration easier than the Pakistani sample, and that, furthermore, their higher level of education may have had an influence on them having greater expectations as to the benefits they might obtain by migrating. In commenting on these findings, Littlewood and Lipsedge (1989, p. 141) added that the lower scores among those from Pakistan may also be attributable to the fact that Islam has 'proved more resilient in Britain than has Hinduism, which is primarily an Indian national religion'.

The above studies display two striking features. Firstly, the inconsistency of the evidence regarding psychiatric hospital admissions among Asians, and secondly the range of untested hypotheses used to explain these findings. With respect to the latter, theories of migration are invoked without any apparent consideration of the migration experiences of those included in samples. Generalised statements to the effect that, for example, Indians may have an easier selection process for migration than do Pakistanis are, without any supporting evidence, little more than mere conjecture. Studies of migration from the Indian subcontinent to Britain indicate that there are wide differences in the circumstances in which people migrate, which are crucially influenced by factors such as gender, socio-economic status and social and economic changes within the regions from which people migrated. Several commentators have pointed to the existence of a range of what have been characterised as 'push or pull factors' affecting migration to Britain and operating within different regions of the Indian subcontinent in different time periods (Aurora, 1967; Robinson, 1986).

A widely reported pattern of migration is one in which an Asian man has initially travelled to Britain for work and, after establishing himself in the country, then arranges for his family to join him (Ballard 1977; Rack, 1982; Robinson, 1986). On the basis of Cochrane's hypothesis, a 'selection' process could arguably operate to determine which Asian males make the initial journey. It would be implausible to extend this theory to the men's families (unless of course one assumes that 'well adjusted Asian males' will always have 'well adjusted' families). Moreover, as Mahmood (1987, p. 13) has observed, the theory of selection is crucially deficient as, 'there has been no published research validation to indicate whether migrants are a negatively or positively selected group in comparison to the non-migrants remaining in their country of origin'.

The view put forward by the psychiatrists Littlewood and Lipsedge (1989, p. 141) to the effect that the resilience of Islam in Britain may be a factor in explaining the apparent low level of psychiatric morbidity among Pakistani Muslims as compared with Hindus is similarly highly speculative. The findings cited by Littlewood and Lipsedge only differentiate between Indians and Pakistanis and the assumption here that all Indians are Hindus is obviously misleading, given the substantial proportion of Indians who are Muslims. Moreover, the authors do not explain in what ways the existence of durable religious traditions help to prevent mental ill-health. The merits of this hypothesis are further eroded by evidence suggesting that, while one can little doubt the resilience of Islam in the British context, Hinduism too has proved to be both durable and adaptable (see Burghart, 1987).

## HOMOGENISATION AND THE MYTH OF A 'LEVEL PLAYING FIELD' IN SERVICE DELIVERY

Besides the fact that the above studies contain a number of unsustainable hypotheses, they give rise to more general and substantial concerns which relate to the context in which the evidence presented is placed. By locating their findings in the context of a wider debate about migration and mental health, or in a broad consideration of the extent to which Asians are more or less likely than members of the indigenous white population to have mental illness, the researchers have often failed to address more specific issues relating to the localities in which their research was undertaken. In reviewing these studies of hospital admissions, Rack (1982, p. 162) concludes that 'in the case of Asian patients there are some seemingly irreconcilable contradictions', while Ineichen (1987, p. 2) has observed that 'the mental health of people of Asian origin produces no clear pattern'.

In my view, what is striking here is not so much the apparent 'inconsistencies' in the evidence produced, but that research is persistently directed towards seeking to identify an overall pattern on which to base generalised statements about Asians as a more or less homogenous group. Besides the fact that the researchers pay scant attention to the characteristics of Asian groups included in their studies (beyond a broad differentiation between Indians and Pakistanis), in the course of formulating hypotheses the possible impact of patterns of service provision in particular localities is not taken into consideration. Is the fact that Asians in Manchester are more likely than whites to enter psychiatric hospital on a first admission attributable, to some degree, to the pattern of service provision in that locality? Reported differences in the rate of psychiatric hospitalisation of Asians between Manchester and Bradford, which suggest that the latter city has lower rates could, arguably, be attributable to the fact that Bradford had developed some specific mental-health services for Asian groups which may have had a preventative function (Rack, 1982, p. 266).

A further objection is that psychiatric hospital admissions may be a poor indicator of levels of morbidity in the community, particularly in the context of black and minority ethnic groups. In recent years there has been considerable debate with respect to the psychiatric hospitalisation of black people and, in particular, the use of compulsory admission under section 136 of the Mental Health Act (1983). Pilgrim and Rogers (1993, p. 50) have noted that recent research on Section 136 has shown that rates of detention for Afro-Caribbean people are up to two and a half times the rate for white people. A study conducted in Bristol also indicated higher rates of compulsory admissions among Afro-Caribbeans (Ineichen *et al.*, 1984). According to Ineichen and his colleagues, these admissions were likely to follow a public disturbance and involve police officers. In a recent study it is also suggested that Asian men are more likely than whites to enter hospital through this route (Barnes and Bawl, 1989). Of further relevance is the fact that the same study suggests that a proportion of Asians, in particular young Asian women, may be inappropriately admitted to hospital. In the report's conclusions the comment is made that 'the percentage of young Asian women admitted inappropriately because of the non-availability of appropriate alternative resources is striking'. Furthermore, on the basis of a comparative study of inappropriate or 'preventable' admissions across ten local authority areas, the report highlights substantial differences in the extent of preventable admissions of Asians in different areas of Britain. These findings suggest that while in some areas there may be appropriate, community-based services for Asians which may prevent hospital admissions, in other areas these services are absent. These apparent inconsistencies in the level of services provided in the community for Asian people may account for some of the variation in rates of psychiatric hospital admissions referred to above.

Furthermore, admission to psychiatric hospital may depend on a wide range of factors. Littlewood and Lipsedge (1989, p. 92) have argued that admission depends on 'the facilities offered, how serious the condition appears to be to the patient, his family and his doctor, and also the amount of support the community can offer'. Goldberg and Huxley (1980) have identified four filters which individuals normally pass through before they are admitted to a psychiatric hospital. The passage through these filters is dependent on a number of factors in addition to the clinical condition of the patient. For example, the attitudes of the patient's relatives and the availability of local medical services may influence the extent to which the patient will seek help from a general practitioner (GP). Subsequent referral to a psychiatrist will depend on the extent to which GPs are able to detect the disorder. Even when patients have been referred on to a psychiatrist, a decision to admit them to psychiatric hospital may be influenced by a number of non-clinical factors such as the availability of hospital beds.

These filters or pathways to care, which culminate in admission to psychiatric hospital, may present particular obstacles to members of Asian communities. Ahmad *et al.*'s (1991) study of GPs' perceptions of Asian and non-Asian patients suggests that GPs tend to regard their Asian patients as being more likely than non-Asians to present with 'trivial' complaints and to use up more of the GPs' time. While empirical evidence suggests that there is no factual basis for this perception, it nevertheless appears to be widespread and reinforced by guidelines to GPs aimed at supporting their work with Asians (see Rack, 1990). A perception of Asians as being likely to present with trivial complaints may lead to a reluctance to refer them for specialist help and, as such, inhibit passage from the second to the third filter identified by Goldberg and Huxley.

## ANTHROPOLOGY AS EVIDENCE

Further research on the mental health of Asians in Britain has been more qualitatively orientated, and has focused on exploring various concepts of mental health and illness present in British Asian communities. These studies can appropriately be set in the broader context of research on Asian communities in Britain conducted principally in the 1960s and 1970s. A principal focus of these studies was the extent to which Asian culture was persisting and adapting in Britain. This concern was articulated in the context of a debate revolving around the question of assimilation and the extent to which this process was occurring in different Asian communities.

Studies of this kind typically consisted of two phases. Firstly, fieldwork would be undertaken in India or Pakistan within villages and towns from which Asian communities in Britain had migrated. The purpose of this initial fieldwork was to acquaint the researcher with customs and practices found within Asian settings. Knowledge of these would enable the researcher to conduct the second phase of the work in which she or he would seek to determine the ways in which particular customs and practices had been continued in Britain and then adapted to a new setting. In several studies attention was focused on potential intergenerational differences in addressing the hypothesis that younger Asian people who were born in Britain would adopt British customs and values which would lead to conflict with older 'first-generation migrants' (for example, Khan, 1979). Jefferys' (1976, p. 7) study of Pakistanis in Bristol is an example of the approach described above. Preliminary fieldwork in Pakistan is justified on the grounds that 'it is not possible to understand the behaviour and aspirations of my informants in Bristol without a close consideration of their lifestyles and life chances in Pakistan'.

Jeffery (1976, p. 5) had initially hoped to study conflict between first-generation migrant parents and their daughters with respect to 'their parents wishes to maintain purdah in Britain and to arrange the marriages of their children'. Such conflict she assumed to exist as a consequence of a process of assimilation. However, in this instance, the line of enquiry proved to be fruitless. Jeffery (1976, p. 5) writes, 'I soon realised that there were few conflicts between the girls and their parents, and I was very much struck with the way in which the migrants were able to maintain a "Pakistani" identity'. This realisation led to Jeffery shifting the focus of her study to the social processes involved in non-assimilation and the maintenance of ethnic boundaries.

An aspect which is missing in this account is a consideration of the reasons behind the formulation of the original hypothesis. The anthropologist assumed intergenerational conflict would be present and the study of this would constitute the parameters of the research. The presence of intergenerational conflict was perceived as being in opposition to the maintenance of Pakistani identity, with the implicit assumption that the presence of Pakistani identity among the young precludes the prospect of conflict between parents and their teenage daughters. A simple dichotomy is thus assumed, according to which first-generation migrants embody cultural norms and values which are at variance with those found in Britain, while their children growing up in Britain find themselves between two cultures in a situation of considerable stress and potential conflict. Such assumptions were commonly made in studies of the relationship between health and social services and ethnic minority groups conducted in the late 1960s and early 1970s (Fitzherbert, 1967; Triseliotis, 1972).

This potential for conflict is, according to Tambs-Lyche (1980, p. 19), mitigated in the context of Gujaratis in Britain by the adoption of Western dress and behaviour within a public sphere while still keeping, 'for certain occasions, codes to communicate their ethnic distinctiveness; and they still judge their behaviour and that of their caste-fellows according to value standards that are peculiarly theirs'. In elaborating on this distinction, Tambs-Lyche differentiates between what he terms the 'encompassed' and the 'encompassing' society, the latter referring to British society while the former refers to the particular social milieu in which his informants are located and from which they derive their particular value system.

Inasmuch as there is an attempt here to identify the particular ways in which a Gujarati community relates to broader British society and how this interrelationship differs from that found within the community studied, it marks an advance on many previous and subsequent studies of Asian communities in Britain, in which the quality and impact of the relationship between Asians and British society is barely addressed. Jeffery (1973, p. 213), for example, states simply that the relationship with British society reproduces the same forms of boundary maintenance as are found within Pakistani communities in Britain. Robinson (1986, p. 84) elaborates on this point in the following statement,

> It seems that Indian and Pakistani migrants in Britain not only avoid contact with the indigenous population, but also minimise the need for interaction with other Asians whom they feel to be members of out-groups (on whatever criteria appear appropriate at that time). They employ similar strategies for both purposes and these strategies produce similar spatial, social, and institutional outcomes.

It is perhaps significant that Robinson makes this rather sweeping statement in the context of reviewing research findings deriving from anthropological studies undertaken on Asian communities in Britain in the 1960s and 1970s. In the latter, there appears to have been little focus or reflection within anthropological literature on the relationship between Asian communities in Britain and the range of British institutions with which they have regular contact. This situation changed, to some extent, with the publication in the late 1970s of a number of studies, conducted principally by anthropologists, which explored the relationship between Asians and agencies concerned with the provision of health and social services.

These studies tended to be targeted at white professionals working in these agencies and aimed at heightening their sensitivity to the cultures of clients from black and ethnic minorities. Examples of this approach are Ballard's (1979) study of social-work practice in respect of ethnic minorities and MacDonald's (1987) work on health-promotion activities directed at Gujaratis living in London. In Ballard's study, an assimilationist hypothesis is explicitly rejected on the grounds that the 'immigrant' minorities are sustaining culturally distinctive patterns of social relations, which are a product of their experiences in Britain, quite as much as of their roots overseas.

As in Jeffery's study, Asians are presented as living in communities whose norms and values may be at considerable variance with those found among white populations. Ballard (1979, p. 149) goes so far as to describe the experience of social workers (who are assumed to be white) as being akin to those of Alice after she passes through the looking glass: 'once across the ethnic boundary . . . they can never be quite sure whether things really mean what they seem to, or rather what they would have done had the rules of the more normal and familiar world continued to apply'. Ethnic minority cultures are here defined as 'coherent systems' or as 'systematic totalities' (Ballard, 1979, pp. 149, 151) to which the anthropologist may provide a map to assist the professional. In addressing the position of South Asians, Ballard (1979, p. 155) puts forward an implicitly essentialist perspective according to which South Asians live in communal groupings in which 'obligation to others is always expected to override personal self-interest'.

The apparently supportive nature of Asian communities is here presented as a reason why they may have less need for social-work services than do the white population. Furthermore, the ideological position of social work which, according to Ballard (1979, p. 155), stresses the values of individual freedom and self-determination, may make it, as presently constituted, an inappropriate agency to help Asian people. 'Paradoxically', he argues, 'the more South Asians move towards the values enshrined in social work theory, the more they will find themselves in need of social workers.' The model of Asian settlement in Britain, according to which Asians live in supportive communities which maintain strict boundaries with wider British society, has been influential in the way in which health and social services have been organised for Asians, particularly in the light of the key policy objective of developing community care, and may have a significant impact on the particular way in which programmes of care are developed for Asians by British health and social services.

Research on the area of mental health and Asians in Britain has been directed primarily at Asian women and has been focused on the latter's expression of symptoms associated, in broad terms, with the Western nosological category of 'depression'. This focus does not appear to be the result of clear epidemiological evidence suggesting that Asian women suffer from these disorders any more than do other groups in British society. In introducing her study of concepts of mental illness among Pathan women in Bradford, Caroline Currer argues that there is evidence to support the view that depression among Asian women is particularly high in Britain. However, the sources she cites consist largely of anecdotal evidence (1986, p. 184).

In the absence of substantial and consistent epidemiological data, there may be two reasons behind the high degree of interest in this area. Errol Lawrence has argued that Asian women are the subject of what he terms 'common sense assumptions' in white British society to the effect that they are both 'passive' and 'isolated' (1982, p. 121). This stereotypical image of Asian women in Britain has been, according to Lawrence (1982, p. 118), promoted by the writings of the anthropologist Verity Khan, who has described Asian families as a locus of 'stress ridden relationships' which in turn hampers their access to social life in Britain. Philip Rack, the Bradford-based trans-cultural psychiatrist, confirms these stereotypes in an essay on the psychopathology of Asians. According to Rack (1990, p. 290) there are:

> Asian women whose days are spent in loneliness and social isolation, cut off from family and neighbourhood networks. Many older Asian women speak little or no English. Some are confined to their home, by their husbands or their own timidity, and are seldom seen; and others may become surgery-haunters – perhaps because a visit to the doctor is one of their few opportunities for a culturally sanctioned outing.

The fact that this view is expressed in the context of a handbook for GPs can only help to reinforce the latter's view of Asian people as malingering despite, as Ahmad and his colleagues have reported (1991, p. 54), there being no objective evidence to support this view. Suman Fernando (1988, p. 29) reports that within mental health services Asian women are seen as 'isolated because of their traditional customs and views of the world' and that this view is linked to an expectation that there will be high rates of depression in this group. Thus stereotypical views of Asian women can be seen as underpinning, or at least providing an impetus for, research into depression in this group.

This is explicit in Currer's work, in which a link between isolation and depression is presented as an opening hypothesis, and a justification for focusing her study on Pathan women, who she describes as being among the most isolated of Asian groups. According to Currer,

> Pathan women do form an extreme, and one that could be expected to illustrate the issues to be explored more clearly. (1986, p. 186)

A further reason for focusing on Asian women in this context may be one of what could be termed 'methodological expediency'. A number of researchers in this field have reported difficulty in establishing contact with Asian men, despite having initially planned to include them in their study (Meg McDonald, personal communication). This was attributed to the fact that men were sometimes more wary of researchers and spent substantial amounts of time out of the home. Asian women, by contrast, particularly those with young children, could be contacted with relative ease. This limitation may be an important consideration, particularly in instances where general statements are made about the beliefs of a particular Asian group.

Currer (1986, p. 184) justifies her focus on Pathan women on the grounds that as a particularly secluded Asian group, through the practice of Purdah, they could best illustrate links between 'isolation' and 'depression' as 'seclusion is seen as leading to isolation, and this to depression'. However, the relationship between 'seclusion' and 'isolation' is problematical, and it is arguable whether this study of Pathan women is a suitable focus for considering isolation among Asian groups. 'Isolation' can be seen as operating on three levels. Firstly, there is isolation from public life, which Currer defines as 'seclusion', and which certainly appears to be present among Pathan women. Secondly, isolation could be defined in the context of an absence of social networks and, thirdly, as what I would describe as 'personal isolation' in which an individual may, ostensibly, have access to a wide social network but may be personally ostracised. While Pathan women appear to have been 'isolated' in the first sense, they would generally not in the second sense in that they had, according to Currer (1986, p. 196), 'social networks which were supportive in a practical sense' (p. 196). In this context also, Pathan women may be far from typical of other Asian groups in Britain. Indeed, Currer suggests that the very practice of Purdah itself may contribute to the development of support among the women involved as 'their very conformity united them within a very real community' (p. 198). Thus seclusion in this sense, far from leading to isolation, can be viewed as a factor in increasing social support among women. One could argue, by extension, that where such socially and religiously sanctioned practices do not exist, as in the case of the bulk of Asian people in Britain, the development of this sort of social network would not be present. Currer argues that the most clearly depressed women were 'members of close networks in which interaction was frequent, but within which they were rejected personally' (p. 197). However, she does not comment on the quality of this interaction, nor on whether the feelings of depression were seen as a result of this personal rejection or whether the latter followed the woman's development of depressive symptoms. Consideration of these matters would have been valuable in ascertaining the extent to which Pathan women in this context functioned as a supportive community in instances where individuals suffered from mental ill-health.

My central criticism of Currer's study is that it may serve to reinforce the stereotypical views of Asian people described by, for example, Lawrence (1982, p. 113) while providing insufficient justification for selecting a group which were, in Currer's own terms, an extreme case. The description of the women contained in the study conforms remarkably closely to the account of British racial discourse on Asian women presented by Parmar (1982, p. 236). For example, according to Currer, 'the women's value, in their own eyes and those of their community, lay in their ability to care for their husbands and children and manage the home' and 'the important thing was not whether or not the women felt unwell, but that they should fulfil their obligations to the family'. (1986, p. 189). Illness, where it occurred, was viewed as a form of social dysfunction in which the woman could no longer fulfil these routine household tasks and a return to health was defined in terms of a return to work. Despite Currer's appeal that such findings should not be taken as typical for Asian women, the view that health and illness are related to the ability to undertake required routine tasks, is echoed in other studies of Asian's mental health. For example, according to Rack,

> The important criterion of health is the ability to carry out one's obligations, do one's work, fulfil one's role. If you can do these things you are well, if you are unable to do them you are ill, and no more needs to be said.   (1982, p. 110)

This implied lack of introspection on the part of Asians has been used, according to Fernando (1988, p. 166), to justify the view that Asians may be inappropriate subjects for psychotherapy, a view that has been strongly challenged both in theory and in practice by Kareem (1992) on the basis of their own psychotherapeutic work with Asians.

## SOMATISATION AND THE CLINICAL GAZE

Investigations into cultural aspects of mental illness among Asians in Britain have also been undertaken by psychiatrists with an interest in anthropological techniques. One particularly influential study was Philip Rack's *Race, Culture and Mental Disorder*, which was published in 1982 and which I have referred to above. In it, Rack identifies what he views as 'cultural pitfalls' in the recognition of mental illness among ethnic minorities in Britain. By gaining knowledge of ethnic minorities' cultures, the clinician will, according to Rack, be in a better position to recognise and treat mental illnesses appropriately. As such, Rack's book can be regarded, at least to some extent, as a diagnostic tool for psychiatrists and other professionals working in the mental-health sphere. With the introduction of cultural knowledge of ethnic minorities, clinicians can, to use Foucault's expression, sharpen their 'clinical gaze' correctly to identify the signs and symptoms presented by their ethnic minority clients.

One particular 'cultural pitfall' Rack associates with Asians is a tendency to 'somatise' psychological distress. This refers to the perceived frequency with which Asians present psychological problems to their doctors in the form of physical aches and pains. As a result of this, according to Rack (1982, p. 182), the uninitiated clinician can waste valuable clinical time by ordering 'unnecessary investigations, X-rays and specialist referrals'. Rack suggests that there may be three reasons why Asians somatise. Firstly, it may be because they view the doctor's role as being related to physical illness and therefore only bring to the latter complaints which they think are appropriate to this role. Secondly, the somatic complaint may be a metaphor used because Asian languages do not have sufficiently rich vocabularies for expressing emotional distress. This view has been supported by the psychiatrist Leff (1973), who argued that Asians may have an inability to have access to a verbal idiom of emotional distress. A third possibility put forward by Rack is that physical symptoms may be the only ones acceptable to patients, who will repress or deny psychological problems.

The apparent tendency of Asians to somatise psychological distress has been challenged by Krause (1990) who, on the basis of a comparative study of Punjabi and English respondents attending a health centre, concludes that 'the Punjabi tendency to somatise more than white British emerged as a non-significant trend and white British patients also presented somatically' (1990, p. 114). Krause rejects Rack's and Leff's hypothesis that somatisation was used by Asians owing to an absence in Asian languages of an idiom for expressing emotional states, and concludes that 'Punjabi patients are as able as their British counterparts to express themselves psychologically'. Furthermore, she adds that this ability is not the result of 'westernisation', as the patients included in this study were of first generation and 'made sense of their lives using traditional Punjabi concepts and ideas of health and illness' (1990, p. 116). In an authoritative paper on the subject Lipowski (1988, p. 1359) has defined somatisation as occurring in instances when the somatising person does 'not recognize, and may explicitly deny, a causal link between their distress and its presumed source'. Furthermore, Lipowski argues that somatisation occurs in instances where the patients perception is in terms of an actual or threatened disease of or damage to the body. In instances where this is not present, he concludes, the term does not apply.

It is interesting to consider Lipowski's definition in the light of charac-terisations of Asians somatising in the context of British psychiatry. According to Rack, somatisation may be the result of an attempt by Asians to 'mask' or 'repress' psychological problems. He suggests that somatisa-tion may be a 'hysterical manouevre' whereby internal conflict is con-verted into physical symptoms. In substantiating this view he cites Kleinman's (1980, p. 7) example of a Chinese patient who presents soma-tically apparently because his psychological problems are so unbearable to him. Interestingly, Rack here moves from generalisations about Asians to generalisations about 'non-Europeans'. It is notable that even in this example, it is questionable whether this patient is somatising in accordance with Lipowski's definition. The patient here explicitly identifies his financial problems as being the key aetiological factor in his illness. Thus a social cause is identified for the physical complaint, a phe-nomena which Lipowski argues is not normally associated with somatisa-tion. Asian patients in the British context will explicitly indicate that a range of psychological and social factors are responsible for their physical condition. These aetiological assumptions may be made explicit in con-texts in which the patient is dealt with in a sensitive manner by a worker who speaks an appropriate language (Fernando, 1989; Watters, 1994).


CONCLUSION

The above inquiry suggests that within the context of British mental-health services, people of South Asian origin are represented in particular ways which may have an impact on the treatment they receive. Underpinning these representations is a view of Asians as being a largely homogeneous group about whom meaningful statements can be made regarding psychi-atric morbidity. Essentialist perspectives on the nature of Asian people and of Asian people and Asian communities are apparent in much psychiatric literature. In these perspectives, Asian culture is reified and located in the context of customs and traditions emanating from the Indian subcontinent. As such, psychiatric and mental health literature displays many of the characteristics which Rattansi (1992) has identified as constituting a multi-cultural approach. Within a clinical context, Asians are presented as soma-tising psychological problems, as wasting disproportionate amounts of clinicians' time and as regarding themselves as cured if they can perform routine duties. Asian women are presented as being lonely and isolated if they do not have relatives nearby, and thus prone to depression, while being subject to high degrees of stress if they live in an extended family context (Bavington, 1986, p. 89).

The material presented here suggests that specific representations of Asians may be ubiquitous in literature relating to mental health. Given the clinically orientated and applied nature of much of the literature discussed here, it may be assumed that these representations are formative, in that they influence the nature of the services which Asian people receive. Ahmad *et al.*'s (1991) study of GPs' attitudes to Asians suggests that specific representations of Asians may inform the treatment which Asian people receive in the context of GP consultations. The present study suggests that a shift of focus from studying Asians as a discreet grouping, displaying particular forms of morbidity, to one which focuses on the dynamic interaction between Asians and psychiatric services would be both appropriate and timely.

## References

Ahmad, W., Baker, M. R. and Kernohan, E. M. (1991) 'General Practitioners' Perceptions of Asian and non-Asian Patients', *Family Practice*, 8: pp. 52–56.

Aurora, G. S. (1967) *The New Frontiersman: A Sociological Study of Indian Immigrants in the United Kingdom* (Bombay: Popular Pakistan).

Ballard, R. (1977) 'The Sikhs: The Development of South Asian Settlements in Britain', in Watson, J. L. (eds), *Between Two Cultures* (Oxford: Blackwell).

Ballard, R. (1979) 'Social Work with Ethnic Minorities', in Khan, V. (ed.), *Minority Families in Britain* (London: Macmillan).

Bavington, J. and Majid, A. (1986) 'Psychiatric Services for Ethnic Minority Groups', in Cox, J. (ed.), *Transcultural Psychiatry* (London: Croom Helm).

Barnes, M. and Bawl, R. (1989) 'Race and Mental Health: S.S.R.G. Monitoring Report', University of Birmingham.

Burghart, R. (1987) *Hinduism in Great Britain* (Cambridge: Cambridge University Press).

Carpenter, L. and Brockington, I. F. (1980) 'A Study of Mental Illness in Asians, West Indians and Africans Living in Manchester', *British Journal of Psychiatry*, 137: p. 201.

Cochrane, R. (1977) 'Mental Illness in Immigrants to England and Wales: An Analysis of Mental Hospital Admissions, 1971', *Social Psychiatry*, **12:** p. 25–35

Cochrane, R. and Stopes-Roe, M. (1977) 'Psychological and Social Adjustment of Asian Immigrants to Britain: A Community Survey', *Social Psychology*, **12:** p. 195

Currer, C. (1986) 'Concepts of Mental Well- and Ill-being: The Case of Pathan Mothers in Britain', in Currer, C. and Stacey, M. (eds), *Concepts of Health, Illness and Disease* (Leamington Spa: Berg).

Dean, G., Walsh, D., Downing, H. and Shelley, E. (1981) 'First Admissions of Native Born and Immigrants to Psychiatric Hospitals in South East England, 1976', *British Journal of Psychiatry*, **139:** p. 506–12.

Fernando, S. (1988) *Race and Culture in Psychiatry* (London: Croom Helm).

Fitzherbert, K. (1967) *West Indian Children in London* (London: Bell).

Goldberg, D. and Huxley, P. (1980) *Mental Illness in the Community: The Pathway to Psychiatric Care* (London: Tavistock).

Hall, S. (1992) 'New Ethnicities', in Donald, J. and Rattansi, A. (eds), *'Race' Culture and Difference* (London: Sage in association with the Open University Press).

Hitch, P. J. (1975) 'Migration and Mental Illness in a Northern City', PhD thesis, Bradford University.

Ineichen, B. (1987) 'The Mental Health of Asians in Britain: A Research Note', *New Community*, 4: pp. 1–2.

Ineichen, B., Harrison, G. and Morgan, H. S. (1984) 'Psychiatric Hospital Admissions in Bristol', *British Journal of Psychiatry*, **145:** pp. 600–11.

Jeffery, P. (1976) *Migrants and Refugees: Muslim and Christian Pakistani Families in Bristol* (Cambridge: Cambridge University Press).

Kareem, J. (1992) 'The Nafsiyat Intercultural Therapy Centre: Ideas and Experience in Intercultural Therapy', in Kareem, J. and Littlewood, R. (eds), *Intercultural Therapy: Themes, Interpretations and Practice* (Oxford: Blackwell) pp. 14–37.

Khan, V. (1979) *Minority Families in Britain* (London: Macmillan).

Kleinman, A. (1980) *Patients and Healers in the Contexts of Culture* (Berkeley, CA: University of California Press).

Krause, I. B. (1990) 'Psychiatric Morbidity among Punjabi Medical Patients in England Measured by General Health Questionnaire', *Psychological Medicine*, **20:** pp. 711–19.

Lawrence, E. (1982) 'Just Plain Common Sense: The "Roots" of Racism', in *The Empire Strikes Back: Race and Racism in 70s Britain* (London: Hutchinson, in association with the Centre for Contemporary Cultural Studies).

Leff, J. (1973) 'Culture and the Differentiation of Emotional States', *British Journal of Psychiatry*, 125: pp. 336–40.

Lipowski, Z. (1988) 'Somatisation: The Concept and its Clinical Application', *American Journal of Psychiatry*, 145: pp. 1358–68.

Littlewood, R. and Lipsedge, M. (1989) *Aliens and Alienists* (London: Unwin Hyman).

MacDonald, M. (1987) 'Communicating Health Care Information: Child and Maternal Health among Gujaratis in East London', *South Asia Research*, 7: 1, pp. 25–37.

Mahmood, S. (1987) 'Life Stress and Symptoms: A Comparative Study of Pakistani and English Women', in Dent, H. (ed.), *Clinical Psychology: Research and Development* (London: Croom Helm), pp. 111–17.

Parmar, P. (1982) 'Gender, Race and Class: Asian Women in Resistance', in *The Empire Strikes Back: Race and Racism in 70s Britain* (London: Centre for Contemporary Cultural Studies/ Hutchinson).

Pilgrim, D. and Rogers, A. (1993) *A Sociology of Mental Health and Illness* (Buckingham: Open University Press).

Rack, P. (1982) *Race, Culture and Mental Disorder* (London: Tavistock).

Rack, P. (1990) 'Psychological and Psychiatric Disorders', in McAvoy, B. R. and Donaldson, L. J. (eds), *Health Care for Asians*, Oxford General Practice Series 18 (Oxford: Oxford University Press).

Rattansi, A. (1992) 'Changing the Subject? Racism, Culture and Education', in Donald, J. and Rattansi, A. (eds), *'Race' Culture and Difference* (London: Sage in association with the Open University).

Robinson, V. (1986) *Transients, Settlers and Refugees* (Oxford: Clarendon Press).

Sperber, D. (1975) *Rethinking Symbolism* (Cambridge: Cambridge University Press).

Tambs-Lyche, H. (1980) *London Patidars: A Case Study in Urban Ethnicity* (Routledge: London).

Triseliotis, J. (1972) *Social Work with Coloured Immigrants and their Families* (Oxford: Oxford University Press for Institute of Race Relations).

Watters, C. (1994) *Asians and Psychiatric Services in Britain: Avenues of Access and Parameters of Treatment*, PhD thesis, School of African and Asian Studies, University of Sussex.

# Part III
# Citizenship, Rights and Inequalities

# 7 Difference in the City: Locating Marginal Use of Public Space

## Karen Evans and Penelope Fraser

The following chapter arises out of work on the ESRC-sponsored research project 'The Public Sense of Well-being – A Taxonomy of Publics and Space' based in the Sociology Department of Salford University. Our research is concerned with constructing what we have called a 'grounded exploration of urban use and urban experience in relation to two particular cities in the North of England' (Evans *et al.*, 1993, p. 3). We have noted that much recent literature on the city has failed to locate *differences* in urban experience, often presenting a view of the city which is held by a particular person or social group – offering little to our understanding of the inequality and diversity of life in cities. We are also concerned to highlight differences between particular conurbations in terms of their actual patterns of use, being at the same time attentive to any differences in social composition which impact upon this use.

We question writings which suggest that there is a reading of the city which can be applied to *all its population* or all those who use its space. We wish, instead, to offer some explanation as to how a city is actually *lived* by its populations and, in particular, how such feelings as anxiety and unease affect groups differently. We are also interested in how these feelings are 'accepted' and 'routinised' into everyday behaviour; in short, how people 'go to town' (Evans *et al.*, 1993). We have spoken to different populations encountered in the two North of England cities of Manchester and Sheffield, about *their* experiences of using *public space* in these cities.

We are concerned in this chapter to uncover some of the ways in which the different populations in the city are forced by economic necessity, inaccessibility or lack of well-being in public spaces, amongst other reasons, into a marginalised use of public space. Despite initiatives which aim to plan out difference, such as the shopping mall which purports to offer a 'democratic' space in which total shopping experiences (consumption and leisure) are available to all with an amount of money to spend, however small, and time on their hands – regardless of class position or consumer power, the public spaces of our cities are used in a myriad of ways. Through their use of these spaces the individuals who make up the city's marginalised populations adopt strategies which help to mediate the effects of their marginalisation. Through this process they become less like the passive consumers of marketing literature and take on a more active role in shaping their experience of the city. We present four case-studies in which populations that we consider in some significant sense to be marginalised in public space, demonstrate very different responses to their marginalisation. For some, activities as diverse as bargain-hunting or hanging around on the streets become the strategies through which these populations take control, albeit in a very limited way, of their use of public space; for others the solutions are less satisfactory, resulting at times in avoidance of these spaces.


## THE RESEARCH METHODOLOGY

In order to capture presently existing difference in the two cities in which we chose to work – Manchester and Sheffield – we were concerned to develop a research design which would not take the concepts of 'Public' and 'Well-being' as uncontested. We set out to discover who uses the public space in our cities and for what purposes, how people experience different places at different times and the feelings generated by these places, as well as the strategies which are employed to manage unease, fear or anxiety in the city.

We have defined public space here as those public arenas where a wide range of the perceived needs of a city's population are met through private enterprise or public funding; where shopping, leisure, information and transport facilities are concentrated and where use of these facilities is pre-sumed to be shared. The presumption is that a library exists for all a city's population to use, transport facilities and interchanges serve all parts of the city – whether middle-class suburbs or working-class housing estates – and banks, financial agencies and travel agents, are no longer required by salaried professionals alone but now serve everyone in the 'classless society' who calls on their services.

People in Manchester and Sheffield were initially contacted through street interviews in various locations. Predominantly housing areas and the streets which serve them have not been chosen for this research, but city and town centres, out-of-town shopping areas and major thorough-fares, which attract people for a whole number of activities, have been chosen as our survey sites. Interview times were chosen to discover patterns of use of public space as different groups of people 'laid claim' to an area at different times of the day or on different days of the week. The information we collected in this way allowed us to construct a view of the city which emphasised the mundane and routinised nature of much of its everyday street-life (Evans *et al.*, 1993). The majority of our respondents were in these public spaces either to work, in the case of Manchester or, in Sheffield, to shop and this was mainly for basic necessities such as food and household goods rather than clothes or leisure goods. In both cities leisure use (mainly drinking in pubs) came a poor fourth, being outnumbered by those passing through an area on the way to some other place.

Smaller numbers were subsequently invited to attend 'focus-group' discussions. Participants in these discussion groups have been drawn from the different sorts of people found to be using public space and have also been conducted with significant groups of the population who were *not* using the streets in any great number. Each focus-group discussion drew on the experiences of the participants, encouraging them to share and to debate their individual 'spatial stories' through which they organise their use of urban space. Through narratives about places, the participants were encouraged to:

> make the journey, before or during the time that the feet perform it. (De Certeau, 1984 pp. 115–6)

During the discussions, we explored areas of shared perception in the city and different experiences and attitudes to the streets and those who populate them. Focusing discussion in this way enabled us to 'unpack' the survey responses, to get beyond possibly superficial answers and more fully to understand the attitudes expressed.

At all stages of the research we have observed street activity, talked to managers of public space (including conducting focus-group discussions with police officers working in areas around our chosen survey sites) and representatives of non-statutory organisations working in each area. This has given us an insight into other significant areas of activity on the streets, such as areas where youth or the elderly 'hang around' or 'sit and relax', thus changing the nature of an area for other users. We also worked in a number of schools and conducted a survey and focus-group discussions with school students aged 13–15 years – a group little considered in recent writing on the urban experience (but see Anderson *et al.*, 1994) and a population which cannot be contacted through the street interview for ethical reasons, but which adds its own particular dimension to the areas where young people congregate.

From the data collected, we have been able to build up a picture, albeit a snapshot, of life on the streets in these cities in August 1992. We are aware that the public streets are an ever-changing arena and that the concerns of their populations will not remain constant – at certain times particular concerns will emerge as predominant, as with present issues concerning levels of youth crime or the safety of young children in the wake of the abduction of Jamie Bulger in February 1993. It is apparent that many of these concerns are both a reflection of, and are reflected by, local news coverage. From a reading of the local press throughout the duration of the research we are aware that had we repeated the exercise in August 1993, the character of some of the places identified as significant for sections of the population may have changed considerably.

## MARGINAL PLACES, MARGINAL ACTIVITY AND MARGINAL PEOPLE

In analysing the responses of the people we spoke to on the streets, it became increasingly obvious that the philosophy of planning for a class-less and (two-thirds) contented society cannot encompass the diverse uses which are concentrated in our public spaces, or meet the needs of the actual population of our two researched cities. The tendency, criticised by Sennett (1991), to create a space characterised by 'blandness', which aims to wall off the differences between people on the assumption that

> these differences are more likely to be mutually threatening than mutually stimulating   (Sennett, 1991, p. xii)

or which serves to 'de-politicise' public space and the differences between people (Lefebvre, discussed in Saunders, 1981, p. 156), which is said to be typical of North-American society, does not translate simply to the populations of Manchester and Sheffield. In these cities *we* feel that public space remains a contested arena, with different groups vying for the privilege of its use. These groups rub up against each other sometimes, accommodate each other at other times, and even celebrate each others' differences. To some degree we would agree with the urban theorists who regard space as the 'primary urban aesthetic' (Jameson, 1984) in mid- to late-twentieth-century culture, and as a scarce commodity in and of itself.

Different strategies exist to manage marginal groups or marginal activity in the city. The homeless who are found sleeping on the streets are one such example, as it is widely believed that their presence causes anxiety and concern amongst other members of the public, although, as citizens, they are merely using the public domain for their own particular purpose. In some English city centres the 'problem' of the homeless or 'vagrants' has been reformulated as one primarily to do with their drinking alcohol in the street and has resulted in the enactment of a number of local by-laws prohibiting the consumption of alcohol in a public outdoor space (for example, Coventry and Bath). Although aimed at curbing the consumption of alcohol in the city centre by 'vagrants', homeless people and those begging for money, such measures have, however, proved very difficult to enforce – the individual may only be prosecuted if he or she continues to drink after a police warning. Town planners, publicans, cafe owners and restaurateurs have been equally frustrated, as the by-law has effectively prohibited the consumption of alcohol at tables outside pubs and cafes. Not only do the police find it time-consuming to enforce but it potentially frustrates attempts to create a more 'cafe-culture' European feel to English cities with more outdoor activity in the city centre.

Police forces around the country are responding in different ways to the problem of homelessness itself. We have evidence that some forces are reluctant to acknowledge that the problem of 'genuine homelessness' actually exists – both Greater Manchester and South Yorkshire forces set up a 'Clean Sweep' campaign to clear the city centre of those sleeping on the streets in the run-up to Christmas 1992. Clearly the scale of the problem is currently greater in London, and the Metropolitan Police campaign in relation to homelessness appears quite different. 'The Police have a duty to every householder' was the heading on a poster depicting a young Londoner living in a 'bash' in London's 'Cardboard City'. The lengthy text accompanying the picture explained the Met's approach to the problem of homelessness in terms of management rather than clearance. It stated that 'We [the Police] owe a duty to these citizens too' and described the local station officers' work with the young homeless, from talking to them to assess their needs, and directing them to hostels and free kitchens, to inter-agency work with social services, voluntary organisations and housing officers. It talked of 'easing the problems of homelessness' and invited the public to understand more and condemn less.

We wish to illustrate some of the possible, though contested, marginal activities, people and places (construed as marginal despite being a part of all cities), by reference to the following examples in Manchester and Sheffield:

(1)  Youth
(2)  Gay Men
(3)  Shoppers
(4)  Women

**Youth in the City**

Young school students in our cities experience a different world to that of adults. The same outside influences and stimuli exist for both groups, but the young person has fewer resources through which to experience life around her or him. As non-wage earners, the economic resources which allow experiences to be felt – through their purchase – are unavailable to all but the very few. However, maybe more importantly, young people have not developed fully the human resources which enable us to make sense of the world around us – the maturity to understand fully what is happening outside of ourselves, the confidence to deal with potentially threatening situations or those which create a sense of general unease. Increasingly, from around the age of thirteen they begin to explore the world around them, not as children but as adolescents entering the adult world. Their private, home environment offers less scope for this necessary activity and becomes more of a place of isolation from the outside world. To some this is still a haven in which to retreat, but to others the streets are a place to find refuge from family, inequality and childhood.

The school students we have spoken to exhibit varying degrees of comfort with these outside, public spaces. They are troubled less by *places*, (although dark, unlit areas are uninviting and seen as the haunts of the drug pushers and those who 'use'), but outside, in the light, they feel threatened by the different types of *people* whom they encounter – the 'hippies', 'druggies', 'beggars' and 'people who sing and ask for money'. Even street-traders and paper sellers are frequently cited as people to be avoided. They have not developed the skills which would enable them to deal with these intrusions – dark places can always be avoided, but adults and people who are older are supposed to be respected and listened to. Young people therefore hang around in groups; not confident enough of their own individual presence and the rights attached to this, they congregate and gain confidence in their group identity instead. In so doing they are invariably seen as 'gangs' and potential 'troublemakers'. They are moved on from place to place, can be evicted from enclosed shopping centres like Meadowhall in Sheffield and are often asked to split into smaller groups by shop security staff. Management and security firms in malls such as Meadowhall are aware of the 'predicament' they face when including leisure facilities in the mall (an example at Meadowhall is the

'Videowall'). Whereas the aim is to maximise spending potential by offering a retail/leisure mix attracting as many different groups of the population as possible, management must also strive to ensure that groups of teenagers, attracted by the leisure dimension, 'spend rather than simply socialise' (Harrison, 1990, p. 31).[1] Young people often feel that they are denied the experience of enjoying a shopping trip or sitting down in a cafe together because of policies which exclude them.

Many of the 13–15-year-olds we spoke to are acutely aware of the existence of gangs of older youths. Some are able to enter their ranks, perhaps because an older brother or sister is part of the group; or, in the case of young girls, because they are used to mixing with boys older than themselves. When outside of the group, however, it is a threatening situation to come face to face with one such 'gang', as it is feared you may be 'taxed', have your baseball cap stolen or be threatened with physical violence. As Paul Willis observes in respect of young men, 'Far from their threatening it, the street threatens them' (Willis, 1990, p. 103). Gangs are to be avoided by crossing over to the other side of the street, but not by avoiding 'town' altogether. If town *is* avoided at any time it is at night or during the evening, when other factors which provoke unease for this age group come into play.

In one of our survey sites the older youths were able to establish their own space entirely. This was immediately outside the entrance to a much-used bus station in the centre of the town and directly adjacent to one of our survey sites – a major thoroughfare. Observation of the area quickly showed that the youths were involved in the buying and selling of drugs. Indeed, a number of those involved in this activity agreed to be interviewed by our researchers and openly admitted that they were involved in illegal activity. They were keen to tell their stories and add their voices to the survey – they were involved in this activity, whether actively or as observers, to meet friends, because they had no money and because there was nothing else for them to do in the area. 'Giroday' was the only day they would be found elsewhere, maybe on a shopping trip into Manchester city centre, taking in the old architecture and visiting the 'top' clothes shops.

The presence on the street of this group of young people was acknowledged by other users of that public space. The school students, especially girls, talked in the focus-group discussions of the 'dealing' which took place there, and some had personal friendships with the group members. The local police were also well aware of the situation, pointing out that the place furnished the drug sellers with a number of necessary facilities – phones, shelter and public toilets – in which to conduct the deal. Ironically, the recent improvements to the area had added raised beds and foliage where drugs could be hidden or discarded if police entered the area.

Here, a public place planned for routine use as a bus station has been appropriated for a marginal activity by youth who have created their own space. Other youths, and presumably some adults too, will choose to catch their bus from stops further along the route during the evenings to avoid these groups of people. However, for those involved in 'dealing', its location, with clear views of all streets leading to it, makes the place ideal for their transactions.

Young people in their early teens progress from their previously privatised existence within the family to a more adult knowledge of the public domain by learning from the experiences of, or from general contact with, older youths. This is accomplished without help from the adult world, where they are likely to encounter hostility and are marginalised from the spaces planned for adult use.

### Gay Pride in 'The Village'

A section of the gay community in Manchester has developed a space where clubs, pubs and cafe-bars catering for this group have increased considerably in recent years. The area is known as 'The Gay Village' or simply 'The Village' and has centred itself around two or three pubs which were frequented by gay men for many years. It has developed into a safe area for gay and heterosexual alike (although it has fewer facilities for lesbians and is therefore less used by this section of the population) which is regarded as the gay community's own place. It has a thriving club scene, cafes and shops. Lesbians and gay men are attracted to Manchester from all over the country at weekends because of this gay space. It has opened up a network of streets characterised by old industrial warehouses, the city's canal network and narrow backstreets to the south of the city centre into a brightly lit, well-populated arena. The area lies behind Manchester's Chorlton Street Bus Station and includes the red-light district of the city where prostitutes and rent boys work the streets throughout the day and evening.

'The Village' has become the most 'European' area in the city; cafe-bars and pubs have encouraged their patrons to spill out onto the streets to drink and they have been designed with balconies and plate-glass facades which encourage drinkers to look outwards over the canals. The area immediately outside these bars has subsequently been pedestrianised and permanent benches have been fixed outside, legitimising drinking on the street. Patrons from nearby pubs mingle with the cafe-bar drinkers on the street, there is a shared understanding of the street culture here and an openly expressed pride in having an area of the city where the gay lifestyle has 'come out'.

There is little doubt that the existence of 'The Village' has given confidence to a community which is discriminated against in heterosexual society. Many lesbian and gay organisations operate inside the area and the lesbian and gay community in Manchester is known to be much involved in campaigning around political and social issues which they consider relevant. Manchester has seen a 20 000-strong march for gay rights and boasts the best facilities for people with HIV and AIDS outside of London. Policy-makers have also reacted to the existence of this gay space. In May 1993, Greater Manchester Police appointed their first Lesbian and Gay Officer, at the level of Inspector, to liaise with the gay community in the city and the city council includes a lesbian and gay sub-committee. The influence of 'The Village' stretches beyond its borders and gay men have told us that they feel safer in most of city centre Manchester as they feel more accepted by Manchester people than they do by the inhabitants of any other UK city. London has a thriving gay scene but this is spread throughout the city; in Manchester the quite closely defined area means not having to step outside of the area at any time during an evening out – rather than being seen as a 'gay ghetto' it is seen as a gay developed space, a place of ownership, a place of which to be proud.

**Budget Shoppers**

There is a widespread belief, especially in Sheffield, that Meadowhall, a shopping centre geographically on the margins of the city which opened in 1990, will become an alternative city centre. This American-style mall contains 223 stores, occupies 1.5 square miles and was visited during its first year of opening by twenty million people. Several articles in the national press over the past three years have opened with such phrases as,

> Shoppers are increasingly forsaking high streets and traditional town centres for vast, out-of-town shopping centres built on sites that are legacies of Britain's industrial past  (*The Independent*, 18 November 1991)

or

> Sheffield lunchtime. Bus stops trail ropes of cold-looking people; streets are clogged with cars. Some shop windows wear bright commercial smiles, others – far too many – are blank and empty, like broken teeth in a new set of dentures. . . . Sheffield is suffering, not just from the recession but from the effects of . . . Meadowhall  (*The Independent*, 22 February 1992)

contrasting this with portraits of the cleanliness and convenience of Meadowhall's malls. Modern shopping centres are portrayed as undeniably viable alternatives to the traditional city centre, the implication being that no right-minded person would prefer the streets of our cities, with their bad weather, homelessness, traffic pollution and other visible signs of depression or neglect.

In the second of these two articles, a Geography lecturer at the University of Sheffield suggests that developments such as Meadowhall create a 'geographic dichotomy', splitting society down the middle, into those who can afford to shop at Meadowhall (which, in its own admission, caters for the more 'upmarket' shopper) and those who are left to negotiate the declining, neglected city centre. Our own research very much supports this claim – those residents of Sheffield for whom a shopping trip consists of seeking out everyday necessities, purchased at the lowest-cost outlets and markets, rather than the purchase of clothes, electrical or leisure goods, are very much in evidence in the city centre of Sheffield. Although many of them cite Meadowhall as one of the assets to living in the city, we would suggest that, for the majority of these people, such a statement has more to do with city image than with their own use of the mall. If they *have* visited the mall it has probably only been once or twice since it opened two and a half years ago. In no way can Meadowhall be described as an 'alternative city centre' for these people, for whom shopping is a mundane and necessary activity, yet who are being reconstituted as the marginal shopping population in this 'geographic dichotomy'.

Much of the debate concerning the success of Meadowhall at the expense of Sheffield city centre assumes that the bulk of shoppers at Meadowhall are actually residents of Sheffield and its immediate surrounds and are, therefore, former users of the city centre for the majority of their shopping. According to Meadowhall's own research bureau, Mall Research Services, around 37 per cent of visitors to Meadowhall live within a five-mile radius of the mall, although 85 per cent have a Sheffield postcode, which includes Barnsley, Rotherham and Chesterfield. However, according to Sheffield's Urban Development Corporation, 75 per cent of visitors to Meadowhall are not from Sheffield itself. Mall Research Services also estimate that the number of visitors from the Sheffield area is declining – the number of shoppers from within a five-mile radius of Meadowhall dropped to 25 per cent during the 1992 pre-Christmas period.[2] The findings from our own survey of Meadowhall users suggest that the loss of trade in the city centre as a result of the attraction of Meadowhall may be exaggerated. The majority of respondents there (58 per cent) came from towns or cities outside Sheffield and claimed not to know its city centre at all; their alternative shopping and leisure locations were their own home towns, not Sheffield. Meadowhall users who *were* from Sheffield (42 per cent) invariably cited the city centre as their favourite alternative shopping site, and were no less positive about the city centre shops than those people we interviewed in the city centre itself.

There is a possibility, on this evidence, that the impact of Meadowhall on Sheffield city centre may have been the subject of some hype and exaggeration and have been based on the assumption that the behavioural patterns of English citizens can be predicted by reference to the United States. Meadowhall is undeniably popular and well-visited, but the centre of Sheffield does not appear to be experiencing the effects of a mass exodus of people to Meadowhall, despite boarded up shops in many parts of the city centre.[3] During the daytime in the two weeks of our survey, the city centre streets were busy during shopping hours and respondents often commented upon the crowds in the centre. In suggesting the marginal nature of the traditional town centre in relation to 'temples of consumption' such as Meadowhall, some journalists have ignored the fact that many people in our towns and cities are marginalised from the type of consumption that is encouraged in Meadowhall due to unemployment, a declining welfare system and rising public transport costs.

The claim that Meadowhall can become an alternative city centre assumes a very narrow view of the function of the traditional city centre – as somewhere for consumption alone. It ignores the wide range of other uses that people may have for the space that constitutes the 'City Centre', whether purposive activities such as working, signing on, going to the pub or library, old-time dancing in the City Hall or demonstrating in civic space, or the less purposive, for example sitting and watching the world go by, showing friends or relatives around, hanging around with a gang of schoolfriends, changing buses or indeed finding one's home on the street.[4] Are all of these activities to be considered marginal to the central function of our Meadowhall 'city centres' of the future? The *Out Of Hours* work by Comedia, the urban consultancy organisation, considers some of these issues and comments that, of the people to whom they spoke, it was perhaps the older generation who felt most marginalised from shopping malls (in this case city-centre indoor malls), because there was seldom anywhere just simply to sit without spending money in a fast-food outlet (Comedia, 1991, p. 40).

Although the findings from our survey in Sheffield do not bear out this assertion that aged people are marginalised from shopping malls (there was no difference between the proportion of people aged 65 or over who answered our questionnaire at Meadowhall and those who answered it in our other survey sites in Sheffield), it is nevertheless difficult to imagine the Meadowhalls of the future fulfilling this sort of basic social function for any section of the community.

## Women

Perhaps our survey's least surprising finding was that the percentage of respondents who were male and who were using public space exceeded the female percentage (overall, 53 per cent were men and 47 per cent women). This proposition is identical for the cities of Manchester and Sheffield; however, there are two important qualifications in respect to this finding. Firstly, the differences between male and female use of our survey sites was most marked during the evening. Furthermore, three sites which elicited the most comments concerning fear, safety and the bad reputation of the area showed the most marked differences in male and female use during the daytime, producing ratios of male to female of 55 : 45; 58 : 42 and 67 : 33. Across both cities, differences between daytime and evening use by males and females were remarkably similar. During the daytime (9 a.m.–6 p.m.) in Manchester, women constituted 46 per cent of the population whereas during the evening (6.30–8.30) they constituted 29 per cent. For Sheffield, excluding Meadowhall, the figures were 45 per cent (daytime) and 32 per cent (evening). Moreover, the survey was conducted during the summer month of August and we believe that this may have resulted in a higher percentage of women using public space in the evening than might be expected during the darker winter evenings, as many women we spoke to made it clear that they would not use the areas in which we met them, after dark.

All respondents were asked if they ever avoided the city centre spaces in which we interviewed them and, if so, to state their reasons. The percentages of women in both cities reporting that they avoided city centre spaces for reasons associated with fear or personal safety were similar (25 per cent in Sheffield and 28 per cent in Manchester) as were the percentages of men avoiding the same spaces for this reason (14 per cent in Sheffield and 18 per cent in Manchester). Clearly, women can be considered as marginalised from use of urban public space both during the daytime and especially in the evening, and they are far more likely to avoid these spaces for reasons connected with fear and personal safety than men.

Public transport is an important dimension to the use of public space by women. Use of public transport necessitates use of public space (at bus stops for example) as well as producing its own set of anxieties and concerns (Pickup, 1988; Taylor,1991 , p. 15 and *passim*). Questions exploring use of different means of transport on the day of the interview revealed many differences in men's and women's experiences of *public* transport. Public transport in Manchester and Sheffield is used by significantly greater numbers of women than men: 60 per cent of all women interviewed as opposed to 48 per cent of men had used public transport (bus, train or tram) on the day of the interview. In addition, a greater number of women had used public transport because they had 'no alternative means' of getting to where they wanted to be. Forty per cent of women as opposed to 33 per cent of men gave this as their primary reason for choosing public transport on that day. For buses only, the percentage gap was slightly greater (44 per cent of women as opposed to 36 per cent of men).

Although, overall, women are more significant users of public transport than men, this use is heavily influenced by the time of day. For instance, although only 40 per cent of all bus passengers from our sample throughout the day (until 6.30 p.m.), were men, during the evening (6.30–8.30) the position is reversed, with only 40 per cent of all bus passengers being women. An interesting finding is that it is unlikely to be public transport itself that deters women from using it for access to public spaces during the evening, as the ratio of *private* car users during the evening is even more biased towards men (79 per cent of all car users in the evening were men compared with 21 per cent who were women, despite female car users marginally outnumbering male car users throughout most of the day).

However, of all public transport users, more than twice as many women as men stated that they would avoid using this form of transport on any evening or at night (13 per cent of women compared with 6 per cent of men). When asked the reasons they would avoid using *public transport* at these times, three times as many women users as men said they would do so for reasons of personal safety or 'because of the sorts of people around' (9 per cent of women compared with 3 per cent of men). Taking all means of getting around in the evening or at night (i.e. private transport and walking included), avoidance was still a greater issue for women – 16 per cent of women and 8 per cent of men said they would avoid that form of getting around at these times.

Given the reluctance of women to use even private transport during the evening, it is unlikely that women-only transport schemes such as exist on Merseyside and as proposed in Sheffield (Sheffield *Star*, 8 June 1993) in and of themselves, would achieve a great deal in encouraging women to make fuller use of city centre spaces.

We also feel that proposals made by councillors in Manchester to create 'safe taxi havens' for women at bus stops late at night after buses have ceased operating also miss the mark (see *Manchester Evening News*, 31 December 1992). Many of our women respondents and focus-group discussants expressed considerable anxiety about waiting at bus stops and bus stations during the evening and at night. Indeed, following a survey finding reported in the Sheffield *Star* that 83 per cent of all women would rather not use buses alone at night, a Crime Prevention Officer from South Yorkshire Police advised women not to stand for too long at bus stops and to use stops in a 'well-lit area' (*Star*, 8 June 1993). The conflicting advice offered out by police and other public authorities merely seems to emphasise what women know already – that being in public space at night-time causes anxiety which is exacerbated by having to wait around conspicuously for *any* form of transport at a bus-stop.

The kinds of spaces that are associated with *all* forms of transport (badly lit, concrete-built car parks, bus stations and stops, often in streets which are located away from main thoroughfares) combine with a general sense of unease for many women at being out anywhere in the evening or at night, to exclude them from our cities' public spaces. Our findings reinforce the view that women are more likely to be found in the private area, *in this survey* stating fear for their personal safety and lack of alternatives as major reasons for this (but see Stanko, 1985, 1990 on women's lack of personal safety in the private sphere).

## CONCLUDING REMARKS

Each of these case-studies illustrates how populations in the two cities can become marginalised and shows how people can adopt different strategies to mediate unease and anxiety. Two groups – youth and gay men – have responded by developing their own spaces within the public arena. Ultimately, the latter have been far more successful in creating an atmosphere of tolerance and acceptance in the city of Manchester (although certain other central and residential areas are still seen as unsafe by gay men) through their development of an established and well-defined 'gay space' accessible to gay and non-gay alike. Economic power, the 'pink pound', has to some extent allowed gay users to 'buy' the space essential to their strategy. Groups of young people in public areas are still seen as potentially threatening to many others and are likely to be subject to intervention by custodians of that space. The option to 'buy' space is not available to young teenagers who have little disposable income of their own;

their need for spaces in which to congregate and from which to begin to negotiate the wider world is not considered by the city planners. Hence the transition from childhood ways of seeing the city to adult, remains confusing and confrontational.

Our second two groups, budget shoppers and women, have tended to adapt more to their fears and anxieties rather than seek to impose their patterns of use onto the street scene. Shoppers manage the city for their own needs, emphasising the facilities which are available to them at little cost, socialising, mixing with other shoppers like themselves and avoiding the expensive shopping areas. They recognise the limitations of consumer-oriented spaces for people like them and look to maximise alternative uses for those spaces. Many women visit public spaces at times when they feel most at ease, or arrange to go with friends or partners – they stress the importance of knowing an area well and use tried and tested 'routes' to move through the city streets. For many women the issue of transportation or *access* to public spaces is also a significant limitation. We have shown that although women are more reliant on public transport than men, they are also more anxious about using it for fear of harassment or assault. The non-availability of reliable public transport, particularly during off-peak times in some parts of the city, apprehension about making use of it when it is there and the perception that the city centre during the evening or at night is not really geared towards their interests or well-being, combine to restrict women's use of the city centre, above all during non-daylight hours.

It is young people and the gay community who are more readily identified as distinct groups with common cultural interests (even though there is actually a range of different interests *within* these groups) than women in general or budget shoppers. These first two groups have, in the experience of our study, adopted a more collective solution to feelings of unease and anxiety. The latter and less obviously marginalised groups, have adopted responses which are more individualised. Lacking economic power or that which is related to group cohesion and identity, their strategies are least successful of all, in that they do not lead to an increased and varied use of public space, but result, instead, in the limitation of use and a degree of avoidance.

Dennis Smith offers the definition of place as somewhere that is 'full', 'fixed' and 'replete with meaning' and 'well-established human relations'. Places take on these characteristics because 'particular communities reside in or frequent them'. By contrast, spaces are 'areas perceived in terms of their potential for being acquired or occupied by members of either your own or some other potentially threatening group or category'. Spaces are 'potential voids', 'possible threats' or 'areas that have to be feared, secured or fled' (Smith, 1987, p. 297).

Within the context of the marginal urban spaces on which we have focused our attention in this paper, Smith's definitions and distinctions are of some use. The case-studies which we have outlined show groups adapting their relationship to 'place' and 'space'. On the evidence of our research, many women can find certain urban spaces fearful precisely because such spaces are without the (real or perceived) security provided by 'well-established human relations'. Gay men in Manchester's Gay Village have succeeded in 'securing' their own space – as a result they have constructed a place 'replete with meaning' which extends beyond the confines both of the city and of the gay population. Groups of young people compete with others for use of public space, whether these are other groups of young people, adults or forms of organised adult authority, such as shopping-centre security. Budget shoppers who use the increasingly residualised downmarket shopping and market areas of the city centre may not articulate a positive attachment to such areas, yet they continue to use them out of necessity. These areas retain 'meaning' for them despite the gradual erosion of familiar landmarks, whether in the form of long-established shops, markets or bus routes.

Marginal spaces and people will not disappear from the central urban core of our cities despite the zoned, gentrified and regenerated areas; they will persist in defining the spaces in between. We are mindful of the fact that such *spaces* can take on different appearances and atmosphere as they become *places* in which different groups interact. This may involve an element of conflict, however our research suggests that this acquisition or occupation of space can be both creative and productive.

## Notes

1.    In this report by the Royal Institute for Chartered Surveyors, it is declared that, '[a]t the Metrocentre (Newcastle), management use electronic surveillance equipment to identify youths who are attracted by the leisure facilities as a place to coalesce in groups and socialise rather than to spend; they are then asked to leave the premises. This predominantly monitoring policy ensures that shoppers are not intimidated by high levels of policing or by disorderly leisure customers' (Harrison, 1990, p. 31).
2.    Personal communication with Mall Research Services, 2 April 1993
3.    It is considered by many Sheffielders to be significant that Cole Brothers, the long-established family-run department store in the city centre, has not yet relocated to Meadowhall. It was felt by some of our focus-group participants in Sheffield that the day this happens will really mark the demise of the city centre.

4.  The reaction of those we have termed 'budget shoppers' to Meadowhall was encapsulated by a group of unemployed Pakistani women we spoke to, who were learning English in a community centre in Sheffield. They were very much in favour of Meadowhall – in principle preferring it to the city centre – yet considered that it would be greatly improved were it to accommodate a fresh produce market, along the lines of those found in the city centre. Ironically, if Meadowhall was to include a 'genuine market', this would be contrary to the very principles of ordered, sedate consumption on which such malls are founded. Meadowhall might then attract precisely the sorts of people associated with the unruly city centre markets, which 'upmarket' shoppers go to Meadowhall to avoid.

## References

Anderson, S., Kinsey, R., Loader, I. and Smith, C. (1994) *Cautionary Tales: A Study of Young People and Crime in Edinburgh* (Aldershot: Avebury).

De Certeau, M. (1984) *The Practice of Everyday Life* (Berkeley, Cal.: The University of California Press).

Comedia (1991) *Out of Hours: A Study of Economic, Social and Cultural Life in Twelve Town Centres in the UK* (London: Comedia).

Evans, K., Fraser, P. and Taylor, I. (1993) 'Going to Town: Routine Accommodation and Routine Anxieties in Respect of Public Space and Public Facilities in Two Cities in the North of England', paper presented to International Conference on the Public Sphere, Manchester, January.

Harrison, J. (1990) *Leisure Facilities in Shopping Centres: an Analysis of the Management Input Required to Optimize the Benefits of Integration* (London: The Royal Institute of Chartered Surveyors).

Jameson, F. (1984) 'Postmodernism or the Cultural Logic of Late Capitalism', *New Left Review*, 46, pp. 53–92.

Pickup, L. (1988) 'Hard to Get Around: A Study of Women's Travel Mobility', in Little, J. and Peake, L. (eds), *Women in Cities: Gender and the Urban Environment* (Basingstoke: Macmillan Education).

Saunders, P. (1981) *Social Theory and the Urban Question* (London: Unwin & Hyman).

Sennett, R. (1991) *The Conscience of the Eye: The Design and Social Life of Cities* (London: Faber & Faber).

Smith, D. (1987) 'Knowing Your Place: Class, Politics and Ethnicity in Chicago and Birmingham 1890–1983', in Thrift, N. and Williams, P. (eds), *Class and Space: the Making of Urban Society* (London: Routledge & Kegan Paul).

Stanko, E. (1985) *Intimate Intrusions* (London: Routledge).

Stanko, E. (1990) *Everyday Violence* (London: Pandora Press).

Taylor, I. (1991) 'Not Places in Which You'd Linger: Public Transport and Public Well-Being in Manchester', report to the Greater Manchester Passenger Transport Executive, August.

Willis, P. (1990) *Common Culture: Symbolic Work at Play in the Everyday Cultures of the Young* (Milton Keynes: Open University Press).

# 8 No Key – No Door? Young People's Access to Housing

## Gill Jones

A Minister for Housing recently described 'the homeless' as 'the sort of people one stepped over on the way out of the opera' (Sir George Young, in 1992), and thus confirmed that the current government's emphasis on a return to 'traditional values' meant a return to Poor Law attitudes. As long as individuals are scape-goated for the problems of society, their ability to exercise their rights as citizens will be diminished, and they will be regarded as 'the undeserving poor'. This chapter considers whether young people have the right not to be homeless, but to be recognised as independent citizens and to be housed. It also considers the responsibilities of parents in this context. How many young people get the key to any door at 18, these days? Is the concept of independent adulthood at 18 years, the legal age of majority in Britain, anything more than an irrelevant abstraction?

Rights in youth are problematic because young people are in the process of transition from dependent childhood, when they derive their citizenship from their parents, to independent adulthood when they become citizens themselves (Jones and Wallace, 1992). During the period of transition, the concept of rights is a murky area needing clarification. The problem is exacerbated as current education, training and social security policies effectively extend the period of dependency into youth. Young people are treated in the legal system and in government policies variously as children or as adults, and there is no overall framework constructing the transition to adult citizenship.

Housing in youth provides an example of this confusion, and of the ways in which it is handled by social policies, parents and young people themselves. In this chapter I shall argue that, in default of legal rights, the claim of young people as a social group to housing requires an appeal to social justice. Thus, there will only be independent housing provision for young people when the circumstances in which they leave home are socially legitimated (Burton *et al.*, 1988, 1989). There are particular prob-

lems in obtaining housing when appeals are not made on the basis of normative behaviour (Jones, 1993a, b).

As the youth housing market shrinks and the period of economic
dependency is extended, access to housing has become more difficult. All
young people leaving home are more likely to have problems entering and
competing in the housing market, but there is polarisation between those
whose rights are recognised and who have social support, and those
leaving home without support, who may become marginalised and
excluded by society. As argued elsewhere (Jones and Wallace, 1992), two
processes have been at work over the last two decades: the position of
young people as a social group has weakened, while at the same time
inequalities between young people have increased.

There is, however, a further problem. While direct access to citizenship
is increasingly withheld from young people as their prospects for economic independence fade, so indirect access via their parents also becomes
more problematic. Government policies assume that as state support for
young people is withdrawn, parents will take up the slack and extend the
period during which they provide support (including housing) to their
young. Dependent children have the right of abode in their parents'
homes, but is this still the case during the period of quasi-dependence,
quasi-independence which constitutes youth? This issue will also be discussed. Young people's rights *vis-à-vis* their parents may prove to be as
problematic as their rights *vis-à-vis* the state.

In a context of increasing homelessness in youth, it is important to
understand the process of leaving home in terms of the social legitimacy
ascribed to it and the degree of social support and housing provided. It is
equally important to clarify whether young people have a right to return
home after they have left it. Most of the research on young people's
housing has failed to explore the link between leaving home and becoming
homeless. The concepts of citizenship rights, social legitimation and social
justice provide a framework for understanding this link.

THE RESEARCH

The research on which the chapter is based was part of a two-year project
*Young People in and out of the Housing Market*. The research was multi-
method, using quantitative and qualitative data from a number of sources
(see Jones and Stevens, 1993). Findings are presented from two school-year

cohorts of the Scottish Young People's Survey (SYPS), surveyed at average age 16¾ years and again at 19¼ years, in 1987/9 and 1989/91 (Brannen et al., 1991; Brannen and Middleton, 1994). The chapter also draws on findings from a 1992 survey of 246 homeless young Scots, which was carried out for the project. Some qualitative data is included from survey questionnaires and interviews with a subset of SYPS respondents at the age of 22 years. Further findings from the project have been produced as a set of working papers and are discussed further in a recent book on leaving home (Jones, 1995).

## ON THE MARGINS OF THE HOUSING MARKET

Where do young people live? Most of those who have left home are on the margins of the housing market, and some are excluded altogether. Analysis of the SYPS (Jones, 1993c) indicates that by the age of 19, around one-third of young Scots have left home, though of these, 28 per cent have returned to live in their parental homes again. There is unequal access to housing provision, whether through the private market, through the public sector or through the family. Young people vary in their housing circumstances according to their economic and marital/parental status. Access to housing is, therefore, not only age-related, but most young people are in what can be described as a *youth housing market*. This consists mainly of private rented accommodation, in which 41 per cent of 19-year-olds who have left home live, often with insecure tenure. A few, mainly dual-earning couples or other more affluent young people buy their own homes (perhaps with parental help). The dwindling housing stocks in the public sector are increasingly targeted at 'deserving cases' – social housing for lone parents or low-income couples with children. There is specialised housing for students, nurses and those in the armed forces, for example, but this is 'tied' (job- or course-linked) and not in an open housing market. And right on the very fringes of the market there is 'transitional housing' (Jones, 1987) – the limited provision, in the form of bedsits, lodgings, hostels and so on, for the single person in the labour force, on low pay, on a training allowance, or on income support.

It is not surprising that many people return to live with their families after they have left home, when access to secure housing is apparently so difficult. But there are young people whose right to housing is apparently not recognised, who do not gain access to independent housing, and who cannot turn to their families for assistance. These may become homeless.

## THE PROCESS OF LEAVING HOME

By examining trends and cross-national variation in patterns of leaving home, we can explore the issue of social legitimation and identify normative and non-normative patterns.

One of the main sources of cross-national variation in patterns of leaving home lies in the boundary of responsibility between the family and the State. In countries where families retain their 'traditional' functions, they, rather than the State or the local authority, are still seen as the main providers of housing to young people. The trend is not necessarily towards more state provision in these countries: in Spain, for example, the government (as in Britain) has extended the period of economic dependency on their families to 26 years; in consequence, young people are prevented from living independently, and there is overcrowding in family homes, especially in areas of social housing. This appears to be a general trend in Europe (Burton *et al.,* 1989), but is particularly the case in Britain, where the responsibilities of parents have been extended – and the rights of young people withdrawn – under successive Conservative governments, anxious both to reduce juvenile crime and to reduce the social security budget (Jones and Wallace, 1992).

Though entry into the housing market is increasingly difficult for anyone leaving home in their teenage years, the provision of housing for young people may relate to the level of social legitimation, and thence support, given to reasons for leaving home. In most countries, the traditional and most 'legitimised' way of leaving home was to marry, so that the individual moved directly from the parental household to the matrimonial one. Leaving home is an integral part of the transition to adulthood, so factors affecting other transitions to adulthood (for example, to economic independence and family formation) therefore also affect patterns of leaving home. Across Europe, there has been a weakening link between leaving home and marriage, even if cohabitation is included (though the link remains strong in the countries of southern Europe). We thus find an increase in the incidence of single person households (Schwarz, 1983). This trend is associated with the availability of housing stock (Kiernan, 1986), a hypothesis supported by the situation in Denmark, where young people leave home earliest, the link between leaving home and marriage is weak, and housing stock is more available because the housing needs of young single people are recognised (Haywood, 1984). In the UK, there is still a strong link between leaving home and marriage or cohabitation, especially among women (Kiernan, 1986), though this is weakening, and the incidence of single and peer-group households has therefore increased (Jones, 1987, 1990).

Recent decades have been characterised in many countries by an extension of the period of economic dependency in youth, caused by an extension and expansion of education and training, shrinkage of the youth labour market, and a reduction in state support (Jones and Wallace, 1992). The increase in numbers going on to higher education accounts in part for the decreased link between leaving home and marriage (Kiernan, 1986). Leaving home to go on a course is the most common reason overall in the UK for leaving home by the age of 19 years (Jones, 1987, 1990). The legitimacy of leaving home in order to study or start a job is recognised in many countries, for young men at least (according to Bloss *et al.*, 1990, who refer to these as the 'scholastic' and 'professional' routes). Both are associated with career progression. It is likely that leaving home to go on to higher education has speeded up the whole leaving home process (Kiernan, 1986), and raised expectations of independent living among other groups. Leaving home to go on a course depends, however, on having the financial resources to do so. Students in Britain are increasingly forced to seek financial support from their families, as their economic circumstances deteriorate.

Income opportunities for school leavers are even more sparse. The 1988, social security regulations have withdrawn the right of under-18s to Income Support, and only provide adult rates of benefit to those over 25 years of age. Income support has been replaced with a 'training guarantee' (see Maclagan, 1992 for a critique), and a small allowance which assumes that living costs are subsidised by parents. Those in insecure or low-paid employment must also find rising housing costs hard to meet. Yet *'to take up a job'* is the main reason men under 18 years of age in Britain give for leaving home, both according to the NCDS (Jones, 1987), and more recently the SYPS (Jones, 1990, 1993b). As incomes fall below the level required for independent living, parental responsibility (into young adulthood) has been implicitly extended and the availability of parental support has been assumed by policy makers.

Young people are, however, increasingly leaving home in order to gain independence prior to forming partnerships. This has been noted in Australia (Maas, 1986), West Germany (Mayer and Schwartz, 1989), France (Bloss *et al.*, 1990), Britain (Jones, 1990) and the Netherlands (de Jong Gierveld *et al.*, 1991). Young (1984, p. 54) identifies this as a new stage in transition to adulthood, 'a stage of independence between living with the parents and becoming married to begin a new family'. Similar observations have been made in Europe (Galland, 1990; Bloss *et al.*, 1990). De Jong Gierveld and colleagues (1991) found that those leaving home to gain independence tended not to have a close relationship with their parents, but at the same time, successful transition to independent living depended on their parents' ability to provide financial help. What happens to those who seek independent housing, but are unable to draw on family economic resources to create more favourable conditions for leaving home? The legitimacy of this new stage of independent living is not fully established, as Burton *et al.* (1989, p. 19) point out. Leonard (1980) found that setting up 'home' alone or with peers was a contradiction in folk terms.

Finally, leaving institutional care, leaving the parental home to look for work, or because of family relationship or economic problems, are perhaps the least socially legitimated and supported reasons for leaving and the most likely to lead to homelessness. The commonly used expression 'runaway' carries with it negative connotations. These reasons may represent individual strategies for survival, but may not gain social legitimation: 'running away from something', in comparison with 'progression towards something' (marriage, course or job), is not seen in a positive light.


DELAYED DEPARTURE?

The extension of the period of dependent youth has made leaving home more difficult. Some writers argue that as a result, the age at leaving home has increased. There has been fluctuation over the decades. In the Netherlands, the age at leaving home rose in the period after the war, then decreased again during the 1960s and 1970s with the increase in economic prosperity and changes in norms and values. Since 1980, however, it appears that there has been a slight increase in the age at which men leave home in the Netherlands (de Jong Gierveld *et al.*, 1991), and this has been found also in West Germany (Mayer and Schwarz, 1989), France (Godard and Bloss, 1988), and the USA (Heer *et al.*, 1984/5).

A number of explanations have been put forward. First, the widespread economic recession, with the loss of jobs, stagnating incomes and withdrawal of social security benefits, means that most young people no longer have the financial resources needed for independent living (Keilman, 1987). A French study (Leridon and Villeneuve-Gokalp, 1988), and a British one (Wallace, 1987) both found that the unemployed were likely to postpone leaving home, though this may also depend on the economic status of their families, since those affected by unemployment are least able to support jobless teenage children (Jones, 1991). Secondly, it has been argued that, as a result of changing parent–child relations, smaller family size and more space in the family home, young people can have more personal freedom and space without having to leave home (de Jong Gierveld *et al.*, 1991), though this explanation may apply mainly to wealthier families. Finally, it is argued that the changing pattern is a response to lack of housing opportunity and dwindling housing stocks (Kiernan, 1986; Burton *et al.*, 1989).

Are we really sure that the age at leaving home is increasing, though? The process of leaving home has become more complex of late (Goldscheider and LeBourdais, 1986). People leave home more than once – mainly because their course or job has come to an end, and for financial reasons (Young, 1984; Jones, 1987). Bloss *et al.* (1990) suggest that education and employment routes to social autonomy, being more tentative and experimental than the matrimonial route, are more associated with returns to the parental home. For many young people, leaving home is a process rather than a one-off event (Jones, 1987). Young (1984) found that in Australia, it was mainly early leavers who returned home: one-third of men and one-half of all women who left before they were 18 years of age. The research suggests that the new transitional phase of single independence, though desirable in theory, may be difficult to negotiate in practice.

We should, therefore, consider the changing patterns of leaving the parental home in relation to the changing patterns of returning. It is possible that more people (and especially younger ones) are returning home as independence becomes more difficult to achieve. It is important to clarify this issue in order not to over-estimate the age at first leaving home and thus under-estimate the level of housing demand in youth.

Trends data from three successive cohorts of the SYPS (Figure 8.1) show that increasing numbers of young people are leaving home by the age of 19 years. This is the case among both men and women. The proportion who had not left home by the age of 19 decreased from 69 to 63 per cent among men and from 61 to 58 per cent among women. The gender difference is thus maintained. However, the chart also shows that increasing numbers are returning home. Proportions had more than doubled between 1987 and 1991: from 5 to 11 per cent for both men and women. We can assume that these will leave home again, and perhaps more permanently, later. It seems then that young people are *first* leaving home earlier than they did in the mid-1980s, but that they *last* leave home later.

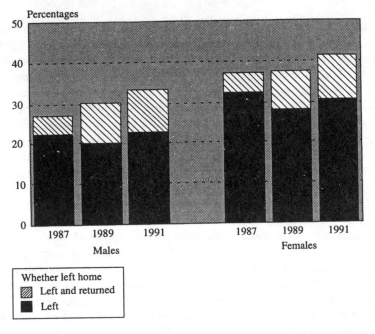

FIGURE 8.1   *Changing pattern of leaving home: 1987, 1989 and 1991 surveys*
SOURCE   SYPS, 1987a, 1989a, 1991a.

Which of these events – as Young (1984) asked – is the more significant? Well, in terms of housing, the first one is. Young people make their first demands for housing when they *first* leave home; though they may return, their housing needs should be recognised from the time of this first leaving home event. Increased youth homelessness suggests that this is not the case.

In the next few pages, I shall examine other policy assumptions. First, I shall address the issue of 'premature' departure from the family home, and consider whether leaving home can be regulated or 'delayed'. Next, I shall discuss returning home, whether the family home is a 'safe haven', whether parents do accept the increased and extended responsibilities now placed upon them, and what happens when they do not. In an age when the state intervenes less and less to redress structural inequalities, inequality in access to family support becomes one of the most crucial factors affecting young people's life chances.

## 'PREMATURE' DEPARTURE

The belief has been expressed that if young people were to 'delay' leaving home, the incidence of youth homelessness would be reduced (though as Burton and colleagues have indicated, it may only be postponed for some people). Underlying the concepts of 'premature' and 'delayed' departure from the parental home are implicit assumptions about normative patterns, which do not relate to actual behaviour. First in terms of age: the median age at leaving home in Britain is around 20 years for women and 21.9 years for men (Jones, 1987). The SYPS, one of the few sources of recent data on leaving home in the teenage years, indicates that over one-third had left home by about the age of 19, and of these, 13 per cent had left home before the age of 17, and 25 per cent at the age of 17 years (Jones, 1993b). But age is not the only factor. Leaving home is not always a matter of choice, and young people cannot always choose the most propitious time to leave, or leave for the most socially approved reasons. While the discussion above indicated some factors which constrain leaving home, we shall see that there are also factors constraining staying there.

Reasons for leaving home vary with age and sex (Figure 8.2). Few at this age leave home to marry or cohabit, even among young women. It is only later, as we know from the NCDS and other data sources, that men and women tend to leave home in order to live in a partnership (Jones, 1987). The 'scholastic' and 'professional' routes (Bloss *et al.*, 1990) are, however, well represented here. Over the age of 17, both men and women tend to leave home in order to start a course. Some leave home earlier for work-related reasons: under the age of 17, young men mainly leave home in order to take up a particular job (over 50 per cent). Though these may be socially legitimated reasons for leaving, the age at which they have left is likely to create particular problems. Students' incomes and housing benefits have been cut, and students are finding it increasingly difficult to live away from home. Trainees receive no allowance towards housing costs. Even workers are likely to be on low wages which prevent them from competing in the housing market, and increased job insecurity puts them particularly at risk.

Other reasons for leaving are even more problematic, as suggested earlier. Some people left home because there were no jobs in the home area, and others reported that they left because they *'didn't get on with the people at home'*. Both reasons were most commonly given by younger leavers, indicating that leaving home was at least as much a matter of constraint as of choice. Twenty-nine per cent of women (and 10 per cent of men) who left home at 16 said they had done so because of problems at home.

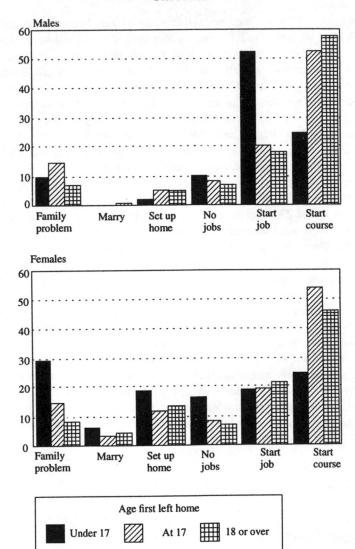

FIGURE 8.2 *Reasons for first leaving home by age, first left and sex*
SOURCE SYPS, 1989a.

Around 8 per cent of respondents to the NCDS in 1981 said that their main reason for leaving home was to set up home (Jones, 1987). While this was relatively rare among men in the SYPS, 19 per cent of women who left home at 16 did so because they *'wanted to set up a home of [their] own'*. This is sometimes associated with family conflict. Nearly 30 per cent of women who left home before they were 17, did so because of problems at home (*'didn't get on with the people at home'*). In all, 23 per cent of women who had left home by 19 because of family problems also said they had left to set up homes of their own, compared with 11 per cent of those who had left for other reasons. Leaving home for independence and because of problems at home can either be regarded as a positive move, towards a 'better' and more responsible adult life, or a negative one, an escape from the responsibilities of family living and the supposedly caring environment of the family household.

Leaving home for 'problem' reasons rather than socially legitimated, 'traditional' ones is more associated with risk in the housing market. Table 8.1 shows that 23 percent of those who left home for problem reasons (because there were no jobs in their home area or because they did not get on with the people at home) had later experienced homelessness, compared with only 2 per cent of those who left home for traditional reasons (to marry, to study or to take up a particular job). Leaving to set up an independent home was not associated with risk of homelessness. Age adds a further dimension though: young people who left home at 16 or 17 because of problems at home were more likely to have experienced homelessness than those who left for the same reason later. This was not the case for those who left home for traditional, or normative reasons. However, the table also indicates that leaving home for independence is more risky for people under 18 years of age than it is for those over 18. These findings suggest that more housing is needed for young people leaving home for problem reasons and who may not be in any position to 'delay' their departure.

TABLE 8.1     *Becoming homeless by type of reason*

| | Percentage who experienced homelessness | | |
|---|---|---|---|
| Type of reason for leaving | Left at 16 or 17 | Left at 18 or over | All |
| Traditional | 2 | 2 | 2 |
| 'Problem' | 25 | 19 | 23 |
| Independence | 11 | 3 | 6 |
| Other | 10 | 5 | 7 |
| All | 7 | 4 | 5 |

SOURCE     SYPS 1989/91.

## FAMILY HOMES AS SAFE HAVENS?

The problems which may affect young people's ability to remain in the family home and economically dependent on their parents include family poverty and family breakdown. Many young people have to cope with family breakdown. It has been suggested that, if present trends continue, 20 per cent of present-day children will have experienced a parental divorce by the age of 16 (Kiernan and Wicks, 1990). This may result in the loss of a parent, but many also have to re-negotiate their family relationships to allow the introduction of a step-parent and perhaps step-siblings. In these circumstances, there is enormous scope for family conflict, both before and after the breakdown itself. But conflict is also exacerbated by poor economic circumstances. There are higher divorce rates among families experiencing unemployment (Haskey, 1984), and family breakdown can be associated with lone parenthood and further poverty. Additionally, by stressing parental responsibility, government policies can increase the potential for conflict (Maas, 1986, p. 12), particularly in more 'fragile' family situations.

Having a step-parent at 16 was one of the main predictive factors associated with leaving home by 19 (Jones, 1993). The extent of this effect on the age at first leaving home is shown in Figure 8.3. Those with a step-parent (around 4 per cent of the whole 1987/9 SYPS sample) are far more likely to leave home at 16 and 17, and by 19 years, 44 per cent of those with a step-parent, compared with 33 per cent of those with a lone parent (13 per cent of the sample) and only 27 per cent of those with both parents, had left home. When asked why they had left home, nearly 23 per cent of men and 40 per cent of women with step-parents gave family problems as a reason (Jones, 1993b). Indeed, among women, this was the most common reason. The cause of relationship problems in step-families is likely to be complex, but the result is quite plain: step-children are disproportionately represented among early home-leavers, as Ainley (1991), MORI (1991) and Kiernan (1992) have also found. They are even more disproportionately found among homeless young people: at least one quarter of those in our Homeless Survey had a step-parent, more if we extend the category to include 'mother's boyfriend'.

Figure 8.4 shows the reasons for leaving home among the 86 respondents to the SYPS who had experienced homelessness and the respondents to the Homeless Survey. In both cases family problems (*'didn't get on with the people at home'*) was the main reason given, by nearly 60 per cent in both groups. *'Other reasons'* were spelled out by 64 respondents to the Homeless Survey. They tended to be associated with difficulties in

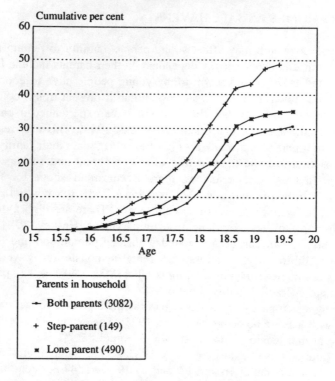

FIGURE 8.3   *Age first left home by household at 16 years*
SOURCE   SYPS, 1987s, 1989a.

family relationships, ranging from 'I got kicked out' (*n* = 17), to sexual or physical abuse of the young person (*n* = 13). In some cases, respondents said it was their parents who were at fault, for example, through drinking, or 'could not cope with mother nagging', 'family arguments and nagging'. In other cases, the respondents took the blame on themselves: 'I was thrown out for smoking hash', '[my] gambling problem was out of control', 'I was out of control', 'did a few daft things – had to go', 'threw [sic] out for not working'. Occasionally there were practical reasons, such as 'house getting overcrowded', or financial problems 'no money to pay rent to parents'. Many young people had left home in order to go into local authority care and had not returned home since.

Around one-third of the respondents to the Homeless Survey had been in local authority care since the age of 14 (see also Department of the Environment, 1981; Liddiard and Hutson, 1991). Six said this was because of truancy or their behaviour at school, and ten said they were beyond

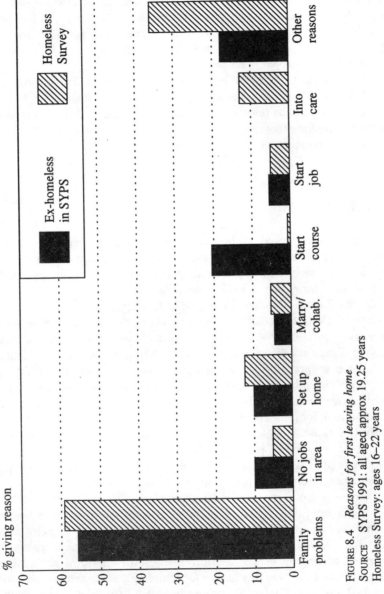

FIGURE 8.4   *Reasons for first leaving home*
SOURCE   SYPS 1991: all aged approx 19.25 years
Homeless Survey: ages 16–22 years

control. Sexual abuse was given as the reason in six cases and physical violence was an element in nine others – the latter usually, but not always, on the part of a parent: 'I hit my mother because she treated me like dirt and didn't look after my gran properly', while another said they had been 'coming home drunk, fighting'. Violence at home may not have involved the young person directly: 'My mother was badly beaten up by my uncle and my mother was put in hospital'.

These comments suggest a home life ranging from the uncomfortable to the dangerous. For some young people, the economic viability of leaving home may not be the priority consideration. Several of those interviewed described packing their bags and leaving home in the middle of the night and with no preparation, after being told to leave.


RETURNING HOME

For many young people, the first entry into the housing market is tentative and their presence even on the margins of the market only temporary. The first leaving home event is often only part of a process leading eventually to household formation and independent housing.

Table 8.2 is based on the SYPS 1989/91. Respondents could have been affected (before they reached the age of 18) by the 1988 change in social security regulations, which effectively withdrew entitlement to State support if they lost their jobs, as well as withdrawing students' entitlement to income support during the vacations, and to housing benefit. Many young people at this time were forced into a resumption of dependence on their parents. Those most likely to have been affected were people leaving home to look for jobs, and indeed 65 per cent of this group returned home again. Of those who left because of problems at home, 44 per cent returned home, and 38 per cent of those who left to start a particular job also returned. It is likely that many of those who left to go on a course will return when older, as previously observed (Jones, 1987).

There is a close connection between the reason for leaving and the reason for returning. Leaving to start a course, job or partnership, are mainly associated with returning because the course, job or partnership has ended. '*Family wanted me back*' was the most common reason for returning among those who had originally left because of problems at home (41 per cent gave this reason for returning). Some returned because they had problems finding housing or financial difficulties, which mainly affected those who left to set up their own homes or because of family problems. Some people were having problems sharing with flatmates.

TABLE 8.2    *Reasons given for returning home (indented), by reasons given for leaving (in bold), among those who have ever left and returned* (n = 411)

| Reason for leaving | % | phi | Significance P≤ |
|---|---|---|---|
| **Problems at home** (44% returned) | | | |
| Family wanted me back | 41 | 0.34 | 0.000 |
| Financial reasons | 34 | 0.20 | 0.000 |
| More convenient | 28 | 0.15 | 0.005 |
| Couldn't find anywhere to live | 23 | 0.28 | 0.000 |
| Didn't get on with flatmates | 14 | 0.22 | 0.000 |
| Partnership broke up | 10 | 0.12 | 0.05 |
| Job finished | 5 | 0.13 | 0.01 |
| **Wanted to set up own home** (18% returned) | | | |
| Financial reasons | 50 | 0.20 | 0.000 |
| Didn't get on with flatmates | 41 | 0.44 | 0.000 |
| Family wanted me back | 41 | 0.17 | 0.000 |
| More convenient | 36 | 0.12 | 0.05 |
| Became unemployed | 23 | 0.14 | 0.01 |
| Partnership broke up | 18 | 0.16 | 0.005 |
| **Looking for work** (65% returned) | | | |
| Only left temporarily | 56 | 0.15 | 0.005 |
| Lonely | 17 | 0.12 | 0.05 |
| **Starting a particular job** (38% returned) | | | |
| Job finished | 48 | 0.53 | 0.000 |
| Became unemployed | 14 | 0.15 | 0.005 |
| Financial reasons | 11 | 0.11 | 0.05 |
| **Starting a course** (16% returned) | | | |
| Course finished | 50 | 0.64 | 0.000 |
| Only left temporarily | 27 | 0.11 | 0.05 |
| Family wanted me back | 5 | 0.17 | 0.001 |
| **Getting married** (13% returned) | | | |
| Partnership broke up | 43 | 0.25 | 0.000 |

SOURCE    SYPS 1989/91.

It would seem from these findings that leaving home is often tentative and experimental, and that many people do return home if problems arise. However, it seems in many cases that it is the family of origin which holds the key to the door of the family home and, especially in the case of family conflict, has to make the first move. We have seen from the survey findings the importance of the 'invitation' to return home. The qualitative data collected during our interviews suggest that in many cases it is difficult for young people to ask to come home – or in other words, to claim their right to return. Where there is a lack of trust between them and their parents, other family members might be used as mediators to talk with the parents and facilitate the all-important invitation home (see Jones and Gilliland, 1993). Stand-off situations can easily occur, as Jill, one of those interviewed reveals: 'She [mother] was waiting for me to ask to come back and I was waiting for her to ask me to come back' (Jones and Gilliland, 1993).

It seems (as Maas, 1986, has also found) that some young people leaving home because of conflicts with their parents do return home after a period away and that their initial departure may simply reflect the need for some 'time out'. Superficial assessments are dangerous, though (Burton *et al.*, 1989): it would be simplistic to assume either that young people living with their families are 'hidden homeless' (Rauta, 1986) and in need of housing provision, or that those apparently in favour of living with their parents would not leave if they could. One of our interviewees, who left home after a dispute and returned when she had housing problems, reveals some of this ambivalence, but also had an impression of 'right' and 'wrong' ways of leaving home:

> It wasnae actually that bad coming back to stay here. ... After that I thought 'I'm gonna get a nice job and save up money and get a flat myself and start all agin, and do it the way I should have done it. (Patricia, quoted in Jones and Gilliland, 1993)

Others, though, do not get a second chance, and find themselves stranded without family or home. (Figure 8.5). Only 10 per cent of respondents to the Homeless Survey said they were thinking of going back home. Some of the others gave practical reasons for not returning, such as that their parents could not afford to have them back (6 per cent), because there was not room for them (13 per cent) or because there were no jobs in the area (4 per cent). Some had lost contact with their parents, or did not like to ask their parents if they could return. By far the main reason for not returning (given by 43 per cent) was because they still did not get on with people back home. Respondents could write in the 'other reasons' why they could not return home. The main reason given was that they liked their independence (*n* = 15), though some just said they 'did not want to go home'. Several said that their parents would not have them back, and in four cases there were court injunctions preventing them from returning. Fear of abuse or violence was the reason given by eight people. Drink and

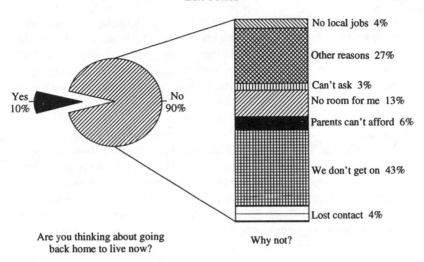

Are you thinking about going          Why not?
back home to live now?

FIGURE 8.5   *Reasons for not returning home among homeless*
SOURCE   Homeless Survey, 1992.

drugs (which could be on either side) were once again a factor in some cases. Others simply said there was 'nothing there'.

These findings suggest that young people's rights *vis-à-vis* their parents are as problematic as their rights *vis-à-vis* the state. Parents appear to have an obligation, though not a duty, to continue to help their adult children (as Finch and Mason, 1993, indicate). This means that parental support needs to be negotiated between family members, and young people do not have an automatic right to it. Where family relationships are bad, the scope for negotiation, even through a mediator, may be diminished. The homeless young people surveyed in particular provide evidence that the assumptions underlying social security policies are erroneous, and that family support may not be available for a variety of reasons.

## THE ROLES OF THE FAMILY, THE MARKET AND THE STATE

However much young people may want to, or need to, live independent lives, their freedom of action is limited by the structures of the family, the State and, increasingly the market, which interact, regulating housing provision and attempting to regulate housing demand. Young people leaving home in their teenage years are likely to be in the least favourable positions in the housing market, all the more so when leaving home at this age is described as 'premature'. Social legitimation of leaving home among this age group might increase their opportunities in the housing market. It is, therefore, timely to re-consider the concepts of 'premature' and 'delayed' departure from the family home.

There are many circumstances when the timing of leaving home is not a matter of choice. This applies as much to students going away to college as it does to young people escaping abuse. While there is social approval in the former case, leaving home because of problems at home – despite superficial recognition that such problems might include physical or sexual abuse – is still not fully legitimated. If it were, it would not be necessary for young people who have left home for these reasons to have to re-live their distress in DSS offices in order to obtain financial support for accommodation (Peelo *et al.*, 1990; Kirk *et al.*, 1991) and there would be fewer young people sleeping on the streets.

'Norms' of social behaviour often turn out in practice to reflect white middle-class patterns, and it is these patterns which are most likely to receive support – both in terms of leaving home and in terms of returning to it. It is a very middle-class pattern to leave home to go away to college at around 18 years, and parents are likely to define their student sons and daughters as 'living away' from home (see Leonard, 1980, on the distinction here). This denies the possibility that they may have left it. It indicates that the door of the family home is always open for them, and indeed many students do go home during vacations or when their course is over. The working-class practice, on the other hand, was to leave home in a more final way, and usually in order to marry. Returning home was not common. Economic factors, including the nature of the housing market and lack of housing provision, are causing a rise in the numbers returning home, particularly among young people from less affluent families. People who traditionally 'left home' permanently are now leaving more tentatively and facing greater risks. They are not only less able to compete in the housing market, but they are also less able to draw on long-standing practices and return home. As indicated above, young people who have left home do not have an automatic right to return.

The formal extension of dependency in youth means that access to the rights of citizenship – including the right to participate in the markets as consumers – is withdrawn. As long as young people are seen as dependents in normative nuclear families, they have no direct citizenship rights –

because, it is assumed, their parents' rights are indirectly transmitted to them (Jones and Wallace, 1992). Not all families can or will support young people, and provide them with housing, during such a protracted period of youth.

The many young people who risk homelessness in Britain need the State to resume some of the responsibility currently handed to parents. Government policies still assume that families are intrinsically 'safe havens', but research is increasingly showing that this is frequently not the case. The effective functioning of the family in providing shelter for young people, and thus regulating patterns of leaving home and housing demand, also depends on its effective functioning in other respects. Not all families are able or willing to care for their young, but as long as 'the family' is upheld in ideology as supportive, while young people are maintained in positions of dependence, then their right to independent citizenship will be denied.

# References

Ainley, P. (1991) *Young People Leaving Home* (London: Cassell Educational).

Bloss, T., Frickey, A. and Godard, F. (1990) 'Cohabiter, Decohabiter, Recohabiter: Itineraires de Generations de Femmes', *Revue Française de Sociologie*, XXXI: 4, pp. 553–72.

Brannen, K., Jones, G., Middleton, L. and Robertson, L. (1991) *Scottish Young People's Survey 1989 (Autumn): Technical Report* (Edinburgh: Centre for Educational Sociology).

Brannen, K. and Middleton, L. (1994) *Scottish Young People's Survey 1991 (Autumn): Technical Report* (Edinburgh: Centre for Educational Sociology).

Burton, P., Forrest, R. and Stewart, M. (1988) 'Growing up and Leaving Home', an information booklet prepared for The European Foundation for the Improvement of Living and Working Conditions, Dublin.

Burton, P., Forrest, R. and Stewart, M. (1989). 'Urban Environment, Accommodation, Social Cohesion: The Implications for Young People', Consolidated Report, SOAS, University of Bristol.

de Jong., Liefbroer, A. C. and Beekink, E. (1991) 'The Effect of Parental Resources on Patterns of Leaving Home among Young Adults in the Netherlands', *European Sociological Review*, 7: 1 pp. 55–71.

Department of the Environment (1981) *Single and Homeless* (London: HMSO).

Finch, J. and Mason, J. (1993) *Negotiating Family Responsibilities* (London: Routledge).

Galland, O. (1990) 'Un Nouvel Age de la Vie', *Revue Française de Sociologie*, XXXI: 4, pp. 529–51.

Godard, F. and Bloss, T. (1988) 'La Decohabitation des Jeunes', in Bonvalet, C. and Merlin, P. (eds), *Transformation de la Famille et Habitat, Actes du Colloque* (Paris: Presses Universitaires de France).

Goldscheider, F. K. and LeBourdais, C. (1986) 'The Decline in Age at Leaving Home', *Sociology and Social Research*, 70: pp. 143–5.

Haskey, J. (1984) 'Social Class and Socio-economic Differences in Divorce in England and Wales', *Population Studies*, 38: 3, pp. 419–49.

Haywood, I. (1984) 'Housing in Denmark', in Wynn, M. (ed.), *Housing in Europe* (London: Croom Helm).

Heer, D. M., Hodge, R. W. and Felson, M. (1984/5). 'The Cluttered Nest: Evidence that Young Adults are more likely to Live at Home than in the Recent Past', *Sociology and Social Research*, 69: pp. 436–41.

Jones, G. (1987) 'Leaving the Parental Home: An Analysis of Early Housing Careers', *Journal of Social Policy*, 16: 1, pp. 49–74.

Jones, G. (1990) *Household Formation among Young Adults in Scotland* (Edinburgh: Scottish Homes).

Jones, G. (1991) 'The Cost of Living in the Parental Home', *Youth and Policy*, 32: pp. 19–29.

Jones, G. (1993a) 'Young People's Right to Independent Housing: A Question of Legitimation?', Working Paper 1, *'Young People in and out of the Housing Market'* research project, Centre for Educational Sociology, University of Edinburgh and Scottish Council for Single Homeless.

Jones, G. (1993b). 'The Process of Leaving Home: Regulated Entry into the Housing Market?', Working Paper 2, *'Young People in and out of the Housing Market'* research project, op. cit.

Jones, G. (1993c) 'On the Margins of the Housing Market: Housing and Homelessness in Youth', Working Paper 3, *'Young people in and out of the Housing Market'* research project, op. cit.

Jones, G. (1995) *Leaving Home* (Buckingham: Open University Press).

Jones, G. and Gilliland, L. (1993) ' "I Would Hate to be Young Again": Biographies of Risk and its Avoidance', Working Paper 4, *'Young People in and out of the Housing Market'* research project, op. cit.

Jones, G. and Stevens, C. (1993) 'Researching *Young people in and out of the housing market*: About the Project', Working Paper 5, *'Young People in and out of the Housing Market'* research project, op. cit.

Jones, G. and Wallace, C. (1992) *Youth, Family and Citizenship* (Buckingham: Open University Press).

Keilman, N. (1987) 'Recent Trends in Family and Household Composition in Europe', *European Journal of Population*, 3: pp. 291–325.

Kiernan, K. (1986) 'Leaving Home: A Comparative Analysis of Six Western European Countries', *European Journal of Population*, 2: 2, pp. 1177–84.

Kiernan, K. (1992) 'The Impact of Family Disruption in Childhood on Transitions made in Young Adult Life', *Population Studies*, 46: 2, pp. 213–34.

Kiernan, K. and Wicks, M. (1990) *Family Change and Future Policy* (London: Family Policy Studies Centre, with Joseph Rowntree Foundation).

Kirk, D., Nelson, S., Sinfield, A. and Sinfield, D. (1991) *Excluding Youth: Poverty Among Young People Living Away from Home* (Edinburgh: Centre for Social Welfare Research, University of Edinburgh).

Leonard, D. (1980) *Sex and Generation: A Study of Courtship and Weddings* (London: Tavistock).

Leridon, H. and Villeneuve-Gokalp, C. (1988) 'Les Nouvaux Couples. Nombres, Caracteristiques et Attitudes', *Population*, 43: pp. 331–74.

Liddiard, M. and Hutson, S. (1991) 'Homeless Young People and Runaways – Agency Definitions and Processes', *Journal of Social Policy*, 20: 3, pp. 365–88.

Maas, F. (1986) 'Family Conflict and Leaving Home', *Bulletin of the National Clearinghouse for Youth Studies*, 5: 1, pp. 9–13.

Maclagan, I. (1992) *A Broken Promise: The Failure of Youth Training Policy* (London: Youthaid and The Children's Society, on behalf of the Coalition on Young People and Social Security).

Mayer, K. U. and Schwarz, K. (1989) 'The Process of Leaving the Parental Home: Some German Data', in Grebenik, E., Hohn, C. and Mackensen, R. (eds), *Later Phases of the Family Cycle* (Oxford: Clarendon Press).

MORI (1991) 'A Survey of 16- and 17-year-old Applicants for Severe Hardship Payments', research study conducted for Department of Social Security, July.

Peelo, M., Stewart, G., Prior, A. and Stewart, J. (1990) 'A Sense of Grievance. Homelessness, Poverty and Youth Offenders', *Youth Social Work*, 2: pp.12–13.

Rauta, I. (1986) *Who Would Prefer Separate Accommodation?*, OPCS, Social Survey Division (London: HMSO).

Schwarz, K. (1983) 'Les Menages en Republique Federale d'Allemagne: 1961–1972–1981', *Population*, 38: 3.

Wallace, C. (1987) *For Richer, For Poorer: Growing up in and out of Work* (London: Tavistock).

Young, C. M. (1984) 'Leaving Home and Returning Home: A Demographic Study of Young Adults in Australia', *Australian Family Research Conference Proceedings*, Canberra, vol. 1: *Family Formation, Structure, Values* (Institute of Family Studies, Melbourne) pp. 53–76.

# 9 'Island Homes for Island People': Competition, Conflict and Racism in the Battle over Public Housing on the Isle of Dogs
Janet Foster

## INTRODUCTION

It is well documented that residents, even in poor and run-down urban neighbourhoods, often feel a strong sense of attachment to the areas in which they live (Abrams, 1986; Bulmer, 1986; Young and Willmott, 1972). The Isle of Dogs in the heart of London's Docklands is no exception. This chapter, which is largely descriptive and exploratory, describes the conflict and emerging racism which occurred on the Isle of Dogs between white working-class residents, some of whom had a strong sense of place and history perceived to be under threat, and the predominantly Bengali population who were forced by changes in local authority housing allocation to move into the area.

## THE ISLE OF DOGS

Nobody knew where the Isle of Dogs was when we moved here. . . . I was so thankful for *East Enders* when it came on because now I say – 'You see that bit that goes like that' [the 'U' of the River Thames in the opening titles of the programme] 'I live down the bottom there.'

As this resident suggests, most people have never heard of the Isle of Dogs. A woman brought up a short distance from the Island, told me: 'Whenever anyone mentioned the Isle of Dogs I imagined it to be in the

Orkneys somewhere!' Yet, this little-known part of London became the centre of the most intense urban development during the 1980s where modern high-rise office blocks replaced the dying and derelict docks.

Prior to the development, the geographical features of the Island made it a largely self-contained and isolated area with a relatively homogeneous white working class population (see Cole, 1984, p. 296). Those born and bred on the Island (29 per cent of residents in 1987; see Wallman, 1987) were proud of their Island heritage and fiercely independent: '[Islanders] fight for their existence' a woman whose family had been in the area for four generations told me:

> They've always had to fight for their existence and they fight for what is theirs. . . . It's their Island and they don't intend to let anybody take their Island away from them.

During the 1960s and 1970s, slum clearance and new public housing developments led to an influx of 'outsiders', largely white working-class families from other parts of the East End. Such groups were initially resented:

> When I first came down here . . . [in the 1970s] we were foreigners and I was born just at the bottom of the East India Dock Road (about a mile away). . . . The likes of me were treated dreadfully . . . you'd sort of go in a shop and you'd hear 'em say 'Bloody hell, not more of 'em', kind of thing, not down 'ere!

Over time these 'newcomers' (who represented 41 per cent of the Isle of Dogs population in the late 1980s; see Wallman, 1987) became more integrated and accepted as others moved in who were perceived to be more threatening. The mid-1980s saw the arrival of affluent residents attracted by the development and the Docklands image (see Foster, 1992). Subsequently Bengali families were moved there as a result of the local authority homeless families allocation policy (see Forman, 1989; Docklands Forum, 1993).

With each 'wave' of 'immigration' the status of existing resident groups changed or was reassessed. Thus, the 'yuppies', themselves the targets of hostility at the outset, became more 'accepted' by indigenous residents as the Bengalis moved to the island (see Foster, 1992, and see Suttles (1972, pp. 41–3) for a discussion of the way such alliances develop in neighbourhood relations).

Consequently, despite its apparent homogeneity significant cleavages existed among Island residents both as individuals and between different groups. The situation was aptly summarised by Cohen (1989, p. 74) who argued 'In the public face, internal variety disappears or coalesces into a simple statement. In its private mode, differentiation, variety and complexity proliferate.' Therefore, in the battle over public housing the struggle became characterised as a simple 'battle' between 'us', the indigenous white working-class (which, for these purposes, now included those who moved to the Island twenty or more years ago) and 'them', the Bengalis, who were perceived to be denying 'local' people access to public housing.

## UNDERSTANDING CHANGE

Before discussing the battle over housing in detail, it is necessary to place the debate within a wider historical framework. Marx's famous dictum is most apt in relation to the Isle of Dogs:

> Men make their own history, but they do not make it just as they please; they do not make it under circumstances chosen by themselves, but under circumstances directly encountered, given, and transmitted from the past.    (Marx, 1970, in Damer, 1989, p. 152)

This is important because the perceptions of the local white working-class population need to be understood within the context of a historic class struggle in which some felt they and previous generations had always been disadvantaged and frequently exploited (see Foster, 1992, p. 171).

The changes which occurred on the Isle of Dogs also need to be understood at a variety of different levels. International, national and local factors all had an impact on events in Docklands. The focus of this paper on the micro-processes of conflict is not intended to minimise the importance of these wider forces. Logan and Molotch (1987, p. 99) remind us that events in individual localities need to be understood within the context of macro factors. However as Payne (1993, p. 29) so aptly stated: 'community study justifies its place by bringing in locality as one component of a total explanation. . . . There is a constant need to balance the elegant simplification of sociological theory with empirical encounters.' What occurred on the Isle of Dogs was consistent with experiences documented in numerous community studies where 'newcomers' (Cohen, 1982, 1989; Bassett *et al.*, 1989; Payne, 1993) moved into established areas. However, local conditions, including the speed of the development process, were also significant in shaping the nature of the particular response.

The research outlined here (based on two years of observations and extended interviews) sought to look at events on the Isle of Dogs from a variety of different perspectives, to obtain a detailed picture of the competing and conflicting forces which shaped the development process. Local residents, from indigenous Islanders to affluent newcomers, were interviewed, as were councillors, local authority officers and community representatives. Key figures in the London Docklands Development Corporation (LDDC) who held positions of power and shaped the course of the development, and representatives from the business community, both small and large, were also included in the study.

I began with an in-built sympathy for the indigenous residents whose lives had been turned upside down by such rapid and dramatic social and economic change in which they had played no part and whose course they could not alter. But as the work progressed, it become increasingly obvious that the situation was far more complex and less clear-cut. There were competing and often contradictory processes occurring in the area. There was no unified view about the development and the impact people felt it had had upon their lives (see Foster, 1992). The positive sense of 'belonging', community and traditional attachment to a way of life valued by some of the indigenous residents had to be weighed against the negativity of a culture which by definition stigmatised, marginalised and was hostile to those who did not 'belong'.

In tackling the complexity of the situation I was struck by Payne's (1993, p. 19) comments about the way researchers of community studies often sanitise their descriptions because of an over-identification with those they study. The reality he suggests is that 'villagers and villages are simply not that *nice*'. A sentiment which will be easy for the reader to identify with as the battle over public housing is described. But it is equally important to appreciate why it was that people did not appear 'that nice' in a climate where groups were competing for scarce resources.

Therefore, in the battle for public housing which ensued, the rights of white working-class citizens were regarded as more important and more deserving of preservation than those of the incoming Bengali population. As Harrison (1991, p. 210) notes, in addition intra-class, age, and gender, 'ethnic divisions and racism are very serious issues for the citizenship debate'.

It was precisely the features which had characterised the struggle for citizenship on the part of the white working-class population (see Turner, 1990) which made extending similar rights and privileges to other groups so difficult, because many felt that by doing so they were losing out. As one woman explained:

> one thing that has always struck me [is] . . . how naturally the instinct of Island people is to see the worst and to see the threat in everything. . . . I can only assume that comes from having been at [the] lower end where horrid things have always happened and big people . . . have always taken decisions which affected their lives which they've been powerless [to influence] and are always in a defence position to have to react and never initiate . . . the dark side is always the one that wins, it's always bad, we've gotta fight this and fight that.

'ISLAND HOMES FOR ISLAND PEOPLE'

[The Isle of Dogs Neighbourhood Committee (predominantly elected labour councillors) said in 1986] quite bluntly 'in future no house would be given to the local community, it would be given to the Borough, Borough wide and more than that it would be given to the homeless'. . . . The Neighbourhood calls us racist. . . . Nonsense we're saying it 'cos they're bleeding dumping people on our patch, irrespective what colour they are, it's totally immaterial.   (ex-docker, community activist)

The houses that become empty are not taken up by Island people . . . the council . . . won't allow sons and daughters to have priority in any way. . . . So that the people who are now coming onto the Island it's just another place for them. It's got no links with the past.   (Islander in his seventies)

Despite a decade of intense development, in which local people had derived little benefit, it was not this which caused most anger to local residents (see Foster, 1992). The key and most explosive issue was access to public housing. Many white working-class residents, especially those with long-established roots in the area, felt they were being forced out. They had witnessed the Development Corporation selling land to private developers for the affluent middle-class which, under previous plans, was intended for rented accommodation (see Brownill, 1990). By 1992 almost 80 per cent of house building in Docklands was for owner occupation (Docklands Forum, 1993, p. 13). The result of which Massey

(1991) notes was 'a total neglect of the state and private rented sectors and of the people in them' (quoted in Hall and Ogden, 1992, p. 153). This, combined with the constraints on local authority expenditure and the 'right to buy' policy, led to decreasing council housing stocks (an estimated loss on the Isle of Dogs of approximately 1500 properties in 7 years (Beckett, 1992, in Docklands Forum, 1993)) generating a crisis in the availability of public housing and rising waiting lists (see Brownill, 1990; Docklands Consultative Committee (DCC), 1990). It was frequently only those with highest priority who were housed, many of whom were homeless families of Bangledeshi origin (see Forman, 1989; Docklands Forum, 1993).

The Labour-controlled Isle of Dogs Neighbourhood Committee operated a needs-based housing policy which offered housing to those across the Borough who had highest priority. The other, Liberal-controlled, neighbourhoods in Tower Hamlets offered a 'sons and daughters' scheme (deemed racist by the Commission for Racial Equality (CRE)) whereby local people with family in the area had some entitlement to housing by virtue of their local connections. As a result, the Isle of Dogs experienced a large influx of homeless families from elsewhere in Tower Hamlets which created resentment and overt racism.

> the vast majority of them . . . are Bengali. There's been a lot of uproar over that for a start because people that live here that are really overcrowded can't get transfers. . . . They keep sayin' they're for homeless families which are Bengali people. And that is beginning to build up. . . . People resent the fact that they've always lived here and they can't find anywhere to live. We have spoken to the LDDC and we've told them they will create racial problems down here if they're not careful but nobody seems to listen. . . . When people have worked for what they've got and they see it all being taken away from them and being given over to ethnic groups, it's not because people are racist it's because they're having what they worked for taken away from them.

As the quotation above demonstrates, what in fact was a complex situation became a simplified battle between 'us' and 'them': 'I have no objections as such to Bengalis families comin' down here' one woman told me: 'but I don't think that the people down here should be pushed out for the other people'.

In almost a decade of development, not a single home for rent had been built on the Isle of Dogs. Housing therefore became a highly politicised issue.

Not surprisingly, the first public housing to be erected on the Isle of Dogs in ten years and on a prime river view site became symbolic of a struggle among some of the white population for 'local' (i.e. white) interests. 'There's two points of view' one of the community representatives of a local organisation explained:

There's the point of view that property developed on the Island, this is the Islanders' perception of it, should be for Islanders, people who lived here and worked here all their lives. The attitude of the local authority is that it's gotta be on a Borough-wide basis. So for example you could have a family living in Bethnal Green who are in desperate circumstances, would be top of the list in housing need, would be nominated to come to the Island and they could end up with one of the river view houses and that's really something that could split the locality if too many of these properties . . . are let to people from outside the Island. That could be very divisive although one can see the argument for giving to those with greatest need on a borough-wide basis there's also a lot to be said for the Island being given special opportunities because of the way that we've had to put up with all the mess and the changes that are taking place around here.

From the indigenous Islanders' perspective, the situation was straightforward: they were being denied access to housing which they felt they deserved. In fact, the situation was very complex indeed. It was certainly the case that those white tenants who had lived on the Island for many years felt they should be entitled to better treatment. But the difficulty lay in balancing the needs of other groups who might have suffered even more than white Island residents. As Ratcliffe (1992) points out, while it is undoubtedly the case that local people rarely benefit from urban regeneration strategies, it is the ethnic minorities who are the most excluded of all. Thus as Smith (1989, p. 181, quoted in Harrison, 1991) highlights: there is 'racially differentiated access to some basic rights of citizenship'.

Despite Islanders' protestations to the contrary, racism played a key role in the battle for housing and it was racism which had strong historical roots (Husbands 1982; Cole, 1984; Eade, 1989; Fryer, 1984): 'The Islanders absolutely loathe and detest what they call "pakis", Asians', a woman with East-End roots and a newcomer to the Isle of Dogs told me: 'They won't have anything to do with 'em, hate beyond, venom . . . there's real venom with that.'

In terms of the contemporary problems of racism and its manifestation in the battle for housing, many white people believed Bengali households were getting preferential treatment even though evidence suggests that ethnic minorities received the very worst deal (see CRE, 1988). The few who got fortunate housing allocation (in terms of the type of accommodation) were vastly outweighed by the many who experienced lengthy waits for housing in cramped bed and breakfast hotels only to be allocated council housing that was inadequate for their needs (Phillips, 1985 in Docklands Forum, 1993).

However, the myth persisted that ethnic minority households were getting preferential treatment and being provided with housing and services at the expense of whites. The comments of the Islander below demonstrate the ingrained prejudice and misinformation.

We're not racialists not by any means. Well you can tell we're not racialists because everybody's got feelings haven't they and it's not their fault if they're given things. They come to expect it without working for it. We know that what we want we've got to work for but they come over here and it's given to them. . . . For all they know we're gettin' the same as them. But we're the ones that know we're not in' it. You can't blame them if it's given to 'em.

Vociferous campaigns were mounted by some local residents and led to the creation of a pressure group called the '*Isle of Dogs Action Group for Equality*' designed not to get equality of housing for all 'but to ensure that new homes go to "Island" people' (*The Islander*, July 1992). A recent report (Dockland Forum, 1993, p. 11) suggested that local councillors were 'pressurised to introduce policies which would discriminate against Bangladeshi families' and that such pressure influenced local authority allocations. For example, one particular scheme, initially built for private ownership, but then given over to housing associations and local authority control, was initially allocated to homeless families. This policy was later reversed and properties were allocated to those on the transfer list so that homeless families filled the properties vacated by tenants who were transferred. Although this policy served a dual function, it actually denied homeless families access to better properties (Docklands Forum, 1993).

The irony of the housing situation on the Isle of Dogs was, as the Docklands Forum (1993, p. 11) noted, that 'whilst people in need of housing fight with each other about who gets access to housing, there are many more sites which remain empty which could be used for social housing on the Isle of Dogs'.

## COMING TO A HOSTILE COMMUNITY

Most of the Bengali family living here, most of us were homeless. Council policy has [it] that homeless only get one offer. This is why we come to this area. None of us likes to come here.   (Bengali resident housed on Isle of Dogs).

I'm not welcome on Island, no matter how much I try to integrate. (Young Bengali man)

As the preceding discussion graphically demonstrates, the Isle of Dogs like many other parts of the East End had a considerable racist reputation (see Husbands, 1982; Tompson, 1988) which had foundation in fact. Not surprisingly, Bengali families who moved on to the Island were often fearful. They frequently had good cause to be. One Bengali man described how he was confronted as the estate officer showed him a flat by a white tenant shouting: 'don't give any flat to any Bengali families because we won't let them stay here'.

One of the first families to move in received a far from welcoming reception. A pig's head was left outside the front door and the telephone lines to the flat were cut on two separate occasions. One Bengali man summed it up: 'we are suffering'.

The fear of violence and the hostility which some families received had an impact on most Bangladeshi families moved to the Island, as this community worker explained:

They're afraid of racist attacks and that's because they hear about some of the things that go on. . . . In a way whether it does or doesn't [happen] is neither here nor there it's the fear of it because it stops people going out and it stops people being as friendly as they might be with white people. I think it's being off their territory because if you live in Spitalfields it's ok, there are plenty of Bangladeshi people about, you feel safe. Down here you're that much more isolated.

Through an interpreter, one of the Bengalis I interviewed said that his family were unable even to walk across the road to the local shops after seven in the evening because:

> teenagers gather around and they just swear and throw something, sometimes even stones. Now the school there, lunchtime he's saying if you go there girls from the school they have some chips and something like that and if they see him going through they might throw chips or something, whatever they're eating.

These were not isolated incidents. Although recorded figures of racial harassment undoubtedly underestimate the extent of the problem, the figures for the Isle of Dogs were startling. In 1987, when 260 families resided on the Isle of Dogs, 104 incidents of harassment were reported (Docklands Forum, 1993, p. 8). In 1991, the Safe Neighbourhoods Unit conducted a survey and found considerable physical and verbal attacks on the Bengali population (Docklands Forum, p. 8).

Attacks even of a serious nature were frequently dismissed by many white people in the area. This was aptly demonstrated in comments made by one of the Parent/Governors at an Island school, who described the reactions of some of her fellow parents when they heard about a serious incident of racial harassment on a young Bengali:

> 'a couple of boys beat up this Indian boy, like nearly killed 'im. He was in hospi'al for weeks [They said] 'Oh well they're Pakis, what does that matter?'. . . . Some of 'em have said 'oh that was bad because they really went too far'. He should have had a whacking, for nothin', it's alright givin' him a whack, but not to put 'im in hospi'al for like four weeks and fracture his skull and nearly kill 'im. Don't nearly kill 'im.

Another woman expressed similar feelings when she challenged a local youth who was harassing a Bengali family on her estate: '"Only Pakis" he says, "Only Pakis". I mean what are these people?'

Although there was a considerable degree of racism amongst the white population, there were some like the two women above who sympathised with the Bengalis plight.

Despite the awful experiences which some families had endured, many of the Bengali residents I spoke to sought to differentiate between racists and other white people pointing out that some had shown them kindness and assistance. One Bengali girl wrote (reproduced in her own words):

I like living in the Isle of Dogs. . . . I think it's a nice place to live even though there are racist people [who] cause problems. But they're not all racist. I [k]now people who are very nice friendly. Most of them are white. Even though I am Bengali when people say everyone is racist round this are[a] I don't agree because there are some very nice people who are helpful, kind and understanding. There are some unfortunate people who don't like other colour people. They don't even try to get to [k]now people. . . . Even though we are different colour, different religion but me they should remember is that what we are all human being no matter where we come from or who we are.

Some of the Bengalis described how their white neighbours had intervened to prevent harassment by talking to those youths responsible. It was not always clear what their motivations for intervening in these incidents were. Was it deterring youths against behaving in such a way *per se*, or simply not tolerating disturbances on their own doorsteps? The difficulty of interpreting people's behaviour was expressed by one Bengali man who said: 'There are some good people on the estate which I think a majority of people on this estate are, you know, good not racist' but he also felt that white people knew what was going on but were turning their backs on the problems, unwilling to get involved or to challenge the perpetrators: 'Why don't they speak up, why are they so quiet?' he asked.

Some Bengalis questioned the motives of those white people who expressed a concern for their plight partly because, as this young Bengali explained, there was always a conflict of interests.

When they see that Bengali families are victims they're saying I'm sorry about this happening but when the time comes to give practical help or if they see the Bengali families are getting . . . any help and resources and things like that then [they] are not sympathetic anymore. They just think that it's them being let down. So it's hard to judge people who really are on your side or not.

Differences existed between Bengalis in terms of their experiences of racism. Many of the older generation, particularly men who had worked in Britain for twenty years or more argued that they had experienced little or no harassment prior to moving onto the Island. Their links with Britain in some cases went back to the Second World War, a factor which, if known by white residents on the Island, was never acknowledged.

The younger generation took the view that many of their older counterparts did not understand the nature of racism and often did not perceive themselves to be victims even when they were. As this young Bengali man explained:

> The environment they had and the environment we had is different. . . .
> When they were living here and working in the factories and things like
> that, at that time the problem was that they weren't able to communicate
> with anybody and not just that they didn't face any problem because
> they were working most of the time and . . . very few Asian people was
> over here. Wasn't much concern of racism or something like that. The
> tension wasn't so high at the time. As families moved in to join them,
> now the people who are mainly racist find that it's a problem for them
> and they're trying to do something about it. Nowadays, even still, old
> people don't understand what the perpetrators are saying. It's the kids
> who goes to school [who] can understand it.

It was also the case that the older generation were not competing for council accommodation to the same extent, because residence rules limited opportunities for blacks to 'register' for housing (see Docklands Forum, 1993, p. 3).

> At that time people very hardly live in council flat, the old people, who
> were young at the time, 1950s . . . worked in industry. They lived in
> their own accommodation, had rented accommodation. Mostly they
> worked in Birmingham . . . place outside (London). . . . At that time the
> numbers were less and now the numbers is getting bigger because fami-
> lies move in to live with them. . . . [The] number of Asian families
> [that] live in Tower Hamlets are making these perpetrators think that
> this is a problem for them. As they see that most of the Bengali families
> in council flats, they're getting the same facilities as they're having and
> things like that and it's something they can't tolerate.

Despite a wish on the part of some for rehousing in areas with more established Bengali communities, most recognised that in reality there was little
possibility of being moved. As one of the younger members of the Bengali
community commented:

> People feel that this is the place they have to live and they try hard to
> adjust in this community because they can see that there is very few
> chances that they could move outside [the area]. So they try to adjust in
> the community. But once they get involved in any incident the distress
> of that makes them feel that they are not welcome here . . . even I feel

that I would be better off if I moved from that Neighbourhood to somewhere else. It's just terrible for people doing nothing, being harassed
just because of their colour. It's intolerable.

Young, school-age children were often victimised. During a day in the
local secondary school, I asked pupils to write an account of living on the
Isle of Dogs. One of the accounts written by a 15-year-old Bengali girl
included: 'There is a Park called —— where most of the white kids go to
play. But if an Asian kid go by themselves they get called names
sometime beat up.'
    Although racism was of considerable concern to the Bengali popula-
tions, not all Bengali families experienced harassment or perceived the
area as threatening, even when they knew of the problems which others
experienced. One Bengali teenager I interviewed, for example, was among
the first families to arrive but had not been harassed. When I asked him
why he felt some were victimised and others were not he told me:

   I think it's cos I like mixing with the people. I kind of mix in with
   whites and everything. By mixing with 'em you get to know 'em. They
   get to know my dad and it's OK.

There was however a clear belief that it was integrating, that is, playing
down the differences between cultures, which was the passport to acceptance rather than the fact that the Bengalis should have been accepted on
their own terms. As one woman commented:

   This is the sad thing, the only way they're ever gonna integrate is when
   they pull away from their own culture. . . . One of my kids, actually they
   said to me one day . . . 'The Asians could help themselves if they
   stopped dressing like they did because they make themselves targets.'
   I said 'Why should they?'

There was a unified belief that Bengalis should not give in to harassment.
This woman told me:

   a family in —— House . . . did leave because of the harassment, you
   know. . . . They'd shoved I think it was a scaffolding pole through the
   glass door and the fellow was really that scared that he just left his property and went with his family. But I thought that was wrong as well
   'cos if they see that they've done that to one family and they've made
   them move then they're gonna try [it on] all the rest of us, you know,

they try and make us leave as well. . . . I understand that he was scared, you know, he was really scared that this happened to him but I don't think he should have left really.

This may be easy to say, but difficult to achieve in practice, especially in the face of such treatment. However, it was not simply the harassment itself which concerned the community, but the impact that harassment was having on the younger generation.[1] In areas like Spitalfields and Whitechapel where there were larger numbers of Asian teenagers, violence among young people was becoming a serious issue as this young Bengali man explained:

It's gone too far. I don't know how it started but maybe I think they faced same problems as kids now face on the Island . . . and now they just can't tolerate it so as anything the victims get gradually tougher . . . and I regret to say that some Bengali kids in Spitalfields are committing crime now. . . . Sometime they don't fight whites they fight amongst themselves. . . . People always do worry about what's happening in Spitalfields could happen in Island. . . . Older generation are worried about their kids, they really . . . want their kids to get a decent study and get a decent job later on.'

Yet this young man believed that the 'Older generation blamed themselves' not the structural inequalities in British society which had shaped their plight:

They see themselves as total failure because . . . they're thinking about their past if they could have buy a decent house or decent business or something, decent job then their kids could have been brought up in the sort of atmosphere where they wouldn't face that sort of problem. But now even if they wanted to get out of that atmosphere they can't afford it financially. They have to live in council flats. So . . . they feel they are the failure . . . they blame themselves.

Yet these structural factors were significant. Approximately 30 Bangladeshi families had been able to take advantage of shared ownership schemes developed by the LDDC (Docklands Forum, 1993, p. 6) and a mere 1 per cent of Bangladeshis owned their own property, despite comprising almost a quarter of the population in the Docklands area (London Docklands Household Survey – LDDC, 1990; see also LDDC, 1988a, b, 1991). Employment opportunities were also scarce. On the Isle of Dogs, Bengali men made up 11 per cent of the male population but comprised over 20 per cent of the unemployed male population (Docklands Forum, 1993, p. 7).


## BREAKING DOWN PREJUDICE?

I don't know why white families think that Bengali families don't want to integrate. It's mainly the communication problem.   (Bengali community activist)

The preceding discussion has illustrated that in the battle for public housing, indigenous Islanders and many white newcomers felt they should be at the head of the queue. Their Bengali counterparts, who in many respects had suffered more severely, were heavily victimised and became the scapegoats for a frustrated and bitter section of the white working-class population. As the local vicar put it, their arrival was 'one more bit of change that people didn't like but which they felt they could kick against' (Foster, 1992), which was no consolation at all to those suffering the harassment resulting from it.

There seemed to be a strong degree of ignorance on the part of white people on the Island about the plight of the ethnic minority families there. Some felt this was simply a convenient front as this tenant explained:

When we put forward this report on the racial attacks to our TA . . . you know, a lot of them were horrified and said 'does it really happen?' I've spoken to what I class as decent people, you know, down here and they 'aven't got a clue, you know, about the extent of these attacks that are being committed. But . . . if I'm honest the majority of people, if you said to them about the state of the Bengalis, you know, the majority of people on the Island . . . [and] I'd say 'ell of a lot of people in the East End as well, . . . they would say 'so what?' 'It's their own fault, shouldn't 'ave so many kids and we didn't ask them to come 'ere in the first place, they come over 'ere and they're just taking resources what we need' and that would be the attitude of the majority . . . a lot of 'em wouldn't say it to me, but that's what . . . people think.

However, another argued:

you don't think about these things you see, and I didn't even realise that . . . it was happening, naive probably . . .[But] you can't blame other people for not realising but you don't, not unless you think about it.

Never having been in another country where I couldn't speak the language, I didn't understand.

The woman quoted above lived next door to a Vietnamese family and openly admitted that she was unhappy when they moved in. It was not until she began to help one of the Vietnamese children with his English that she changed her view:

I said to him one day, 'do some writing I want to see what your written work (is like)' . . . and he wrote about what it was like to be a foreigner. I read that and I thought what must it feel like to come into a country, you don't understand the language, you don't even have a clue because even your writing is different, and what must it be like to come into a society like that. And that's when I started to realise well something I hadn't thought about.

A relationship which was once acrimonious changed dramatically because as her Vietnamese neighbour told her 'we had that level of communication all of a sudden, I'm not the big bad neighbours any more, you see'.

Generating understanding was frequently difficult in a climate where some were deliberately stirring up conflict and transmitting prejudice. Non-racist parents expressed considerable concern about the impact that the school environment had on the attitudes of their children:

I don't allow my kids to say things, [like] 'paki'. . . . But even my eldest one [in primary school] now is coming home sayin' 'I hate Pakis they stink.' I really get upset about things like that.

Another woman on the Island reported much the same experience:

I feel that school has a lot to do with it. In fact you know, kids that go to school on the Island they don't know anything else outside it, and the peer pressure down there, people say it's the same everywhere but I think being such a close knit community, it's so insular, it's got to be worse here.

## CONTRADICTIONS AND TENSIONS

There were those on the Island, particularly in community roles, who felt that people were too ready to focus on the bad and that not enough was made of the positive features of the area on which better relations might be built. As this community worker explained:

> There's terrible racism down on the Island and yes there is but there's terrible racism in Stepney and Spitalfields and everywhere else. Somehow because it's an Island they do see it as a different place and they do kind of exaggerate the problems but they don't particularly exaggerate the advantages like I think there's a better sense of community in some ways. It's not always used in a positive way but the fact that people do have a sense of community is a good thing because in lots of areas that's gone. That's something that can be built on even if some of the attitudes that are expressed through that community are not particularly helpful at least they're people who talk to each other, which is much better than working in an area where everybody keeps themselves to themselves.

Despite such optimism, the tension, conflict and competition remained, and striking balances like those proposed by the local churchman below is easier said than done:

> My feeling would be yes, it makes sense to have both a policy that deals with the needs of homeless people and you don't waste money on bed and breakfast and you also need a policy that says particular areas like this, which are really villages in the inner cities, that the place of sons and daughters in the community are vital to the continuing sense of having identity rather than just being like anywhere else in the suburbs which are pretty anonymous. Everybody in the suburbs tends to complain about 'wouldn't it be nice if we had a sense of community'. We've got it here historically but unless you are going to keep people or at least provide the means by which people who want to stay can stay then you're gonna destroy that and you end up with the worse of all worlds.

This quotation captures the tension which existed on the Island. It was special to those who had lived there for a considerable time (and indeed to many including some of the new affluent residents) but on a number of fronts, their way of life was challenged. 'Outsiders' whether they were affluent, homeless, developers, or businesses, were all seen to be encroaching on what Islanders perceived to be *theirs*. None were seen as offering opportunities. They were only perceived as threats.

The battle over housing was the latest in a long line of struggles, and in one sense the Islanders' treatment of the Bengali population was consistent with their attitude towards all outsiders. In other respects, their behaviour towards the Bengalis was quite different. They might have ostracised those who moved to the Island as a result of slum clearance, they might have disliked the 'yuppies' and daubed the walls with slogans telling 'yuppies' to 'keep out' but their behaviour in relation to the Bengalis, forced to move to the Island against their will, was not simply the result of a historic struggle but deep-rooted and unquestioned racism. This begs the question whether preserving a relatively homogeneous white working-class community is positive or desirable, especially as the Isle of Dogs was, as Hostettler (1988, p. 4) points out, 'founded on a melting pot of people with different regional accents, beliefs and customs'.

'It's got a marvellous history this place' one of the residents commented 'But let's move on. . . . The clique want to keep it to themselves. Don't let anybody outside in. . . . It's so inferior of them to think they're not equal to other people. . . . They've got this confidence within a community but in a wider [context they're lost] keep 'em out, block the bridges off again. . . . We don't want strangers in here because they're frightened. It's fear. It's inferiority.'

History had demonstrated time and again that Islanders could not prevent the tide of change either social or economic because it was mostly beyond their control. But this did not mean that they could not resent and battle against it. So that while in some respects the indigenous white working-class were themselves victims of a process from which they were excluded and over which they had little or no power to influence change, their resentment and marginalisation was powerfully exploited in their treatment of the Bengali population.

The possibility of each group having equal access to citizenship rights could not be envisaged, as resources were scarce and one set of claims were regarded as more valid than another. Yet, ironically, 'Islanders', a term reserved for those born and bred on the Isle of Dogs, would, in another decade, include the children of Bengali families whom many of the white working class were trying to keep out.


POSTSCRIPT

This paper was written prior to the electoral success of the British National Party candidate at the Millwall local council election. This result graphically and frighteningly demonstrates the extent of resentment among many white working-class people on the Isle of Dogs and reveals that some were willing to express their dissatisfaction politically via a party who, for them, clearly stated whose 'side' they were on.

## Acknowledgements

This paper is based on research conducted while I was T. H. Marshall fellow at the L. S. E. This fellowship was funded by the *British Journal of Sociology*. I would like to thank the Journal for their financial support and Paul Rock, the editor, for his ongoing help and encouragement. I would also like to thank Stephen Small, who made a number of useful comments following my presentation of this paper at the BSA conference and Martyn Hammersley and Paul Rock who commented on earlier versions of it. Last but certainly not least I would like to thank all those who took the time to talk to me about their experiences of living and/or working on the Isle of Dogs.

## Notes

1.    This concern was also expressed in previous research I conducted in an adjacent area of the East End. In this case though, it had a more optimistic outcome where racial violence and fear was reduced by a combination of an active Bengali community organisation, tenant participation and decentralised housing management (see Foster and Hope, 1993).

## References

Abrams, P. (1986) in Bulmer, M. (ed.), (1986) *Neighbours: The Work of Phillip Abrams* (Cambridge: Cambridge University Press).

Bulner, M. (1986) *Neighbours: The Work of Phillip Abrams* (Cambridge: Cambridge University Press).

Bassett, K., Boddy, M., Harloe, M. and Lovering, J. (1989) 'Living in the Fast Lane: Economic and Social Change in Swindon', in Cooke, P. (ed.), *Localities: The Changing Face of Urban Britain* (London: Unwin Hyman).

Beckett, G. (1992) Minutes of Extraordinary Milwall Consultative Committee, 20 February 1992; quoted in Docklands Forum 1993.

Brownill, S. (1990) *Developing London's Docklands: Another Great Planning Disaster?* (London: Paul Chapman).

Cohen, A. (ed.) (1982) *Belonging: Identity and Social Organisation in British Rural Cultures* (Manchester: Manchester University Press).

Cohen, A. (1989) *The Symbolic Construction of Community* (London: Routledge).

Cole, T. (1984) 'Life and Labor in the Isle of Dogs: The Origins and Evolution of an East London Working Class Community 1800–1980', PhD thesis, University of Oklahoma.

## Janet Foster 167

Commission for Racial Equality (CRE) (1988) *Homelessness and Discrimination: Report of a Formal Investigation into London Borough of Tower Hamlets* (London: CRE).

Damer, S. (1989) *From Moorepark to 'Wine Alley': The Rise and Fall of a Glasgow Housing Scheme* (Edinburgh: Edinburgh University Press).

Docklands Consultative Committee (DCC) (1990) *The Docklands Experiment: A Critical Review of Eight Years of the London Docklands Development Corporation* (London: DCC).

Docklands Forum (1987) *Housing in Docklands* (London: Docklands Forum).

Docklands Forum (1993) *Race and Housing in London's Docklands* (London: Docklands Forum).

Eade, J. (1989) *The Politics of Community* (Aldershot: Gower).

Emmett, I. (1982), 'Place, Community and Bi-lingualism in Blaenau Ffestiniog', in Cohen, A. (1982) (ed.), *Belonging: Identity and Social Organisation in British Rural Cultures* (Manchester: Manchester University Press).

Forman, C. (1989) *Spitalfields: A Battle for Land* (London: Hilary Shipman).

Foster, J. (1990) *Villains: Crime and Community in the Inner City* (London: Routledge).

Foster, J. (1992) 'Living with the Docklands Redevelopment: The Community View', *The London Journal*, 17: 2, pp. 170–82.

Foster, J. and Hope, T. (1993) 'Housing, Community and Crime: The Impact of The Priority Estates Project', Home Office Research Study 131 (London: HMSO).

Fryer, P. (1984) *Staying Power: The History of Black People in Britain* (London: Pluto Press).

Hall, R. and Ogden, P. (1992) 'The Social Structure of New Immigrants to London Docklands: Recent Evidence from Wapping', *London Journal*, 17: 2.

Harrison, M. L. (1991) 'Citizenship, Consumption and Rights: A Comment on B. S. Turner's Theory of Citizenship', *Sociology* 25: 2 May, pp. 209–13.

Hostettler, E. (1988) *An Outline History of the Isle of Dogs* (London: Island History Trust).

Husbands, C. (1982) 'East End Racism 1900–1980', *The London Journal*, 8: pp. 3–26.

Jacobs, B. (1988) *Racism in Britain* (London: Christopher Helm).

Logan, J. and Molotch, H. (1987) *Urban Fortunes: The Political Economy of Place* (Berkeley: University California Press).

London Docklands Development Corporation (LDDC) (1988a) *Report of London Docklands Survey* (London: LDDC).

London Docklands Development Corporation (LDDC) (1988b) *London Docklands Housing Review* (London: LDDC).

London Docklands Development Corporation (LDDC) (1990) *The London Docklands Household Survey* (London: LDDC).

London Docklands Development Corporation (LDDC) (1991) *Report of London Docklands Survey*, unpublished.

Marx, K. (1970) 'The Eighteenth Brumaire of Louis Napoleon', in *Marx–Engels: Selected Works* (Moscow: Progress Publishers, 1970), p. 96.

Massey, D. (1991) *Docklands: A Microcosm of Broader Social and Economic Trends* London: Docklands Forum.

Payne, G. (1993) 'The Community Revisited: Some Reflections on the Community Study as a Method', paper presented to BSA Conference, University of Essex, 5–8 April.

Phillips, D. (1985) *What Price Equality? A Report on the Allocation of GLC Housing in Tower Hamlets*, cited in Docklands Forum (1993), *Race and Housing in London's Docklands* (London: Docklands Forum).

Ratcliffe, P. (1992) 'Renewal, Regeneration and 'Race': Issues in Urban Policy', *New Community*, 18: 3, pp. 387–400.

Smith, S. (1989) *The Politics of 'Race' and Residence: Citizenship, Segregation and White Supremacy in Britain* (Cambridge: Polity Press).

Suttles, G. (1972) *The Social Construction of Communities* (Chicago, IL: University of Chicago Press).

*The Islander* (1992): 'Housing or Masthouse', July, p. 5.

Tompson, K. (1988) *Under Siege: Racial Violence in Britain Today* (London: Penguin).

Turner, B. S. (1990) 'Outline of a Theory of Citizenship', *Sociology*, 24: 2, pp. 189–217.

Wallman, S. (1987) *The Millwall Survey* (London: Department of Geography, University College, London).

Young, M. and Willmott, P. (1972) *Family and Kinship in East London* (Harmondsworth: Penguin), first published 1957.

# Part IV
## Environment, Planning and Bureaucracy

# 10 Contracting Knowledge: Commissioned Research and the Sociology of the Environment

## Elizabeth Shove

Contract work for the grey-suited guardians of government research does little for the research ratings: commercial-in-confidence reports sink without trace and anonymous authors are understandably reluctant to admit their involvement in this seedy side of sociology. Academic careers do not generally depend upon successfully completed contracts or on close contact with the practicalities of policy making. In any case, the tightly programmed environment of commissioned research is certainly not conducive to the careful construction of sociological theory. Yet it would be wrong to dismiss developments within these grubby margins of sociological activity. After all, commissioned projects do represent a potential source of income. Just as important, the organisation and management of contract researching has far-reaching implications for the place of sociological analysis within such fields as health, housing and the environment.

The environment is a good case. The Economic and Social Research Council's Global Environmental Change programme seeks to take 'social science to the heart of the environmental debate'. If this ambition is to be fully realised, sociologists will have to establish a legitimate role for themselves within research and development (R&D) programmes currently dominated by natural-scientific and technological interests. In 1992/3 the Department of the Environment's research and development budget was £86.9 million (DoE, 1992) a further £1.2 million being devoted to non-technical research in the field of buildings and energy conservation. It is impossible to say how much of this went on recognisably social research but the proportion is undoubtedly small. This is unfortunate. Around half the energy used in Britain is consumed in buildings and action is required in this sector if there is to be any significant reduction in associated $CO_2$ emissions. Here we have an area in which the social sciences could make a real contribution and in which sociological analysis is currently missing.

171

Sociologists may have good reason not to engage with (or become ensnared by) this sort of environmental agenda; their absence may reflect 'a deeply-rooted set of theoretical and conceptual difficulties' (Newby, 1991) and there is always the possibility that critical detachment masks a measure of disciplinary laziness. Such explanations focus upon the qualities and characteristics of the discipline itself. Taking a rather different tack, I want to look outwards, examining the organisation and management of environmental research and considering the implications of present funding practices for the development of sociological knowledge. There is nothing especially novel about the idea that funding strategies influence the production of knowledge and there is no shortage of literature on the social shaping of science (Rose and Rose, 1969; Mulkay, 1979). Couched in these terms, debate about the politics of research generally takes place on a rather large scale, covering great sweeps of history and implicitly applying to all areas of science. On closer inspection, the research environments of different disciplines vary systematically and in this context the finer details of research management make a real difference to the potential for interaction between social and natural sciences.

The following review of government-funded research on energy and the environment suggests that current forms of project management effectively prohibit multi-disciplinary responses to the challenges presented by global environmental change. The organisation of contract research has consequences for the development of knowledge and expertise in a wide variety of disciplines but the practical implications of present arrangements are, I think, especially limiting for the social sciences.

This discussion reflects six years experience (from 1986 to 1992) as a contract researcher competing for projects and contracts commissioned by the Department of Energy and, later, the Department of the Environment and the Department of Trade and Industry. During this time I was able to track developments in research funding at first hand, whilst also accumulating documentary material relating to earlier strategies of research management in the field of building science and energy conservation. An Economic and Social Research Council funded project, 'Putting Science into Practice: Saving Energy in Buildings' subsequently provided an opportunity to interview project officers involved in commissioning energy-related research in Britain, France, Sweden and the USA. The events and developments described in this paper are thus based on a selective review of invitations to tender for government-funded research, on personal experience as a contract researcher and on interviews conducted as part of a larger project designed to explore the role of social science within areas currently dominated by technical and natural-scientific interests. The focus throughout is on energy conservation and government-funded building research.

The plan, then, is to document the changing structure of building and environmental research and assess the consequences of such developments for the potential contribution of the social sciences. My three-part review records the shift from in-house research to consultancy and from early forms of project management to present methods of contract control.


## IN-HOUSE EXPERTISE

In the post-war period, building researchers sought to identify genuinely practical solutions to immediate problems in health-building, housing and education. This was thought to require an appreciation of social and economic context and careful, scientific, analysis of building methods and of building materials. The Building Research Station, now the Building Research Establishment, consequently employed architects, quantity surveyors, various sorts of engineers, physicists, mathematicians, economists, psychologists and sociologists. Claims that 'the Building Research Station was one of the earliest examples of a multi-disciplinary organisation depending on the working together of staffs trained in many different branches of the arts and sciences' (Lea, 1971, p. 1) are somewhat exaggerated, but there is no doubt about the perceived importance of a multi-disciplinary approach. As Saint observes, the idea of the public sector 'development group' that is of a 'vanguard removed from everyday tasks to find some radical solution of general applicability to a pressing technical problem', reflected 'pre-war and wartime enthusiasms for science, research, and "group working"' (Saint, 1987, p. 116). Such in-house groups tackled problems of building design without much regard for disciplinary boundaries (Roberts, 1991). Ideas were explored, experimental buildings constructed, and experiences gained during the development of systems such as CLASP – the Consortium of Local Authorities' Special Programme – for school building and 'Best Buy', 'Harness' and, later, 'Nucleus' for hospital planning and design. The context was one which allowed architects to work, in the case of the Architects and Buildings Branch, 'side by side with educationalists, both employed together in the same public service and sharing their accumulating experience' (Saint, 1987, p. 213). Although many harboured unrealistic beliefs about the nature of sociological understanding (especially in the area of social housing), social scientists had a recognised role within the research team.

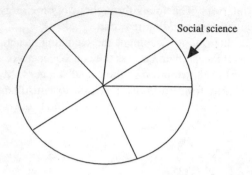

FIGURE 10.1    *In-house expertise*

Picturing this period in pie-chart form (Figure 10.1), we can see that social science has a slice of the action. Each segment represents a different discipline and, as the image suggests, research teams were organised as single inter-disciplinary units. The reality was often less cohesive but the formal structure of research management ensured that team members shared the same tea-breaks.

The pie-chart of research management has since evolved, first turning into a pattern of co-ordinated consultancy and then acquiring the fragmented features of contracting knowledge.

## CO-ORDINATING CONSULTANTS

The second pattern, which I shall call, 'co-ordinated consultancy', did not automatically replace the in-house team, but by the mid-1970s, government research groups were more likely to be managing projects contracted out to private-sector researchers or to universities than they were to be doing the work themselves. Lord Rothschild's 1971 report, *A Framework for Government Research and Development*, emphasised the need to clarify responsibilities for research within government departments and underlined 'the principle that applied R. & D., that is R. & D. with a practical application as its objective, must be done on a customer–contractor basis. The customer says what he wants; the contractor does it (if he can) and the customer pays' (Rothschild, 1971, p. 3). This was something of a landmark. In distinguishing between their role as client (or customer) and as research provider (or contractor), government departments began to dismantle the cosy culture of in-house research. A new breed of project officer emerged. These people represented the customer and it was their job to specify research requirements, select and evaluate potential contractors, and commission studies either from in-house experts or from those outside.

To begin with, this shift from in-house research to co-ordinated consultancy made little difference to the interdisciplinary environment of building research. Some government researchers left to set up new organisations and proceeded to compete for research contracts from the departments and divisions in which they were formerly employed. Those who remained in the civil service acquired new skills, turning themselves into project officers responsible for managing still sizeable programmes, but no longer directly involved in research activity. In-house teams were formally disbanded as research drifted away from the civil service and out to the universities and the private sector but, for a while at least, belief in the importance of a multidisciplinary approach was as strong as ever.

Studies to assess and develop the potential for using solar energy in British buildings provide a clear illustration of this pattern of research management. Having explored the potential for using 'active' systems involving the storage and subsequent use of solar energy, the Energy Technology Support Unit (ETSU), at that time funded by the Department of Energy, turned its attention to 'passive' methods of exploiting the sunshine. Started in 1982 and only now drawing to a close, millions of pounds later, ETSU's Passive Solar House Design Programme was initially designed as a genuinely inter-disciplinary enterprise. The aim was to identify, evaluate and exploit technically and economically viable ways of designing houses to take advantage of solar energy. There were a number of technical options to explore, for the distribution of glazing, orientation, layout and planning were all likely to make a difference to 'useful solar gain' and so to the amount of additional energy required. There was little point in developing theoretically efficient passive solar houses which nobody would build and which nobody would buy. Recognising this, the project officer responsible for the programme devised a research and development strategy encompassing contributions from many different disciplines. Detailed study of experimental houses was thus complemented by computer-based analysis of generic solar features; architects were involved to ensure that technically possible options could be incorporated within real, buildable houses, and private-sector house builders, economists and social researchers (Meikle and Wensley, 1984) contributed to debate about marketability and the social and economic acceptability of passive solar designs and layouts.

In effect, the ETSU project officer commissioned and worked with a multidisciplinary research team whose members were drawn from the outside world rather than from within one centrally funded government research group. The total programme was divided into separate packages of work, each defined in enough detail to ensure that consultants contributed to the overall project, but not so tightly structured as to specify the methods and procedures to be adopted. After all, the development of appropriate methodologies was an important part of the project and contractors were selected because of their expertise in these matters.

Research results were not scripted in advance and there were real opportunities for making and learning from mistakes as the programme unfolded. Some of the first trial houses were, for example, provided with very large south-facing windows, an arrangement designed to maximise solar gain. Heat is also lost though glazing and building researchers were keen to establish exactly how much difference these large windows made to overall energy consumption. Experimental properties were consequently stuffed with monitoring equipment tracking temperature and energy demand in enormous detail. Analysis of the results suggested that something was awry and indeed it was. Faced with large blank areas of glass, occupants hung up net curtains, thus eliminating the best part of the solar gain. As the social surveys were to show, inhabitants were more concerned to preserve their privacy than to save a few kilowatts of energy. The implications were clear. If technologists were to produce really plausible designs they would have to take account of the ordinary conventions of domestic life and they would have to re-think their solar strategies. Optimal technical solutions simply did not work as predicted when adopted in the real social world. Basic appreciation of the practical consequences of householders' desire for privacy does not depend upon any very profound sociological insight but, as this example suggests, social analysis could and did influence the direction of technological enquiry. Estimates of realisable energy savings were revised downwards as a result, and investigation focused upon the potential contribution of other more 'people proof' aspects of design, such as orientation and layout.

As this case suggests, social researchers still had a legitimate role in the formation and development of what was, in the main, technical research. By current standards, the overall budget for the passive solar house design studies programme was huge and slices of funding were large enough to keep individual researchers in work for years at a time. There was a real sense, then, in which people from different organisations worked together on the project team. The ethos was still one of team-work and regular multidisciplinary seminars routinely involved all participating contractors.

Energy research reached a turning point in the 1980s. By this time, building scientists had established a range of simple, cost-effective, energy-saving measures. Having identified these technological solutions, the next step was to 'get the message across' to building professionals and to individual householders. Increasing interest in technology transfer created new opportunities for social scientists and in this relatively open research environment it was possible to explore the social contexts of technical innovation in some depth.

In 1985, the Energy Efficiency Office sponsored a series of seminars and workshops to show local authority staff how they might improve the energy efficiency of their housing stock. In purely technical terms the case was compelling. It was demonstrably easier, cheaper and more effective to adopt a total package of energy-saving measures (insulation, better heating system, draught stripping, etc.) than to make such improvements piece-meal. Before embarking on a full scale national programme of educational events, the Energy Efficiency Office commissioned a market study to establish the needs and interests of the intended audience. This study, which involved long and detailed interviews with a sample of housing managers, engineers, surveyors and architects, suggested that current prac-tice reflected a range of competing pressures which complicated, and in some cases prevented, the simple adoption of technically optimal solu-tions. Local authority staff were, it seemed, perfectly capable of improving energy standards but were unable to apply this expertise because of the organisational context in which they worked. So the problem was one of institutional structure, not of technical ignorance, as was at first supposed. As the authors of the market study concluded, successful 'technology transfer' depended on the social and political environment of technolo-gical choice for it was this which inhibited, and occasionally enabled, the practical application of existing expertise (Shove *et al.*, 1985; Shove, 1989). Although these findings made no difference to the chosen method of dissemination (a national programme of technical, information-packed workshops soon followed), the market researchers had an opportunity to examine the inner workings of local authority departments and to show how ideas and practices were formed and fixed within these bureaucratic structures. Such investigation still involved a process of discovery and exploration, and researchers were still able to develop and defend methodological strategies appropriate to the task in hand.

To summarise, the period of co-ordinated consultancy was one in which terms of reference permitted social as well as technical investigation and in which contractors took responsibility for research design and methodo-logy. In the case of energy-related research, there was scope for negotiation about the way in which problems and issues were framed and addressed and about the ways in which they might be studied. Invitations to tender were cast in fairly general terms, as illustrated by the following extract which relates to a proposed investigation into the cavity wall insulation industry. Cavity wall insulation represents one of the single most effective environmental measures a householder can take, hence the Energy Efficiency Office's interest in the following questions.

J.    *Questions needing answers are:*

2.1    i    *Why are people installing cavity wall insulation and, conversely*
       ii    *Why are people not installing cavity wall insulation*
       iii    *What information do people need to persuade them to invest in cavity wall insulation?*
       iv    *Are there other incentives needed – apart from government grants*

*. . . You are invited to submit a fully developed and costed programme based on this brief . . .*

This extract does, of course, make certain presuppositions about the nature of social research. It revolves around a socially undifferentiated category of 'people'; it assumes that energy-related decisions are determined by personal conviction and it implies that financial investment will follow once people have the right information. Such individualistic assumptions about the rationally acting public do not, in themselves, prohibit investigation of the organisational and economic structure of the insulation industry or of the diverse social situations of its customers (Shove, 1991). In other words, the terms of reference for this nine-month contract were flexible enough to allow for some genuinely exploratory research and for an appropriately wide-ranging analysis of this crucial environmental industry. Tasks were not specified in enormous detail and in developing a costed programme, potential contractors were invited to devise their own research strategies.

In this phase of 'co-ordinated consultancy', contractors expected to make a real intellectual contribution to the research programme. They helped to develop research briefs, they formulated methodological strategies and they were paid to find things out. For their part, project officers relied upon the support and experience of their contractors. Researchers were likely to spend a year or more of their lives on a single project and

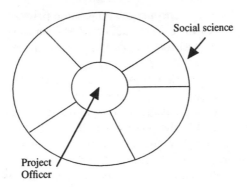

FIGURE 10.2   *Co-ordinating consultants*

the pattern of funding – one in which projects were split into a handful of large contracts – enabled these people to develop something of a research career. Knowledge was divided between organisations, not shared by the members of a single research team as before, but successful contractors were able to retain a critical mass of staff, each engaged on a substantial project. No one could be sure of securing the next contract, but it was clear that the system relied upon, and helped develop, the experience of those involved.

Figure 10.2 shows a second version of the pie-chart which illustrates the central position of the project officer as co-ordinator of consultancy. Although this was an important change, projects were still divided into sizeable contracts, contractors helped to form the research agenda, and social science still had a significant slice of the action.

## CONTRACTING KNOWLEDGE

The pattern of research management has shifted again over the last decade or so. The size and value of individual research projects has decreased, while the number of project officers and the number of contracts has risen. It is impossible to get hold of any figures to substantiate this claim, but the trend is undisputed. The days of £200 000 contracts in the field of energy-related building research are pretty well over, and contractors now compete with each other for projects worth a fraction of that value. Such fragmentation reflects growing pressure for ever more detailed account-ability and for ever tighter project management. This, together with an equally forceful drive to encourage competition between contractors, has serious consequences for the production of new knowledge about energy and the environment and for relationships between government research managers and their contractors.

The trends discussed below remove many of the risks and uncertainties associated with interdisciplinary interaction and creative thought, and conspiracy theorists might plausibly argue that the research process has been deliberately de-skilled to the point where it is now a secure, manageable and entirely predictable bureaucratic function. Whatever the intention, the roles and responsibilities of research managers and contractors have changed dramatically with especially sinister implications for the place of social science within environmental research. From the project officers' point of view, research management has turned into a form of contract control.

**Contract Control**

Each contract represents a burden of ordinary financial and administrative labour and as the number of separate contracts goes up, the daily quota of paper work increases. Engulfed by a rising tide of routine administration, project officers lose contact with the research process. Their ability to retain a strategic view of the total interdisciplinary operation is further eroded by the sub-division of responsibilities between a growing number of fellow officers. In this context, it is simply impossible to develop research strategies which exhibit the scope and vision of wide-ranging initiatives such as the passive solar house design programme discussed earlier. Instead, project managers submit their own bite-sized research topics for consideration by the relevant selection committees. As before, committee members direct the research agenda by picking priorities from a menu of submissions. The difference is that these submissions are now prepared by people who are detached from the realities of research and unable to take a broad view because of their position within a wider management structure. In these circumstances it is much easier to champion personally favoured projects than to become entangled in ambitious multidisciplinary schemes. In any case, the sub-division of research contracts tends to obscure relationships, trends and patterns which would have appeared important under other research-management regimes.

Researchers and project officers used to work together rather more closely than they do now and in helping to shape coherent research programmes experienced contractors had opportunities to steer the 'gravy train' in their direction. The splintering of research contracts has changed all that. From the project officer's point of view, contractors are nothing more than the neutral, intellectually detached, suppliers of research services. Independent contractors bid for separate parcels of work and it is the project officer, not the researcher, who pieces together the 'findings' which emerge from a string of separate contracts. In this competitive environment, communication between commissioned and competing research organisations is potentially problematic, bringing with it the possibility of collusion, price-fixing, interdisciplinary exchange and who knows what else. Researchers working on the same project are therefore kept in ignorance of each other. This is frustrating and often embarrassing for the researchers involved – and it does nothing to promote trans-disciplinary understanding – yet the arrangement makes perfect sense within the prevailing structure of research management.

If they are to advance their own careers, project officers must produce research results on time and within budget. This is difficult, for research is an inherently uncertain business. In an effort to manage such unpredictability, project managers define invitations to tender in increasingly precise terms. Success depends upon tying isolated researchers to a specified schedule of work and on keeping them to time at all costs. Programmes of work, now punctuated by 'milestones', generally conclude in a pile of 'deliverables'. Invitations to tender routinely specify dates by which interviews will be complete, dates by which questionnaires will be returned, dates by which analyses will be concluded, and so on. This highly structured system prescribes the exact duration of each stage of the research, allowing project officers to monitor performance and assess progress. In this environment, contractors have no reason to speak to each other and no reason to look beyond their allotted task. There is no opportunity for discovery; one might even say there is no opportunity for research, for the slightest unanticipated development disrupts the pre-determined programme and hinders progress.

The following contract for a 1991 project illustrates the 'milestone' phenomena and the degree of detail likely to be encountered in even the simplest work programme. The focus of energy-related research has shifted away from technical analysis toward technology transfer, education and marketing, and the Department of Environment is increasingly keen to evaluate the impact of efforts to 'get the message' of energy efficiency across. The brief below relates to a follow-up study designed to assess delegates' responses to a series of educational events on energy and the environment:

*3.4   Delegates views on the seminar will be broken down into:*
- *(a)   overall;*
- *(b)   the talks;*
- *(c)   the delegate information pack; and*
- *(d)   the exhibition (if provided).*

*The contract will take place according to the following timetable:*

| Event | Date |
|---|---|
| *1.   Submission of personal interview details and questionnaire for approval* | *14th January* |
| *2.   Mailing for first questionnaire* | *15th January* |
| *3.   Initial report to be submitted* | *29th January* |

In the past, contractors were expected to provide a report describing their research and assessing its implications at length. Project officers do not now have time to become familiar with all the contracts they supervise and they are not in a position to contemplate the wider relevance of these isolated studies. They are, none the less, expected to present results and summarise conclusions. Contractors are therefore asked to provide 'speaking notes', that is a few pages of text and a matching set of slides, which project officers can use if called upon to talk about the project. Competing researchers are not expected to talk to each other, contractors' skinny 'deliverables' are routinely branded as 'commercial-in-confidence', and, as noted above, isolated findings are finally presented in verbal form. The present pattern of contracting knowledge breeds confidentiality and an insidious secrecy which affects commissioning organisations as badly as it does researchers. In the sector with which I am familiar, the turnover of project officers is very high; there is no central library of commissioned research reports and the collective memory of previous studies quickly seeps away. Each new recruit arrives to identify 'new' projects and to write a 'new' research strategy in almost total ignorance of what has gone before.

The following extracts reveal the recycling of projects and the changing style of brief writing. Both relate to studies of decision-making in social housing, the first in 1989, the second in 1992.

*Housing Associations*

*1.   Examine organisational, and managerial factors which inform Housing Associations views of energy, warmth, and efficiency, and which affect choice about energy efficiency and housing rehabilitation.*

The 1992 version is as follows:

*TOP LEVEL DECISIONS IN SOCIAL HOUSING*

| | | |
|---|---|---|
| *Aims* | *1.* | *To determine how decisions are made at the top level on energy efficiency in landlords housing stock* |
| | *2.* | *To determine the type of information required by the people making these decisions to improve their quality* |
| | *3.* | *To determine the best means of delivering this information* |
| | *4.* | *To assess the success of efforts so far in addressing 1 to 3.* |
| *Deliverables:* | *1.* | *Questionnaire* |
| | *2.* | *Report on aims 1 to 3* |
| | *3.* | *Report on success so far* |
| | *4.* | *Recommendations for future work.* |

Paradoxically, anxiety about accountability and the need to control contractors has fragmented the research process to such an extent that project officers have less idea of what is going on than ever before. Methods of reporting compound the problem, for it is hard to capture the complexity of energy conservation when project output is of so brief a form. It is true that more money is being spent in this field, it is true that there are more project officers, and it is true that there are more researchers but there is a real sense in which less is happening.

**The Research Community**

Present methods of managing and organising environmental research have far-reaching consequences for the research community. It takes almost as much time to prepare a proposal for £20 000 worth of work as it does for a project ten times that size, and the constant financial drain of proposal writing has undermined the economic viability of experienced teams of respected researchers. Projects no longer demand much creative input, and knowledgeable researchers are no more likely to win a contract than their less experienced rivals. Indeed there is a definite pattern of moving work around, preventing those who have gained some expertise from putting it

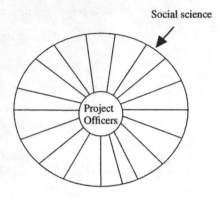

FIGURE 10.3    *Contracting knowledge*

to further use and providing opportunities for other less competent researchers. The chances of securing a really steady stream of small contracts are increasingly remote and contracting organisations find it difficult to sustain a healthy team of researchers on a scrappy diet of short-term projects. For these reasons, energy-related building research is now likely to be done by a research 'temp' hired for the duration of the project by an organisation offering yet another layer of project management, or by a self-employed research consultant working from home. Neither situation is especially conducive to team-working or to interdisciplinary interaction.

A third version of the pie-chart (Figure 10.3) illustrates the proliferation of small contracts and the increasing importance of contract control.

Changing styles of project control have consequences for all disciplines, but in this last section I want to focus upon the implications of contracting knowledge for social-scientific involvement in government-funded environmental research.

IMPLICATIONS FOR SOCIAL SCIENCE

As we have seen, research projects and invitations to tender are now quite precisely specified. The role of social research within building and environmental science therefore depends upon project officers' beliefs about the value of social science and about the areas in which it might make a worthwhile contribution. Current practice suggests that technically oriented research managers share a rather limited view of the potential of sociological enquiry. In effect, sociology is seen as a form of behavioural research, perhaps useful as a means of shedding light on the confounding peculiarities of individual action, but of no wider relevance. There is no place here for the sociology of science, or for sociological analyses of organisations, of professional power, of social structures or of changing environmental cultures.

Notes for potential marketing services contractors underline this individualistic understanding of the social world: 'In the building industry the total number of decision-takers is well in excess of 100,000', hence the aim of targeting key individuals in the hope of converting them to the cause of energy efficiency. By implication, energy-related standards simply reflect the personal preferences and prejudices of totally autonomous, socially anonymous, decision-makers. Project officers are at a loss to explain seemingly irrational reactions to perfectly good technical solutions and this is where social and marketing researchers come in. These experts are widely believed to have special access to the inner secrets of 'how people tick' and a direct line to their 'attitudes'. As such, they have an important part to play in promoting technology transfer.

There is a second area in which the social sciences have a recognised role. In the conventional account, the market may fail to adopt technically proven, self-evidently sensible energy-saving technologies if impeded by what are usually termed 'non-technical barriers'. Perplexed by the confounding irrationalities of the social world, technically trained project officers turn to the social sciences in the hope of finding a way around these obstacles. In the example quoted below, the project officer recognises that the routine pressures of commercial house-building may inhibit adoption of energy saving measures. Understanding of these 'barriers' seems to require some sort of social investigation, but it is not clear what form this should take, nor how such research should be managed and accommodated within the technical programme. The schedule of work for a study of private-sector house-building illustrates this unease, allowing for the detailed investigation of up to three non-technical obstacles:

> *1.3.1   During the course of the project, factors that complicate the optimisation of energy efficient design are likely to be identified. Where these become a barrier which compromise or prevent the adoption of energy efficient measures, investigation may be felt necessary. The intention of this shall be to overcome the barriers and ease the design and construction process. Areas to be investigated must be agreed with and shall be limited in number to three.*

While this is an invitation to explore unspecified social factors influencing the application of energy-related expertise, the idea of arbitrarily limiting such investigation to three agreed areas, together with emphasis on the need to *overcome* barriers, implies that there is some uncertainty about the practical value of such analysis.

It is virtually impossible to escape the narrow roles of market research or barrier analysis and contracts are so closely controlled that there is little chance of redirecting projects to explore the social and economic contexts of individual action. The prevailing view of social research, shared, no doubt, by many other government research managers, effectively precludes sociological involvement. This is so despite the emphasis now placed upon issues of technology transfer, on 'barrier studies', and impact assessment – all areas in which investigation requires the use of social rather than natural-scientific methodology.

In the past, specialist contractors were able to determine their own research strategies. For the sake of efficiency and tighter project control, methodological decisions are now made by people who have no formal training in social research. Market studies and opinion polls provide the unstated reference point and, as the following extracts reveal, invitations to tender frequently define inappropriate and sometimes totally unrealistic research methods. Not surprisingly, issues of sampling are especially problematic.

In this first case, which relates to a study of the perceived benefits of energy-efficient design in proposed private-sector housing developments, the project officer gives a clear specification:

> 2.16   *The contractor shall interview four clients on each development, to include those in all day and those out all day, both with and without children.*

The difficulty here is that the brief relates to a study of six (as yet unbuilt) housing estates, some including no more than half a dozen dwellings. It would be truly remarkable if these small developments each included the required range of respondent types. The following example presents a similarly daunting methodological challenge.

> 3.2   *The sample of approximately 400 respondents shall be drawn from those who currently have unfilled cavities and shall be structured so as to include those living in each of the four areas of rain exposure. It shall also be designed to represent the UK distribution of socio-economic categories.*

It is impossible to tell in advance whether people do or do not have unfilled cavities, the population is unevenly distributed across rain exposure areas and the last minute addition of socio-economic categories compounds an already overwhelming task.

Questions of representativeness present other problems. Again, ill-informed project officers make quite unreasonable demands. Consider this statement relating to a proposed study of the beliefs and attitudes of those involved in making decisions and advising on levels of insulation in new and existing properties.

> 2.3.1 *Interviews will be held with a representative sample of architects, surveyors and others.*

Keen to cover their own backs, project officers pass impossible methodological responsibilities on to their hired contractors. This next case, which concerns a study of energy efficiency in public and private sector housing, exemplifies the pattern.

> 3. *Set up a study group of housing decision-takers designed to represent the market place as a whole.*

In this last instance, the project officer takes a more definite role, specifying the size of the representative sample but without also specifying the terms in which it is to be representative.

> 7. *Select a representative sample of delegates at recent seminars (typically a 10–20% sample) and estimate the impact the seminar has had on this sample.*

The meaning of interviewing also shifts as project officers come to dictate the methodology. Their equation of social enquiry with attitude surveying helps to explain the rising number of ten-minute telephone interviews. Questionnaires are ever more popular and this brings with it its own problems. As noted above, project officers are often unaware of what their colleagues are up to and there is no communication between research contractors. In this context, there is every chance that very similar questionnaires will be sent to the same 'representative' samples of decision-takers. This sets in train yet another layer of control as lists of potential respondents are checked to eliminate embarrassing duplication. In issuing detailed instructions, project officers seek to control the detailed conduct of research, as illustrated by the following notes relating to a proposed telephone survey of development officers employed by housing associations.

> *3.1   Compile lists of people to be approached in the telephone surveys.*
> *Agree lists according to the procedures laid down in Annex 1.*
> *Permission shall be obtained before any individuals or organisa-*
> *tions are contacted in this survey (either by postal questionnaires,*
> *telephone or face-to-face interview)*

Compliance with these rules would, of course, bring the whole research process to an immediate halt. Researchers would be unable to take any action without permission and project officers would be so snowed under with requests that they would be unable to vet suggestions and grant, or refuse, permission in time for the researchers to complete their prescribed tasks according to the agreed schedule of work.

Such amateur management of survey research is worrying enough, but approaches to data analysis and interpretation are even more disturbing. Each new project has to be justified on the grounds that it goes a step further than its immediate predecessor and ambitions escalate accordingly. The first aim of a recent £20 000 contract – again involving a postal questionnaire – was thus:

> *Aim:   To determine how strategic decisions are made on energy*
> *efficiency in housing by Local Authorities and Housing*
> *Associations and predict the effect on these of future changes in*
> *Government funding arrangements.*

Ambitious aims and objectives are matched by equally breathtaking approaches to analysis and report-writing. Wide-ranging conclusions are consequently founded upon limited research material. In the following example, relating to an evaluation of a series of seminars, there is no room for doubt about the legitimacy of drawing conclusions from specific cases or from survey data. Researchers were simply asked 'to prepare a report detailing attitudes and perceived changes in attitude towards energy efficiency' using 'evidence' from one informal discussion group. Contractors are therefore invited – indeed told – to make huge generalisa-tions on the basis of meagre information. Project officers have little methodological conscience and, in the absence of any peer review, poorly designed studies are taken as seriously as those which have some substance.

Doubts about the relevance of social research, together with entirely mistaken beliefs about methodology, generate a curious mixture of demands and claims. Excessive faith in simple social surveying coexists alongside equally excessive suspicions about the practical value of any other form of social analysis. This limited understanding of the nature of social research is especially damaging. The issues involved in conducting basic questionnaire and telephone surveys are barely perceived and there is certainly no appreciation of the theoretical implications of alternative methodological strategies. In this context, it is easy to equate social research with market studies and attitude surveying and in doing so project officers automatically exclude vast reaches of potentially valuable social–environmental enquiry. So the chances of taking the social sciences to the heart of this particular sector of environmental debate look slim, not just because sociologists are unwilling to engage (though that may be so), but because present methods of contracting knowledge conspire against coherent social analysis.

## RESEARCH ENVIRONMENTS

I have suggested that each form of research management – in-house research, co-ordinated consultancy and contract control – has specific implications for relations between social and technical researchers and for their understanding of environmental issues. In short, some methods of research management foster interdisciplinarity while others constrain it. Still operating within the more accommodating framework of co-ordinated consultancy, French and Swedish sociologists (Callon *et al.*, 1992; Klingberg, 1984) have expanded the environmental agenda and extended its boundaries to encompass social as well as technical concerns. In the USA, National Research Laboratories have a key role and although they do not strictly qualify as in-house research teams, they do employ staff with a variety of different backgrounds and these people do work together on sizeable research contracts. Here, too, the structure is such that social and economic researchers have a chance to engage with physicists, engineers and designers (Kempton and Neiman, 1987; Sanstad *et al.*, 1993). In Britain, the old-fashioned interdisciplinarity of the ivory tower and the in-house team has gone forever and research is instead driven by the short-term imperatives of project management. Methods of contracting knowledge do not foster the exchange of ideas between anyone, not between competing researchers and not even between one project officer and another.

There are, of course, other sources of research funding and other less restricting forms of research management. The Research Councils and the European Commission have made deliberate efforts to promote the social analysis of environmental issues: the ESRC's Global Environmental Change Programme is now in its third phase; the SERC recently launched the Sustainable Cities programme; and the EC's DG12 has issued two calls for proposals on Socio-Economic Environmental Research. All adopt a 'honeypot' approach to research funding: that is, they set money aside to support projects submitted in response to a specific brief. Attracted by the pot of gold, researchers prepare proposals which meet the criteria set out in the briefing material. Selection then depends upon an independent process of peer review. Or at least that is the theory. This strategy, deeply rooted in the very different culture of academic research, depends upon a scholarly tradition of specialist comment. While this probably ensures a measure of methodological rigour, it may none the less hamper the development of interdisciplinary understandings of environmental change. Judgements affecting detailed funding decisions mirror the convictions and perceptions of respected and recognised experts and, in this context, proposals which threaten established disciplinary boundaries are especially vulnerable.

Although research funders can encourage interdisciplinary proposals, or proposals which engage with social aspects of environmental change, they have no influence over the content or form of the resulting applications. There is little that can be done if the research community fails to respond to a specific call or if it fails to respond in the way the funding body would like. Because these funders do not commission studies and because they are unable to determine the detailed design of specific projects they have only limited control over their own research agenda. Critical choices are left to applicants who are as likely to gear responses to the presumed preferences of their peers (for it is they who count when it comes to selecting projects for funding) as to the grand ambitions set out in the programme brief. For these reasons, the 'honeypot' approach is of uncertain value as a means of changing established preoccupations and challenging familiar disciplinary boundaries. This time the roles are reversed, for ambitious and creative project officers find themselves at the mercy of conservative proposers and their conventional peers.

Despite their faults, earlier forms of in-house research and co-ordinated consultancy accommodated, and sometimes favoured, sociological involvement in areas traditionally dominated by the natural sciences.

Whichever way wc look at it, current research environments are not especially conducive to interdisciplinary environmental research: present patterns of research management do not encourage such interaction, neither
do proposals for the future.

In the academic sector, the weight of vested interests tends to work
against interdisciplinary innovation and it will be a while before environmental sociology establishes itself as a legitimate enterprise, respected and
valued by academic peers. Until then, the peer-review process and its
anticipated consequences are likely to inspire caution amongst aspiring
socio-environmental applicants. Meanwhile, methods of contracting
knowledge have elbowed social analysis out of key areas of the government's environmental agenda. As we have seen, there is little scope for
significant sociological involvement when policy-oriented project officers
and other policy 'users' take command. In these circumstances, the future
of socio-environmental research depends on the choices and perceptions
of people who have no knowledge of the social sciences and no special
interest in promoting interdisciplinarity. It will take concerted effort to
develop an appropriately trained body of 'users', aware of the potential of
sociological analysis and suitably informed about the practicalities of
social research, yet there is no doubt that this is what is required. There is
not much time left, indeed it may be already too late, for in accelerating
'the operation of market forces in relation to the science and technology
which Government Departments commission' (*Chancellor of the Duchy of
Lancaster,* 1993, p. 44), and in emphasising 'user' needs within the
academic domain, the government is inviting knowledge, and especially
sociological knowledge, to contract even faster.

**Acknowledgements**

This paper is based on work funded under the Economic and Social
Research Council's Global Environmental Change programme: 'Putting
Science into Practice: Saving Energy in Buildings'', Project Reference
Y320253021. The author and editors are grateful to the Building Research
Establishment (BRE) for permission to quote from their invitation to
tender documentation. However, that permission certainly must not be
taken to imply that BRE share the views or opinions expressed in the
paper.

192        *The Social Construction of Social Policy*

## References

Callon, M., Laredo, P., Rabehariosa, V., Gonard, T. and Leray, T. (1992) 'The Management and Evaluation of Technological Programs and the Dynamics of Techno-economic Networks: The Case of AFME', *Research Policy*, 21: pp. 215–36.

Chancellor of the Duchy of Lancaster (1993), *Realising Our Potential: A Strategy for Science, Engineering and Technology*, Cm 2250 (London: HMSO).

Department of the Environment (1992) 'DoE Research Market: 1992', Chief Scientist Group Science and Technology Information Note: 1/92.

Kempton, W. and Neiman, M. (eds) (1987) *Energy Efficiency: Perspectives on Individual Behaviour* (Washington, DC: American Council for an Energy Efficient Economy).

Klingberg, T. (1984) 'Effect of Energy Conservation Programs', National Swedish Institute for Building Research Bulletin M84: 2.

Lea, F. M. (1971) *Science and Building: A History of the Building Research Station* (London: HMSO).

Meikle, J. and Wensley, R. (1984) 'Cost Effectiveness Criteria for Energy Investment in Private Housing', Energy Technology Support Unit Passive Solar Cost Studies, Working Paper 2, Harwell, ETSU, September.

Mulkay, M. (1979) *Science and the Sociology of Knowledge* (London: George Allen & Unwin).

Newby, H. (1991) 'One World, Two Cultures: Sociology and the Environment', lecture given to mark the 40th Anniversary of the founding of the British Sociological Association, London School of Economics, February.

Roberts, M. (1991) *Living in a Man-Made World* (London: Routledge).

Rose, H. and Rose, S. (1969) *Science and Society* (London: Allen Lane).

Rothschild (1971) *A Framework for Government Research and Development*, Cmnd 4814 (HMSO: London).

Saint, A. (1987) *Towards a Social Architecture* (New Haven and London: Yale University Press).

Sansted, A., Koomey, J. and Levine, M. (1993) 'On the Economic Analysis of Problems in Energy Efficiency: Market Barriers, Market Failures, and Policy Implications', Energy and Environment Division, Lawrence Berkeley Laboratory, University of California

Shove, E. (1989) 'Professional Energies: Putting Science into Practice', in Steemers, T. and Palz, W. (eds), *Second European Conference on Architecture: Science and Technology in the Service of Architecture* (Dordrecht: Kluwer Academic).

Shove, E. (1991) *'Filling the Gap: A Social and Economic Study of the Cavity Wall Insulation Industry'*, Institute of Advanced Architectural Studies, University of York.

Shove, E., Sutcliffe, S. and Willoughby, J. (1987) *'Energy, Warmth, Efficiency'*, Institute of Advanced Architectural Studies, University of York.

# 11 Us and Them: The Construction and Maintenance of Divisions in a Planning Dispute

## Kate Burningham

### INTRODUCTION

The building and siting of new roads is an issue at the forefront of contemporary popular debate about the environment. Events at Twyford Down and East London, in particular, highlight the extent of divisions between those involved in disputes about new road schemes. In this paper I draw on data collected during two research projects into the impacts of road schemes to provide a sociological analysis of some of the features of such conflicts.

I begin by describing the projects which generated the data and briefly discuss the existing literature on planning disputes and public inquiries. I then provide an analysis which illustrates the active role played by local people in shaping the dimensions of environmental and planning disputes. Drawing on the work of Edwards and Potter (1992) I aim to show that participants' accounts of the issue are not merely commentaries on an external reality, but are central to the organisation of the conflict. To illustrate this point I discuss a recurrent feature of participants' accounts: the attempt to distinguish self from others and own position from others'. Rather than assuming that divisions between categories of individual (for example, experts/ordinary people) exercise some external influence on their action and interaction, I will explore how participants orient to particular categorisations of themselves and others, and suggest what interactional work this may attend to for them.

### DATA

This chapter is based on work carried out during two projects into the social impacts of trunk road schemes. The first project (1990–1) was funded by Acer Consultants Ltd, a group of consultant engineers who were responsible for designing and assessing routes for the Department of Transport's (DoT) planned 'improvement' scheme of a stretch of trunk road in the south of England.[1] Acer subcontracted the social impact component of the assessment to sociologists at the University of Surrey. The second project is ongoing and is funded by the ESRC. This project aims to contribute to the literature on methodologies for the assessment of the social impacts of developments such as road schemes by undertaking a post-impact study of an area where a trunk road has recently been completed. The bulk of the literature on social impact assessment is anticipatory, based on what local people and researchers believe the social effects of a scheme will be. The current project aims to provide a comparison of the anticipated impacts with the expressed impacts now the road is operational. The road is another stretch of the same trunk road examined in the Acer study, and was opened to traffic in 1988.

As part of the Acer project, interviews were carried out with local informants. These were people who were expected to be able to provide an overview of local concerns such as local councillors, clergy and headteachers, as well as leaders of residents' associations, action and conservation groups and others who could be expected to be adversely affected by one of the schemes under consideration. These interviews provide some of the data to be analysed. The ESRC project has involved the collection of a variety of different sorts of data. Documentary material was collected which provided information about the impacts anticipated before the road was built, and about arguments current at the time of the public inquiries. This corpus includes objectors' submissions to the public inquiries, and extracts from these data will also be analysed. The project has also involved interviews with people who were prominent objectors at the inquiries, local councillors, leaders of residents associations and of action groups set up to campaign about the current problems of the road. Extracts from this corpus are also discussed.

## ROAD SCHEMES AND PLANNING CONFLICTS

Disquiet about the government's transport policy and particularly about the siting of new roads is not a new phenomenon, but has recently become the subject of renewed public debate. Contemporary media critics echo the earlier words of Tyme (1978) and Adams (1981) in their condemnation of the lack of a clear and integrated transport policy and the current Conservative government's championship of the 'car society'. Commitment to private over public transport, and to the use of cars in particular is apparent in the simultaneous direction of resources to improving and increasing the infrastructure of roads while privatising the railways and deregulating bus services. The strength of public feeling (at least about the siting of specific roads) has been evident in the clashes between protestors and representatives of the DoT over the building of the M3 through Twyford Down in Hampshire; in the coordinated action to prevent the East London River Crossing passing through Oxleas Wood in East London; and in the opposition to the M11 extension through East London. Objections to the building of new roads are made on a variety of grounds. Concern may be expressed about the effects on residential areas and on the local countryside, and also about the wider environmental implications of a reliance on transport by motor vehicles which use finite resources and emit pollutants. Debates about the siting of new roads, and whether they should be built at all, provide a clear and current example of conflicts over planning issues.

The public inquiry is the focal point of disputes over road schemes as it provides a forum for objectors to state their case against the plans and to tackle the proponents directly. Consequently, much of the literature on planning disputes concentrates on this stage of the process. Research stretching back to the 1960s has branded the public inquiry system as a 'farce' (Levin, 1969), a 'charade' (Self, 1970) and 'fraud' (Cowans, 1980). The two recurrent criticisms made of the inquiry system are, firstly, that the Department's mind is made up before the inquiry and thus the process is merely cosmetic and, secondly, that the relationship between 'experts' and 'ordinary people' is unequal. Objectors are said to lack the resources of time, money and expertise necessary to provide an effective criticism of the Department's case (Hutton, 1986).

Although academic attention has often focused on public inquiries as the site of planning conflicts, these conflicts usually begin long before the announcement of a public inquiry and, as the incidents noted above have displayed, may continue well after it has closed. As soon as plans to improve an existing road or to build a new one are made public (or when it is perceived locally that a new road is necessary, as in bypass campaigns), local people begin to organise themselves into groups to support or object to the various proposed routes. Groups develop strategies of action and adopt stances towards the DoT and their consultants, condemning or praising their plans. They also develop critiques of other individuals and groups whose views on the road scheme differ from their own.

## SOCIAL CONFLICTS AS DISCURSIVE ACTS

Edwards and Potter (1992) suggest that rather than viewing peoples' talk about social conflicts as commentary on some external state of affairs, it may be more appropriate to regard the discourse as actively constructing and fashioning the conflict itself. This discourse-analytic approach[2] has its origins in the philosophical work of Wittgenstein and Austin, and is influenced by the sociological recommendations of ethnomethodology and conversation analysis. Discourse analysis breaks with the assumption implicit in much sociology that language somehow corresponds to, or can be taken as 'standing for' states of affairs as they 'really are'. Instead of regarding language as a detached commentary on reality, it is viewed as a dynamic medium through which this reality is actually constituted. Edwards and Potter apply what they call the 'discursive action model' to the analysis of public political discourse, concentrating on issues such as how events are described and explained, how factual reports are constructed and how cognitive states are attributed. They argue that in public debates and conflicts 'the events that take place are inextricable from their various constructions' (1992; p. 1).

From the beginning, planning conflicts are played out in spoken and written discourse in a variety of forms. The DoT and their consultants issue press notices and publish and exhibit maps and plans. Individuals are invited to complete questionnaires about the choice of route and to write to the Secretary of State with objections and comments on the DoT's plans. Action and Residents' Groups hold public meetings, put up posters and distribute pamphlets. At the public inquiry, individuals and groups are invited to present written or spoken submissions of objection or support. Finally, the Inspector sums up the arguments made and issues raised in a report. Media, political and public debate continues beyond the inquiry. Planning conflicts are, therefore, discursive acts and consequently it makes sense for sociologists to study the organisation and construction of the language employed.

The practices that individuals and groups deploy to warrant the authenticity of their own account, or to suggest that another's version is untrustworthy, constitute the very site of the dispute. The issue of whether an account appears to be factual, is robust, or insidiously undermines alternative accounts is not simply an issue of academic interest but is something which participants are aware of and take account of. This is perhaps best illustrated within the context of a public inquiry, where it is obviously important for participants that their accounts of how the road will affect them manage to gain the Inspector's attention. One of the interviewees in the ESRC study described the range of potential impacts that the action group he had belonged to had raised at the public inquiry. He indicated that the wide range of objections which they raised were motivated less by real fear or concern that these impacts might come to pass, than by an appraisal of the sorts of strategies which might prove successful within the inquiry context:

> that was really part of our strategy, we will just come at them every single angle we can think of . . . create as much hassle for them, make it [the inquiry] last as long as possible and just hope in doing that we'll dig out, find out the weak chink in their armour.

Thus participants recognise that the way in which they construe the costs and benefits of alternative schemes may have practical implications for the outcome of the dispute.

From this discourse-analytic perspective, divisions and differences between groups holding opposing views are not simply given, but are actively constructed and maintained. Rather than examining how external inequalities of power and resources determine the shape and outcome of the interaction in planning disputes, this paper focuses on the issues of how participants employ particular characterisations of themselves and of each other, and to what ends. That is, the identity of for instance 'ordinary person' or 'expert' comes to be viewed as an accomplishment of social interaction rather than a causal or determinant feature of subsequent events. I explore two ways in which individuals and groups distinguish themselves and their position from that of others: the way in which local people resistant to the DoT's plans distinguish clearly between 'us' and 'them', and how participants at a public inquiry make a distinction between 'experts' and 'ordinary people'.

## THEM AND US

1. They bought the houses ten years ago. They sold them back to the owners, well they sold them anyway. Now they've done the same again, and we don't know what is happening.

2. If that does come here, they will infill here. They'll infill the other side from here to [place name], there's another big field, two fields, two big fields. They'll infill that in no time at all. Well why?

3.    You see with a week to go to the road coming through somebody in power could change their mind. And with a week to go, a month to go, whatever, they could say 'right we've changed our mind, we're going to go the blue route, the pink route, whatever'. So we are hand tied until it actually happens.

4.    And it seemed extraordinary to me that they just come, and they just bulldoze 100 beautiful houses, maybe 200 beautiful houses.

5.    You're talking about I forget how many houses, is it 60 houses that are going to be affected? I mean that's a drop in the ocean to the Ministry of Transport.

6.    There's no question about it this is a popular golf course. But from the point of view of the Ministry of Transport, from the college over there, all the way through this golf course, through the four holes on the other course, they've got uninterrupted road building. No hold ups, no problems. They just move in and take their time leisurely.

All of these extracts are taken from the Acer project, and in each the interviewee is talking about the actions or anticipated actions of 'them', who I take to be the Department of Transport, their consultants and contractors. In the first extract, the speaker is describing the effect that the years of uncertainty about the route have had on residents. The DoT had purchased a number of properties along their preferred route and had then sold them again a number of years later when the original plans were shelved. The plans were later resurrected and the houses repurchased. The respondent presents these events as an inexplicable cycle of buying and selling. The behaviour of the DoT is presented as irrational, leaving 'us' confused and uninformed; 'we don't know what is happening'.

    In the second extract, the respondent is expressing her fear that if the DoT's preferred route is constructed there will be subsequent pressure to develop the countryside surrounding the road. In this case 'they' are not the DoT, but planners, industrialists and businessmen; however, their incursion into the countryside follows hard on the heels of 'their' (DoT's) decision to site the road across this stretch of land; 'if that does come here, they will infill'. Again 'their' actions are depicted as incomprehensible, their destructive action is built up by the repetition 'they will infill' and by the escalating description of the amount of land that they will infill;

'another big field, two fields, two big fields'. The extent of their damaging action is then contrasted sharply with 'our' bewilderment – 'well, why?'.

In both these extracts the construction of 'their' actions takes the form of a three-part list:

1. (1) they bought the houses,
   (2) they sold them back to the owners – well they sold them anyway,
   (3) now they've done the same again;

2. (1) they will infill here,
   (2) they'll infill the other side from here to [place name], there's another big field, two fields, two big fields,
   (3) they'll infill that in no time at all.

In the second example there is a further three-part list embedded within the extract. When the speaker clarifies the amount of land that will be infilled she does this in the form of a three part list:

1. another big field,
2. two fields,
3. two big fields.

The construction of lists in three parts has been found to be a recurrent practice in ordinary conversational materials (Jefferson, 1991). The phenomenon is common in a variety of forms of discourse and suggests that three-partedness may be a culturally available resource for list construction. Atkinson (1984) noted that three-part lists were a recurrent feature of political speeches and were typically used to package praise for the speaker's own position or criticism for that of others. He argues that three-part lists provide a very suitable method for packaging praise or criticism because listing similar items can work to strengthen almost any kind of message. In these data the three-part lists clearly amplify the criticism of 'their' actions, building up a picture of arbitrary destructiveness.

In the third example, the respondent is talking about the effect that alternative routes would have on the local golf courses, and explaining that no redevelopment of the courses can be planned until it is clear which route is to be built and what the details of the route will be. Two three-part constructions are employed in this extract and work to characterise 'their behaviour' as capricious:

1.  with a week to go,
2.  a month to go,
3.  whatever,

they could say 'right, we've changed our mind,

1.  we're going to go the blue route;
2.  the pink route,
3.  whatever'.

Both of these lists are constructed with a 'generalised list completer' – 'whatever' (Jefferson, 1991, p. 65) – occupying the third slot. Jefferson argues that the use of generalised list completers such as 'whatever', 'or something', 'something like that', demonstrates that people orient to the convention of constructing lists in three parts, as they produce three-part lists even when a clear third part is not immediately available. The use of generalised list completers in these data work to accentuate the impression that the DoT can do 'whatever' they want. The list is constructed in three parts but the range of options for the DoT is left open, their options on both the timescale and choice of route are characterised as unconstrained and potentially limitless. This sense that they are accountable to no-one is reinforced by the speaker's claim that they can simply say 'we've changed our mind', they do not have to provide any reasons for their decision. The particular formulation of 'our' reaction to 'their' actions in this extract; 'we are hand tied', provides a neat depiction of the power relationship between 'us' and 'them', 'we' are portrayed as physically bound, captive to their designs.

The final three extracts depict 'them' as having totally different values, and as being guided by a completely different frame of reference from 'us'. In the fourth extract we see again the construction of 'their' absolute power; 'they just come, and they just bulldoze', no explanation is given for their actions, 'they just' do what to 'us' is extraordinary, destructive behaviour. They are characterised as wantonly destroying something of great value to 'us'; '100 beautiful houses, maybe 200 beautiful houses'. The speaker in the fifth extract picks up this theme of the number of houses that will be taken by the DoT's scheme, and argues that the number is 'a drop in the ocean to the Ministry of Transport' providing an implicit contrast between 'their' evaluative framework and 'ours'; in 'their' assessment 60 houses have little worth.

The final extract provides a comparison of 'our' assessment of a piece of land and 'theirs' and characterises 'their' assessment as based on entirely different factors to 'ours'. What is to us a popular golf course is to them the site for 'uninterrupted road building'. Again we have the depiction of their casual power, 'They just move in, and take their time leisurely'.

In his analysis of political speeches Atkinson (1984) notes that assertions which convey positive or boastful evaluations of our hopes, our actions and our achievements stand a very good chance of being endorsed by audiences with a burst of applause. Assertions of 'our' goodness contain an implicit condemnation of 'their' badness. Conversely, explicit criticisms of 'their' values and 'their' behaviour contain an implicit praiseworthy evaluation of 'our' values and behaviour, and also elicit enthusiastic applause.

In the extracts above, respondents provide accounts which clearly distinguish 'them' from 'us'. 'They' are characterised as all-powerful, ruthless and capricious, and 'their' behaviour is constructed as motivated by values distinct from those that 'we' hold. In contrast, 'we' are portrayed as confused ('well why?', 'we don't know what is happening', it seemed extraordinary to me'), constrained ('we are hand tied'), and holding entirely different frameworks of value. It might be that these constructions employ contrasts of 'them' and 'us' to the same ends as politicians in their speeches: to gain sympathy and approval for their position. All the accounts were produced in the context of an interview with a researcher carrying out an assessment of the social impacts of the road schemes. Clearly it is in respondents' interests to gain the researcher's sympathy for their case, to convince her that they are 'hard done by' and that the DoT are proceeding unreasonably. The implicit contrast between 'them' and 'us' works to maximise their complaint that their feelings and assessments of the situation are being ignored.

Bauman has drawn attention to the distinctions that people draw between 'us' and 'them', he writes:

> The image of the enemy is painted in colours as lurid and frightening as the colours of one's own group are soothing and pleasurable .... were they allowed to have it their way, they would invade, conquer, enslave, exploit: openly if they are strong enough, or surreptitiously if forced to hide their true intentions. (1990, p. 46)

The images in the data of 'their' destructiveness of the environment are contrasted implicitly with other references in the interviews to 'our' concern for the value of homes, the countryside and recreation sites. The unnamed individuals and groups who comprise 'them' are depicted as invading and desecrating what 'we' hold dear. This rhetorical strategy is not confined to interview situations, it occurs in other contexts and in relation to other road schemes. It is used in situations where individuals seek to gain sympathy or recognition for their position, and to disparage the actions and beliefs of the planners. For example, a local newspaper article, published before the road examined in the ESRC project was built, reported one resident as saying:

> we get the impression that the road is going to be pushed through whatever we do . . . [village] is going to be decimated, it will no longer be the little village we have known and loved. To ruin the peace and tranquillity of this place is criminal.

And an article which appeared in *You* magazine (November 1991) about a proposed road scheme in Derbyshire had one resident claiming:

> [place name] is a jewel, I see it as a haven from the modern world where we can come and breathe the fresh air and enjoy an unspoiled English landscape . . . this road is an abomination of desolation, cars and lorries will roar through the valley and no-one will give a second thought to what has been lost to the nation.

In both of these extracts, the worth of the area is built up, in the first it is referred to as a 'little village' and a place of 'peace and tranquillity', in the second it is a 'jewel' a 'haven' and 'unspoiled'. The Department of Transport are portrayed as 'criminals', and planners of an 'abomination', their actions will 'ruin' a village and result in something of great value being 'lost to the nation'. The same imagery was apparent in a cartoon which appeared in *The Independent* (2 March 1992) depicting the DoT's choice of route for the M3 over Twyford Down as the rape of the Garden of Eden. The cartoon shows a bulldozer being driven into Adam and Eve with the caption 'I don't care if this is the Garden of Eden, we're coming through!'. Once again, the DoT are characterised as invading and destroying something of great beauty, with no concern for its worth or the feelings of the people who live there. The residents of the area, Adam and Eve in this case, are depicted as powerless to stop the bulldozers wreaking havoc on their home.

This strategy of portraying planners as invading and destroying something which 'we' treasure has also been noted in other sociological studies. Wynne (1983, 1985) reviews the work of Winner (1978), McDermott (1974) and Daly (1970) who describe the fantasies or spectres which ordinary people create in the attempt to make meaningful their lack of control of the forces directing technology. Wynne suggests that such constructions are condensed images which become surrogates for explanations of more complex experiences. He argues that they should be seen as metaphors for the real social relationships which exist; they represent the alien social elites controlling technological innovation. Thus for Wynne, in the data above the 'monster' which will 'just bulldoze' beautiful houses, 'will infill' fields and build roads at its leisure through popular golf courses, should be viewed as a metaphor for the social relationship between planners and the public. Wynne's approach treats this portrayal of planners as alien creatures as revealing something about the 'real situation'. For instance the sentiments expressed in the data above might indicate that there is little communication between the DoT and ordinary people, or if there is, that it is not understood, and that people feel powerless, confused, threatened and invaded in the face of the DoT's plans. In contrast, the approach taken by Edwards and Potter challenges the assumption that what people say can be taken as 'standing for' states of affairs as they 'really are'. This approach concentrates instead on the interactional functions achieved by the use of particular characterisations of actors and events.

## ORDINARY PEOPLE AND EXPERTS

11. You will be hearing from expert pollution witnesses later on in this inquiry. They will be more able than I to provide you with research evidence on the effects of vehicle pollution on schoolchildren. However, I feel it is necessary to draw your attention to the concern of parents and teachers over the risk of pollution. We all know that motor vehicles emit a lot of poisonous and noxious chemicals from their exhausts.

12. I don't know much more than the ordinary parent about the risks of pollution, but what I know makes me very concerned about the proximity of the first school in particular. Much of this school, as I've already indicated; is less than 100 metres from the proposed road.

And this seems to be just the area which is vulnerable to the effects of pollution, particularly lead pollution.

13. I am not qualified to discuss in detail pollution from lead and other chemicals. I do know, however, that there is controversy over both the effects of lead on growing children and the concentrations which cause those effects

14. I have not got the expertise to criticise the principles of the procedure used to evaluate the new road. But I would point out that as far as I know the construction of the new [road] would create a stretch of road from [place name] to [place name] – all motorway or dual carriageway – on which there is no service area.

All of these extracts consist of an explicit refutation of any claim to expertise on the subject under discussion: 'expert pollution witnesses . . . will be more able than I to provide you with research evidence on the effects of vehicle pollution on schoolchildren', 'I don't know much more than the ordinary parent about the risks of pollution', 'I'm not qualified to discuss in detail pollution from lead and other chemicals' and 'I have not got the expertise to criticise the principles of the procedure used to evaluate the new road'. The denial of expert knowledge in each case is followed by a 'but' or 'however' after which the speaker's claim or concern is voiced.

An interest in the way in which speakers describe their activities and themselves as normal or ordinary in order to achieve specifically interactional goals originates from the work of Sacks. He argued that rather than applying the notion of an 'ordinary person' to this or that person it should be considered as the way somebody constitutes themselves:

It is not that somebody is ordinary; it is perhaps that it is what one's business is, and it takes work, as any other business does. (Sacks, 1984, p. 414)

Sack's work focused on how people do 'being ordinary' and explored particularly how people may claim membership of the category 'ordinary people' without making explicit references to it, for instance by presenting their experiences or actions so as to make them appear mundane or usual rather than in any way extraordinary or unusual. Sacks' preliminary observations have been developed in subsequent research. For instance Jefferson's (1984) study of the way in which people who have had extraordinary experiences work to produce unexceptional versions of the events, and Wooffitt's (1992) analysis of how people who claim to have had paranormal experiences warrant their normality. The analysis which follows shares the conviction of this earlier research that speakers describe their activities as 'ordinary' in order to achieve interactional goals.

In the data above, the explicit disavowal of expert status on such matters as pollution and road-scheme evaluation anticipates the criticisms that could otherwise be made of the statements that follow. By presenting their complaints as explicitly not those of experts, objectors request that their submissions should not be criticised in the way that expert statements would be. Challenges from the Department on matters of empirical detail are deemed inappropriate. This could be an effective strategy for objectors; as previous research has documented (Wynne, 1982; Hutton, 1986) it is very difficult for them to compete with the experts on their own terms. They are usually ill-equipped to produce submissions which would stand up to rigorous examination by the Department. By presenting their complaints as explicitly 'not expert' perhaps they endeavour to protect themselves from much of the criticism that they might otherwise be subject to.

The disclaimer (Hewitt and Stokes, 1975) that they are not expert creates a distinct identity for objectors and ensures that their concerns and claims are heard as those of 'ordinary people'. Presenting a concern or complaint as that of an ordinary person may give it a special strength. Expert or pseudo-expert assessments of the danger of pollution lend themselves to easy refutation by the Department of Transport. However the concerns of 'ordinary people' cannot be criticised on the basis of facticity or dismissed lightly. Previous analyses argue that objectors are at a disadvantage because they are unable to challenge the Department's experts, but equally the Department cannot effectively challenge the authority of 'ordinary people' to talk about their concerns for their community. Thus there is a degree of symmetry (not asymmetry as others have argued): the DoT can argue as an expert, an opportunity not open to objectors, while objectors can argue as 'ordinary people' which the DoT cannot.

There are a number of other ways in which objectors invoke their status as ordinary people in their submissions. Statements presented as 'what anyone would say', what is 'common knowledge', and 'what we all know' and including detailed descriptions of everyday local life, are all employed as foils to expert technical knowledge. A very clear example of this is contained in the following extract in which the speaker is arguing that heavy goods vehicles 'thundering past' the local schools will have a detrimental effect on pupils' health and education:

15.  We all know quite well how dirty and noisy these vehicles are. This is the threat which hangs over the peaceful environment of these two schools. Not only will the children be surrounded by polluted air from this new road, but they will also be subjected to continuous loud and unpleasant traffic noise. Is this the right environment for young children from five to twelve years to play in? I don't think one needs any research to prove that this sort of environment cannot be beneficial to our children.

The speaker makes a direct appeal to common knowledge; 'we all know quite well how dirty and noisy these vehicles are' and then goes on to claim that 'I don't think we need any research to prove that this sort of environment cannot be beneficial to our children'. Common knowledge, what ordinary people know, is explicitly posited as an alternative to expert analyses. Ordinary knowledge is elevated over expert analyses, it is suggested that it is a more relevant and reliable source of information. The impression created is that ordinary people are well aware of the dangers of the road and do not need the expertise of the DoT to prove that these dangers are likely – they already *know*. In this sense they are portrayed as 'ahead' of the experts, and expert research is deemed to be an unnecessary waste of time. Objectors can concede that experts know more than they do about the technicalities of road schemes without undermining their case. They can lay claim to expertise in another sphere: their common knowledge which they possess by virtue of being 'ordinary people' enables them to provide alternative assessments of how the road will affect the locality.

Thus 'I'm not an expert, but . . . ' may be viewed as a device which protects objectors' claims from empirical criticism, and sets up the following speech as that of an 'ordinary person', consequently providing a source of legitimate authority for speakers and working to secure the success of their complaints.

CONCLUSION

This chapter has considered three strategies which participants in planning disputes over road schemes employ in order to distinguish their position from that of others. The rhetorical devices used in all of these strategies have been documented in other sorts of data and are common methods for bolstering one's own argument and undermining that of others.

The analysis differs from previous investigations of planning disputes, which have tended to focus on the importance of factors such as differential access to resources and political influence between experts and the public, and between different groups of the public. These analyses have undermined the Government's claims that inquiries are objective 'fact finding' exercises (Department of Transport and Department of Environment 1978) and have concluded that they are an attempt to make the planning system *appear* to be objective and fair. They argue that the inquiry system is biased, and that consequently the developer's preferred scheme is likely to be built whatever the 'factual' case against it (see Tyme, 1978; Cowans, 1980; Adams, 1981).

Both Wynne's (1982) work on the Windscale inquiry, and Hutton's (1986) on the inquiry into the siting of a natural gas liquids plant in Fife, provide detailed sociological analyses of public inquiries and draw attention to the way in which the 'facts' of the public inquiry are socially constructed. However, they concentrate on how the dominance of the 'experts', in terms of external power and relations within the inquiry, enables them to determine what counts as fact and thus ultimately to determine the outcome of the inquiry.

Thus existing studies employ an implicit assumption that divisions between the various parties in planning disputes emerge from features of the background or experience of those involved, or are caused by the institutional setting of the public inquiry. In contrast, this paper has focused on the way in which divisions are worked at by participants. The distinctions between 'ordinary people' and 'experts' and between 'us' and 'them' are viewed as discursively constructed and maintained, rather than simply exerting some external constraint on interaction.

Rather than focusing on the strategies, ploys and tactics of the 'experts' this paper has concentrated on those of the 'ordinary people' affected by the plans. By focusing attention on the power of the experts within planning disputes previous research has tended to create the impression that ordinary people are powerless victims. The planning system clearly favours developers at the expense of residents in a range of ways; however, residents are not merely submissive or frustrated victims, they are active participants in the dispute. Like the experts, they are concerned to distinguish 'factual' from 'fictional' accounts, and to ensure that their position appears more robust and credible than that of others. In addition, this activity is not confined to the public inquiry but extends before and after it. As one interviewee said to me

we're still fighting, we will fight I can assure you.

In this paper I've looked at some of the ways in which they conduct this 'fight'.

## Acknowledgements

This paper is based in part on research funded by the ESRC under grant no. R000233246, and in part on research funded by ACER Consultants Ltd. An earlier version was presented at the British Sociological Association Conference at Essex, April 1993. I would like to thank Nigel Gilbert and Robin Wooffitt for helpful comments on a previous draft.

## Notes

1.  Areas are not named in order to protect respondents' anonymity.
2.  Although the term 'discourse analysis' is used to refer to a variety of analytic approaches in sociology, socio-linguistics, and social theory, in this paper it will be used only to refer to the approach exemplified by Gilbert and Mulkay (1984) and Potter and Wetherell (1987).

## References

Adams, J. (1981) *Transport Planning: Vision and Practice* (London: Routledge).
Atkinson, M. (1984) *Our Master's Voices* (London: Methuen).
Bauman, Z. (1990) *Thinking Sociologically* (Oxford: Basil Blackwell).
Cowans, R. (1980) 'The Public Inquiries Fraud', *Town and Country Planning*, April: pp. 109–10.
Daly, R. W. (1970) 'The Specters of Technicism', *Psychiatry*, 33: 4, pp. 417–32.
Department of Transport and Department of Environment (April 1978) *Report on the Review of Highway Inquiry Procedures* (London: HMSO), Cmnd 7133.
Edwards, D. and Potter J. (1992) *Discursive Psychology* (London: Sage).
Gilbert, G. N. and Mulkay, M. (1984) *Opening Pandora's Box: A Sociological Analysis of Scientists' Discourse* (Cambridge: Cambridge University Press).

Hewitt, J. P. and Stokes, R. (1975) 'Disclaimers', *American Sociological Review*, 40: 1, pp. 1–11.

Hutton, N. (1986) *Lay Participation in a Public Local Inquiry: A Sociological Case Study* (Aldershot: Gower).

Jefferson, G. (1984) 'At First I Thought': A Normalising Device for Extraordinary Events', unpublished manuscript, Katholieke Hogeschool Tilburg.

Jefferson, G. (1991) 'List Construction as a Task and Resource', in Psathas, G. and Frankel, R. (eds), *Interactional Competence* (Hillsdale, NJ: Lawrence Erlbaum Associates).

Levin, P. (1969) 'The Planning Inquiry Farce', *New Society*, 3: July, pp. 17–18.

McDermott, J. (1974) 'Technology: Opiate of the Intellectuals', in Teich, A. H. (ed.), *Technology and Man's Future* (New York: St Martin's Press).

Potter, J. and Wetherell, M. (1987) *Discourse and Social Psychology: Beyond Attitudes and Behaviour* (London: Sage).

Sacks, H. (1984) 'On Doing "Being Ordinary"', in Atkinson, J. M. and Heritage, J. (eds), *The Structures of Social Action: Studies in Conversation Analysis* (Cambridge: Cambridge University Press).

Self, P. (1970) 'A Planning Charade', *Town and Country Planning*, 38: 8, pp. 366–9.

Tyme, J. (1978) *Motorways versus Democracy: Public Inquiries into Road Proposals and their Political Significance* (London: Macmillan).

Winner, L. (1978) *Autonomous Technology* (Cambridge, MA: MIT Press).

Wooffitt, R. (1992) *Telling Tales of the Unexpected: The Organisation of Factual Discourse* (London: Harvester Wheatsheaf).

Wynne, B. (1982) *Rationality and Ritual: The Windscale Inquiry and Nuclear Decisions in Britain* (Chalfont St Giles, Bucks: British Society for the History of Science).

Wynne, B. (1983) 'The Social Viability of Technology', *Futures*, 15: 1, pp. 13–22.

Wynne, B. (1985) 'From Public Perception of Risk to Cultural Theory of Technology', in Covello, V. T., Mumpower, J. L., Stallen, P. J. and Uppuluri, V. R. (eds), *Environmental Impact Assessment, Technology Assessment and Risk Analysis* (Heidelberg: Springer).

# 12 Inter-organisational Negotiations in Political Decision-making: Brussels' EC Bureaucrats and the Environment
Carlo Ruzza

## INTRODUCTION

In recent years, environmentalism has gained momentum stimulating a heightened receptiveness of environmental themes among elected officials, and resulting in more stringent laws and regulations. Environmentalism, as an extensive concern, is now solidly embedded in the institutional realm, while it still manifests the traits of a social movement. The central EC[1] political and administrative decision-making centres are crucial in this regulative process. European Institutions[2] are, therefore, becoming the target of much attention from business and political actors with a direct interest in environmental issues. In this context, this paper examines which models best describe decision-making processes in the European Community.

Environmental decision-making is increasingly a complex process that results from the interaction between the environmentalist movement, multinational firms, and policy-makers. Even a cursory analysis of this process reveals that the conjunction of a rapidly changing normative environment (resulting from the process of European legislative harmonisation) and a newly emerging framework of institutional regulation has contributed to the creation of a particularly dynamic situation. For business and political actors environmentalism constitutes both a threat and an opportunity. An environmentalist focus could provide instrumental advantages with external organisational efforts *vis-à-vis* regulative agencies, and in some cases internal ones pertaining to the development of organisational cultures. Conversely, environmentalism remains a threat for many organisations who would find it more rational to counteract its influence and attempt to block its gains in the legislative arena and the marketplace.

This study was conducted in Brussels where most EC-level environmental decision-making takes place. As a community of policy-makers, consultants, lobbyists and secretarial personnel, Brussels has grown dramatically in recent years. In relation to environmental issues, it has attracted a large number of business lobbyists as well as environmentalist organisation lobbies who have permanent offices and personnel in Brussels.

Two interviewers conducted a set of personal interviews with EC bureaucrats, business leaders, lobbyists and social movement activists in 1992 and early 1993.[3] Contacts were obtained informally through networks of personal connections in each community. All the interviewees operate in environmentally sensitive areas, that is to say in areas that are generally recognised as relevant to the environmental discourse, but that might be treated within several different sectors of the EC bureaucracy or lobbying organisations. A total of 30 formal interviews were conducted, but several informal conversations also took place with actors at all levels of the hierarchy of the various organisations considered.

## POLICY-MAKING IN THE EC AND ITS ENVIRONMENT

First some introductory notes on the EC architecture are necessary. One factor that is likely to impress a new observer of the Brussels' environmental decision-making process is the magnitude of formal and informal lateral contacts between bureaucracies, industrial organisation consultants and scientists in Brussels and from the EC nation states.

Consequently, it is quite apparent from all interviews that the traditional Weberian model – based on fixed and isolated hierarchies – is only marginally applicable. None of the field examined approximated a Weberian bureaucracy. The EC personnel have to play a delicate role of mediation and consensus formation that requires many lateral and non-bureaucratic contacts. Social movement representatives interact on the basis of values of egalitarianism and consensus-seeking that refuse to formally accept chains of command and the steady pursuit of agreed-upon goals. Lobbyists act in an entrepreneurial manner, often only oriented by ambiguous guidelines. Generally, each of the different types of actor have a wider span of control than predicted in traditional Weberian theory.

The field in which these bureaucrats operate is much more ambiguous than a Weberian model would predict. However, many criticisms are still inspired by a desire for yet more flexibility. For instance a functionary said:

Agriculture is responsible for agriculture, and environment is responsible for environment. But agriculture, like environment touches upon everything. So the Commission is too vertically structured for a job that requires lateral contacts; that requires changes in Commission structure. We need many more people working on horizontal coherence which would be to the benefit of the efficiency of this organisation.

This need for flexibility is stimulated by the necessity to operate in different organisational environments that are characterised by different institutional dynamics, but that are constantly connected to varying degrees. For instance, social movement organisations might attempt to control the political and legislative environment through lobbying.[4] They might seek to control the political environment through advertising aimed at influencing the media and the public. Work organisations might promote and finance counter-movements,[5] or use advertising to claim or imply the existence of such movements. Activists might threaten or employ more or less disruptive forms of protest to influence political decision-making.

The strict connection between different organisational environments, and their role in EC decision-making is not accidental. As Peters (1992) has pointed out, the EC has traditionally used strategies of bureaucratisation and fragmentation of negotiations in order to diffuse conflicts and 'technicise' them.

Informal consultations have determined a cohesive decision-making structure. As Williams (1991, p. 160) notes 'Committees of experts, some 500 of them in 1987, over 70 percent composed of national civil servants in non-official capacity, are the architects and builders of commission policy.' Thus the informal process of co-ordination among different political and non-political actors takes place from the beginning of the decision-making process, a style of work which has characterised the EC from its inception.

A constant process of negotiation is explicitly intended by the Commission. Moravcsik (1991, p. 44) notes 'The Commission has long sought to encourage the development of a sort of pan-European corporatist network by granting these groups privileged access to the policy process, though this process has met with little success.'[6]

These considerations point to the fact that the relationships among the different organisational environments involved in EC environmental decision-making are not generally based on controversial stances. Rather, the inspiring principle is a willingness to compromise in order to accommodate different interests. Clearly, for negotiation to reach a compromise is often difficult and protracted and occasionally engenders factious disputes. But in these exchanges a cohesive policy sector is formed, where distinctive values, information-processing mechanisms and goals, emerge and bind a community of specialists.[7] The constraints on each of the actors participating in the exchanges should be considered in the light of their respective operating rules.

## POLITICAL–ADMINISTRATIVE ENVIRONMENTS

In recent years the media has shown a growing awareness – and occasionally criticisms – of the impact of environmentalism on politics.[8] It has become apparent that the growing public support of environmentalism has stimulated a heightened sensibility to environmental themes among elected officials. This has translated into more stringent laws and regulations which are supported even by Commissioners and European MEPs whose political identities are not significantly defined by environmental issues.[9]

In environmental matters different political and economic considerations affect the perception of interests of the northern and the southern states. The wealthier northern states – Germany in particular – are more receptive to stricter environmental legislation. Their public opinion is more supportive of environmentalism, and their economies can afford higher standards. Conversely, southern countries face a reverse situation. As Michelmann notes:

[Nationality] is one of the most pervasive of influences in the Commission, and it is institutionalized in such structures as the cabinets, and in practices [such] as the national quota system. It has its effects in the perceptions of officials. (Michelmann, 1978, p. 30).[10]

Northern countries are significantly more pro-environmental than southern countries, reflecting the different public opinion of their electorate. This creates a significant and persistent split over environmental issues. However, the need for consensus creates a constant availability of compromise.[11] Considering that there is strong formalised and informal pressure for consensual decision-making, one would expect the EC to be a political body less active in the field of the environment. Few countries are generally able to block legislation in controversial areas. This is particularly true for new areas of legislation, as the environment was until recently, and in part still is. To understand why this is not the case I will examine how political pressure is brought to bear on the Brussels regulative environment.

Firstly, two basic principles of EC policy-making should be born in mind. From its inception, the EC has pursued: (1) the strategic goal of 'ever closer union' through a philosophy of *thematic shifts* into areas of least resistance;[12] and (2) in the EC the inevitable tensions *cannot be effectively solved by a vote*. These constraints have traditionally stimulated a climate of repressed conflict, and constant attempts to create consensus through various techniques of diffusion and de-politicisation of controversial issues. Since politicians spend relatively less time in Brussels, they tend to delegate the tasks of consensus-building to high-level bureaucrats that are politically appointed.

Bureaucrats, be they political appointees or not,[13] will gain power whenever they increase their regulatory functions. Hence a first reason why environmental issues gain support is that they are sponsored by professionals with a vested interest in strengthening their role.[14] This vested interest does not need to be intentionally conceptualised and pursued, as it also tends to guide the 'taken-for-granted' assumptions of professional engagement. A second reason is that northern countries are more powerful and thus more able to impose their agenda on the rest of the community. But to gain a full understanding of the issue, a better understanding of the emerging EC bureaucratic culture is necessary. This culture in many ways is a universal Brussels phenomenon that permeates the whole policy-making community, regardless of the many significant splits. For instance, there is almost universal agreement that the environment needs more regulation.

As for thematic shifts, after the EC *impasse* of the 1970s, the environment appeared as a particularly appealing area on which to concentrate regulative efforts and acquire legitimacy for the entire EC project, as it was under-regulated and high on the public opinion agenda. In a hierarchical organisation such as the EC, this agenda-setting task was relatively easy to accomplish.

The second issue concerns rules for decision-making and the scope of consultation procedures, and is at present one of the most frequently debated issues, and one which often defines Left and Right. Nationality is once more an important dividing line. The position of bureaucrats on environmental matters is determined by nationality even more than by other variables, especially at high levels of the hierarchy. The fragmentation of opinions among high-level bureaucrats also has positive effects, for example it invites the opening of political institutions to external bodies which can provide information or occasionally arbitrate conflict.[15] The presence of fragmentation, complexity and the necessity to achieve consensus stimulates the inclusion of external consultants, representatives of other organisations, and technical experts. The *Committee System* has, therefore, become the standard way of working in most fields even at a relatively low bureaucratic level. Furthermore, this has the advantage of connecting bureaucrats and politicians on a steady basis. As Sbragia (1992, p. 91) notes:

> The Committee structure also helps Commission bureaucrats . . . work with the Parliament . . . committees will probably develop some form of symbiotic relationship with the Directorates whose work they oversee, a relationship heightened by the connections of both with European and national interest groups. Policy communities are already forming.

The implications of this decision-making method are very broad, especially when committees are informed by a collegial ethic. This diffuses responsibility to a larger body which tends to develop a distinctive ideology and thus a sense of common belonging. This is especially the case in sectors that can easily be 'moralised' as can the environment.[16] Moralisation, in turn, can re-define conflict away from a national dimension.

At the lower levels, the conflict between national viewpoints is not as disruptive as one would expect it to be. At this level, a sense of dissatisfaction (and occasionally cynicism) with the system, and a desire to improve participation in decision-making is often felt. For instance, a functionary noted:

> It seems to me that if we are to produce efficient environment policy there are several preconditions for that. It has to be an environment policy that can be accepted, widely accepted. The first condition is that there have to be adequate consultation procedures, so whether it is the industry itself, environmental NGO's, whether it is the man in the street, he feels that he must have a chance to express his views and that they be reasonably considered. So, I would argue that new improved consultation procedures taking into account all those actors is a *sine qua non* for improving policy efficiency.

Policy formation is also criticised. It is often seen as a process that, globally, the organisation is unable to control. One interviewee said:

You could also say that efficient environment policy in the Community requires much more dialogue with the Member States themselves and the experts of the Member States prior to the Commission drawing up a proposal. There is a feeling here that too many proposals jump like a rabbit out of a black hat, are put on the table and cause problems to the industry, problems to the Member States and so the whole decision-making process is not efficient.

The problem of responsibility also emerges in the more general context of the role of the EC *vis-à-vis* other institutions. A high-level bureaucrat remarked:

there is a very clear need to make everybody understand who is responsible for what. From the man in the street, to local government, to regional government, to national government and to the Community. And that it's just not clear. And I don't think many people outside Brussels understand.

Because of their international background, bureaucrats are very sensitive to the climate of opinion in several countries, and far less isolated than some of their critics would argue. They are very aware of the Weberian metaphor of the iron cage and its shortcomings, and together with a strong pro-European ideology, often display apprehension on the way the dream is actualised. In the words of a functionary:

The institutional structure in the Community has got to be much more democratic. You could improve the consultation procedure without changing the current architecture. I'd argue that the current architecture has got to be changed.

## ACTIVIST ENVIRONMENTS

There is little doubt that the story of environmental activism has been one of glaring success in influencing public opinion – a fact widely acknowledged in the media, although some scepticism has recently been emerging.[17] The success as well as the cyclical nature of social movements have changed the character of environmentalism over the years. Processes of professionalisation of activists and the institutionalisation of groups have occurred.

Since environmentalism has also been embedded in the regular political realm, the situation confronting most environmental groups has changed. If most have acquired some of the necessary skills to interact with a political environment that is always at least nominally favourable to environmentalism, they are also aware of the difficulties. For instance, Andrew Lees of *Friends of the Earth*, with reference to the parliamentary debate over the Maastricht Treaty, argues that the British Conservative government is invoking subsidiarity to adopt lax environmental regulations.

The Commission must be made far more open and directly accountable to the European Parliament. The present arrangements facilitate informal horse-trading between the Member States' national civil servants and give their ministers too many opportunities to strike political deals at the expense of environmental protection. (Lees, 1992, p. 17)

This scepticism is justified both by the awareness that the regular political environment is a very powerful influence in setting the terms of the game, and by the awareness of the relative weakness of environmental activists at playing that game. This weakness is nowhere more evident than in Brussels. The very limited number of environmental group representatives corresponds to their effective lack of formal power. As Krämer (1992) notes:

The Commission does not ... have generalized institutional relations with any other specialized institutional association or organisation which groups environmental interests.

Often regulators express doubts on the possibility of the environmental movement achieving better representation. For instance, an interviewee said that he would have welcomed a formalisation of consultation procedures with NGO's, but did not expect to see that happening soon.

In addition, the movement is undergoing a process of institutionalisation. A pro-environmental-movement bureaucrat noted as a problem the fact that the movement is excessively institutionalised. He says:

My problem is that I am not waiting for lobbies, I am waiting for movements. What I hope is to have some kind of, let's say, democratic input in my thinking. I know people [in the movement] and they are brilliant, but they are academic, not movement. My point is that I have simply not been approached by these people, although I am actually looking forward to it, and I have tried to be in contact. What I get as contact, it's only from international meetings, where I see them in the same light, with the same clothes I wear, business cards etc., but they don't bring me very much new. I know what they do, what they think, and I cannot use it.

Among environmentalists this state of affairs is commented upon in two opposite ways. Either activists advocate more formalisation, or they propose a return to extra-institutional strategies such as more disruptive action forms and the pursuit of cultural goals of influencing public opinion. Occasionally the two approaches are joint as it is typically the case of *Greenpeace*. The institutionalisation of social movements is an important dimension of most new movements of the 1980s and of the environmental movement in particular. It requires special attention.


## BUSINESS ENVIRONMENT

The *Committee System* is particularly receptive to the representation of business interests. This is intentional, to the point that the European system of representation can be described as a form of neo-corporatism. In the environmental field, the relation between business and the regulators can at times be very strained, but can also be a symbiotic one. Commenting on industries' strategies, a functionary noted that often regulation is actively promoted by industry, especially those large industries that operate with a long-term perspective. A functionary said:

> My view is that we should have a separate committee for industry because I believe the environment has to be a long term major strategic industrial dimension. When you think of renewable energies, of new transport systems, new industrial processes, recycling techniques. These are massive changes. So it is very important that the Community industry is the first in this game, not the second.

Multinational corporations, associations of industrialists and even smaller companies generally have the resources and technical expertise to permeate and influence all the relevant committees. However, many industries, particularly in some countries, are still learning the know-how of lobbying.[18] But, in general, there are close ties with lobbying organisations. For instance, the secretariat of UNICE[19] provides staff support for some committees, but interest groups often prefer to interact with the Commission through more direct channels.[20]

Corporate actors have reacted strategically in their competition for resources. Organisational adaptive behaviour has focused on changing market preferences, the legislative environment, and technological change. Specifically, in the EC there are significant politically mediated resources available to environmentally compliant business actors. As a bureaucrat noted:

> Industrialists lobby the Commission, because don't forget that the Commission has still got to write the proposals. Therefore a document can technically be withdrawn. Maybe this is something they like, maybe it is something they don't like. So we still have an immense amount of power in the decision-making process. So they lobby very hard, they lobby in the services, they lobby through organizations, they lobby through the cabinets of the Commission. If it is a very serious matter they will try to see the Commissioner. And they won't be satisfied in just seeing a Commissioner for the environment, but they will also see other Commissioners. If it is a German company they will go and see Mr Schmidt, an Italian will go and see Rossi.

Clearly the relation with industry is one of the most controversial issues within the EC bureaucracy. For instance a functionary remarked:

> The problem is that some people consider all industry as a black thing [a terrible thing] and these are not very productive positions. So for instance take my colleague x, when he talks with DG11 people they are simply fighting each other all the time. So the DG11 people simply hate him. I know him, I think he is one of the most interesting, I think he has actually the most complete information.

However, conflict also cuts across industries, and alliances can be formed with regulators against other industries:

> But [industries like regulation] if they feel they are in a leading position against their competitors, [they are] maybe the more avant-garde. I think if you look at some of the best-run environmental companies in Europe, the ones that are using very low-levels of fossil fuel or recycling their waste and so forth, they don't mind what the Commission does because they are well ahead of everybody else. The Germans are in this position, they don't mind what comes out of Brussels, they are way beyond that.

Of course, this is not always the case. In another field, a bureaucrat reported that industry is becoming increasingly united and as a consequence 'there is an immense amount of lobbying'.

CONCLUSIONS

This paper has examined the emergence of environmentalism in the institutions of the European Community, and the impact of lobbies and environmentalist organisations. Using a multi-causal model, three factors can be identified as contributing to the prominence of environmental regulation in the institutions of the Community. They are: (a) resource dependency; (b) a strong organisational culture inspired by value orientations; and (c) an organisational architecture that reinforces the taken-for-granted aspect of increasing environmental regulation. Predictably, lobbyists appeared directly influenced by the first factor and environmentalists by value considerations. Regulators often took a procedural approach based on taken-for-granted assumptions on their deliberative role. But it is relevant to note the extent to which all three criteria oriented organisational behaviour in each of the three fields identified – EC institutions, social–movement organisations, and lobbying organisations. Altogether these three actors constituted a macro-organisational field based on often ambiguous rules, which because of their relative novelty and pace of change has yet to be fully consolidated and formalised. As a process of mutual accommodation takes place, these actors are becoming increasingly alike.

   (a)  The first process – resource-dependency dynamics – makes regulation advantageous, on a macro-organisational scale both for the global EC institution and for individual civil servants' careers. Environmental regulation ensures an influential role for EC institutions on the policy-making function of European states. This erodes the power of nation states, but this process is not necessarily resisted by nation states as they often welcome more external regulation. In implementing environmental directives they are also gaining power to regulate new areas without having to expand into them with the difficulty of negotiated political processes.

   Resource-dependency processes are also aided by the non-homogeneity of nation states which facilitates the emergence of supra-national regulation as a new and alternative political arena emerges. Thus, interviews indicate that altogether regulators, industrialists, and environmentalists have a common vested interest in regulating the environment, or at least in controlling the regulative process. Awareness of this clearly emerged, particularly among lobbyists. Resource-dependency explanations are less appropriate for regulators. To them the benefit of increased regulation is rather indirect. Regulation would benefit the entire class, but make little difference to specific individuals.

(b) The congruence between individual and organisational goals increases when individuals identify with organisations on a value basis. This occurs with the majority of civil servants who hold strong pro-European views. In a number of instances they take the global organisational success as one of their goals. In alleging and promoting a value identification with the process of 'European construction', however, they can also pursue their own interests. As Majone points out, regulatory decisions are often related to societal values, hence policy-makers have a vested interest in the cultural milieu (Majone in Downing and Hanf, 1983). This points to the second criteria, value identifications, which is particularly prominent among environmentalists. Badly paid, with little job security and scarce influence, they act on the basis of their commitment. Thus, a value commitment is also a key factor in the impetus towards originating and implementing environmental regulation.

(c) Thirdly, the regulators follow procedures in a taken-for-granted fashion. Careful to maintain personal legitimacy, they follow established procedures. As one regulator pointed out, they work within the system, use the right language, etc.

As for inter-organisational relations, it is important to stress that the organisational environments of Brussels are a fairly recent creation. All of them have undergone transformations that can be conceptualised as processes of institutionalisation. That is, organisations have acquired a stable position in an organisational field with homogeneous rules and modes of operation.

### Notes

1. As at the time of the interviews the European Union was still called the European Community, I will adopt the latter term throughout this essay.
2. By 'European Institutions' I am referring to the political–administrative sphere developed around the organisations of the European Community including both the formal and informal networks in which political influence is exerted.
3. The interview schedule can be obtained from the author. A main schedule was adapted to the specific context of business, social movement or political/bureaucratic actor.
4. In some cases corruption, or a combination of lobbying and corruption, can also be used as a strategy to attain favourable regulation. However, the study of such strategy is beyond my means.

5.  For instance organisations are known to have promoted groups that advocated smokers' rights, or that advocate the employment of nuclear facilities to produce energy.

6.  This view is congruent with the position of Keohane and Hoffman (op. cit., p. 10) who conceptualise the Community 'as neither an international regime nor an emerging state but as a network involving the pooling of sovereignty'. As in other networks, there are processes that push the actors to prefer to interact with each other, reinforcing their bonds over time (op. cit., p. 14).

7.  For the concept of policy style, and the formation of sectoral tendencies see Freeman (1989, p. 482–4).

8.  For instance the cover story of *Forbes* of 6 July 1992 argues that in the American context 'environmental policy is out of control, costing jobs, depressing the U.S. standard of living and being run by politicians, scheming business people, political and social extremists'. Similar concerns are frequently aired in Europe, though generally in a far milder form. See for instance 'Hot Stuff' in *The Economist*, 11 July 1992, p. 67.

9.  However, it should be born in mind that at Community level the reflection of public opinion into legislation is obscured by the particularly complex decision-making process that, in addition to different types of actors, involves distinct and frequently conflicting political communities.

10. It must be stressed that nationality also has a crucial role in the social life of civil servants.

11. For instance, Sbragia notes that 'The Council of Ministers remains the focus of what to Americans seems parochialism in the EC. . . . There are however supranational checks on that nationalism' (Sbragia, 1992, p. 81).

12. See, for instance, Roy Jenkins' *European Diary 1977–1981* who about this principle cites Jean Monnet: 'the lesson he taught me was always to advance along the lines of least resistance, provided that it led in approximately the right direction' (p. 23).

13. A distinction between politicians and bureaucrats is a somewhat artificial one. Top bureaucrats are appointed politically and work in close connection with national polities as well as with national bureaucracies.

14. This line of argument has been particularly developed by rational-actor-model studies of bureaucracy.

15. For instance, Krämer notes:

> Participation in the work of the European Parliament – from time to time the Environmental Committee organizes public hearings on environmental matters to which environmental organizations are regularly invited. (Krämer, 1992, p. 128)

16. For discussions of committees and specifically of collegial forms of decision-making see Baylis (1989) and Waters (1989).

17. For instance *The Economist* writes 'So effectively have environmentalists greened public opinion that it takes an unashamed reactionary to question the wisdom of becoming ever greener and cleaner' (*The Economist*, 8 August 1992). Similarly, *The Independent* ('Hot Air and Global Warming',

7 August 1992, p. 17) questions 'the environmentalist rhetoric that would have us believe that our planet is on its last leg'.
18. See, for instance, De-la-Guérivière (1992) on French lobbying which is described as rather primitive compared to Italian lobbying.
19. UNICE is the federation representing community industries in their role as employers.
20. This is due to conflicting interests among interest groups which make collective representation difficult to achieve. See Michelmann (1978, p. 35).

# References

Baylis, T. A. (1989) *Governing by Committee* (Albany, NY: State University of New York Press).

De-la-Guérivière, J. (1992) 'Le Lobbying Français à Bruxelles', *Le Monde*, 3 November, pp. 32–3.

Downing, P. and Hanf, K. (1983) *International Comparisons in Implementing Pollution Laws* (Boston, MA: Kluwer Nijoff).

Freeman, G. P. (1989) 'National Styles and Policy Sectors: Explaining Structured Variations', *Journal of Public Policy*, 5: 4, pp. 467–96.

Keohane, R. O. and Hoffman, S. (eds) (1991) *The New European Community* (Boulder, CO: Westview).

Krämer, L. (1992) *Focus on European Environmental Law* (London: Sweet & Maxwell).

Lees, A. (1992) 'Maastricht, Subsidiarity and Environmental Protection', *Earth Matters*, 16, pp. 16–17.

Michelmann, H. J. (1978) *Organizational Effectiveness in a Multinational Bureaucracy* (Farnborough: Saxon House).

Moravcsik, A. (1991) 'Negotiating the Single European Act', in Keohane, R. O. and Hoffman, S. (eds), *The New European Community* (Boulder, CO: Westview), pp. 41–84.

Peters, B. G. (1992) 'Bureaucratic Politics and the Institutions of the European Community', in Sbragia, A. (ed.), *Euro-Politics* (Washington, DC: The Brookings Institution), pp. 75–122.

Sbragia, A. (ed.) (1992) *Euro-Politics* (Washington, DC: The Brookings Institution).

Waters, M. (1989) 'Collegiality, Bureaucratization, and Professionalization: A Weberian Analysis', *American Journal of Sociology*, 94, (5), pp. 945–72.

Williams, S. (1991) 'Sovereignty and Accountability in the European Community', in Keohane, R. O. and Hoffman, S. (eds), *The New European Community* (Boulder, CO: Westview), pp. 155–76.

# Index